Catching a Case

Catching a Case

Inequality and Fear in New York City's Child Welfare System

TINA LEE

Rutgers University Press
New Brunswick, New Jersey, and London

Library of Congress Cataloging-in-Publication Data
Names: Lee, Tina, 1976– author.
Title: Catching a case : inequality and fear in New York City's child welfare system / Tina Lee.
Description: New Brunswick, New Jersey : Rutgers University Press, 2016. |
Includes bibliographical references and index.
Identifiers: LCCN 2015028620| ISBN 9780813576145 (hardcover : alk. paper) | ISBN 9780813576138 (pbk. : alk. paper) | ISBN 9780813576152 (e-book (epub)) | ISBN 9780813576169 (e-book (web pdf))
Subjects: LCSH: Child welfare—New York (State)—New York. | Child abuse—New York (State)—New York. | Low-income parents—New York (State)—New York. Social service—New York (State)—New York. | Family services—New York (State)—New York. | Discrimination—New York (State)—New York.
Classification: LCC HV743.N48 L44 2016 | DDC 362.709747/1—dc23
LC record available at http://lccn.loc.gov/2015028620

A British Cataloging-in-Publication record for this book is available from the British Library.

Visit our website: http://rutgerspress.rutgers.edu

Manufactured in the United States of America

Contents

Acknowledgments

I am indebted to the parents who were willing to share their oftentimes painful stories with me and especially to those who allowed me to follow their cases and their lives during my fieldwork. I am also grateful to the caseworkers and judges who talked with me about their jobs and to the attorneys who granted me interviews and allowed me to follow them as they did their work. Judge Susan Danoff opened her courtroom to me and patiently answered all my questions when the family court process was still new and confusing early in my fieldwork. Heather Saslovsky, Ash Nangia, Paula Moore, and Andrea Gangoo provided help in numerous ways, answered follow-up questions, and introduced me to their colleagues.

I could not have completed my project without the assistance of the Child Welfare Organizing Project, an amazing and dedicated group of parents who have struggled with child welfare cases. They provide their expertise and support to other parents and train an equally amazing group of parent advocates each year. Mike Arsham and the organization's board allowed me to sit in on support groups so that I could meet parents and hear their stories. Both Teresa Bachiller, parent organizer, and Sabra Jackson, parent advocate, supported me every step of the way, shared their immense knowledge, and introduced me to parents. I will always be grateful for their kindness, humor, and welcome.

The research also benefited immensely from the financial support of a Wenner-Gren Dissertation Fieldwork Grant.

I am, of course, also deeply grateful for the help and guidance of my graduate advisors, Leith Mullings, Jeff Maskovsky, Kate Crehan, and Ida Susser. Many colleagues along the way also provided insights, helpful comments, and support: Raja Abillama, Christian Anderson, Vivian Berghahn, Rebecca De Guzman, Molly Hurley Depret, Esin Egit, Jen Giesking, Christina Harris, Lynn Horridge, Amy Jones, Nicole Laborde, Abraham Lotha, Adrienne Lotson, Andrea Morrell, Claudine Pied, Ted Powers, Katrina Scott, Nandini Sikand, Vikki Stone, Wendy Williams, Midori Yamamura, Janette Yarwood, and Gabriela Zamorano. I owe special thanks to Andrea Morrell for suggesting that I investigate family court.

Finally, special thanks go to my husband, Damon, and my children, Evelyn and Owen, for putting up with my absences as I finished this book in the midst of my first years as a tenure-track professor.

Catching a Case

1

Introduction

In January of 2006, a few months before my research began, news broke of the tragic death of Nixzmary Brown, a seven-year-old girl living with her mother and stepfather in Brooklyn. She was severely beaten by her stepfather and died from the injuries. She had been reported to child welfare authorities more than once for excessive school absences and bruises, but caseworkers did not thoroughly investigate the reports in a timely fashion. Most of the news coverage presented the story as a simple case of the child welfare system failing in its duty to prevent the tragedy. Such stories commonly appear in the news media and generate considerable public outrage, often leading to reforms of the child welfare system, increased numbers of reports, and more children being placed in foster care. The modern child welfare system is in fact meant to encourage the reporting of such abuse and aims to protect children from it through placement in foster care and services that seek to reform dangerous parents.

Severe abuse is not the main issue that the child welfare system confronts on a daily basis, however. Most cases involve varying degrees of neglect, and the parents who come in contact with the system are likely to be struggling but loving parents who suffer from the negative effects of large-scale social inequalities of race, class, and gender, as do most members of their communities. These parents are certainly not perfect, and they do face issues that can be, and often are, detrimental to their caretaking and their children's well-being. Their problems are also complex, and they are often in need of better housing and education, jobs, and services such as drug treatment or shelter from domestic violence. The child welfare system is simply not able to provide the help these parents need. Instead, it blames them for their problems and tends to deal with them punitively in an attempt to reform their behavior.

Joan,[1] an African-American mother in her forties, was investigated by the Administration for Children's Services (ACS, New York City's child welfare agency) after testing positive for drugs when she was admitted to a public hospital. Caseworkers initially allowed her to retain custody under the condition that she enroll in drug treatment. She lost her job as a nurse's assistant as a result of her case, and consequently she lost her insurance and was not able to enroll formally. She did find a program that would let her attend group counseling sessions until she could get Medicaid, and she traveled hours by subway to attend. When she was unable to provide documentation of her treatment, caseworkers removed her daughter. Salina, a Latina in her late twenties and a former foster child herself, lost custody of her children after admitting to marijuana use but was able to stop using quickly. She was, however, unable to regain custody of her children when caseworkers determined her apartment was unsafe—the wiring was old, and you could see evidence of small electrical fires. She could not find a landlord who would accept her Section 8 housing voucher[2] and thus could not move. Olivia, an African American in her forties, lost custody due to her inability to provide adequate housing for her children. A single mother with little education, she was evicted from public housing after her boyfriend was arrested, and she moved to a former parlor of a brownstone without adequate space for her children. The lock on the front door to her building was broken, and the door to her room was a flimsy interior one. She shared a bathroom and kitchen with others in the building and couldn't leave food in the fridge. Caseworkers wanted her to enter a shelter to regain custody, but she did not want that experience for her children. Instead, she decided to wait for a voucher to get an apartment. Leslie, an African American mother in her forties, lost custody of her children when they were frequently absent from school. When questioned about their absences, she admitted her depression and previous experience with domestic violence to a school social worker who reported her for these issues. She lost her job at a dentist's office partly as a result of her case and then lost custody of her children when she did not access mental health counseling.

These cases are typical and broadly representative of the types of cases the child welfare system deals with on a daily basis in New York City. The problems these mothers faced, and the resources they were or were not able to marshal to deal with them, were profoundly shaped by their race, class, and gender. Yet this context was largely ignored by caseworkers and family court officials; instead, these women were labeled neglectful parents, subjected to state supervision of their families, and faced the placement of their children in foster care. Their attempts to prove their worth as parents in order to end this supervision and/or regain custody were also constrained by these larger social inequalities.

This book focuses both on the day-to-day decision-making practices and definitions of child neglect used in the child welfare system and on the parents' experiences with child welfare and their attempts to regain custody of children placed in foster care. It reflects my findings from fourteen months of embedding myself in the child welfare system in New York City. I spent months observing family courts, interviewed parents and followed them through the system, asked caseworkers for detailed descriptions of their work and their decision-making processes, and discussed cases with attorneys on all sides. Throughout this book, I use "child welfare" and "the child welfare system" to refer to the various state bureaucracies and private agencies that are responsible for investigating allegations of child maltreatment and providing services to families who have been reported for child maltreatment. These include ACS, private nonprofit foster care agencies, service providers, and the family courts. ACS is the state agency responsible for investigating reports of child abuse and neglect and for coordinating services (including foster care) for families that have been reported. Private, nonprofit foster care agencies place children who are removed from their parents in individual foster homes or group homes; such agencies are responsible for both monitoring these homes and coordinating the reunification and/or adoption process. Various other agencies provide services such as counseling and drug treatment for families who have been reported or had their children removed. The family courts are responsible for overseeing these decisions and making sure that the law surrounding child maltreatment and the policies relating to child welfare case practice are followed.

In describing this complicated system and analyzing how it works on a daily basis, I seek to add to our understanding of state practices that shape the lives and behaviors of poor women of color in the contemporary United States. I am guided by an overarching concern with how, and to what extent, state practices build on and re-create stratified reproduction and inequalities of race, class, and gender. I understand reproduction, including raising children, as political in the sense of being inextricably bound up with power and inequalities of power (Ginsburg and Rapp 1991). I use the term "stratified reproduction" to discuss the conditions under which some individuals are valued and supported in bearing and raising children while others are not (Ginsburg and Rapp 1995). Everyday practices in child welfare empower or disempower parents to carry out their caretaking work through the casework and legal processes that grant custody of children to some and not to others, based on notions of what the proper care of children entails and, more important, what kinds of individuals proper parents should be. Child welfare is thus a key arena for drawing lines between "fit" and "unfit" parenting, and these lines often fall along divisions of race, class, and gender. Consequently, I see the child welfare system, which is fundamentally engaged in judging the behavior of individual mothers (and, to a lesser extent, fathers) and making decisions about child custody, as integral to the production and re-creation of stratified reproduction.

I also argue, more generally, that the child welfare system both builds on and helps reproduce race, class, and gender inequalities. I see child welfare as a system parallel to policing and incarceration. Both systems deal with issues that have their roots in inequality through practices of intensive surveillance and punishment rather than distribution of supportive services. Although much has been written about the punitive nature of criminal justice and its use as a way to deal with the effects of increasing inequality (see, for example, Wacquant 2001), child welfare has not been added to this picture. Child welfare involvement is heavily concentrated in the same neighborhoods as intensive policing, and, despite important differences, there are also striking similarities. The level of child welfare involvement in these neighborhoods means that many parents worry about child welfare reports. In fact, large percentages of parents in their communities are or have been reported, creating a widespread fear of "catching a case" in a way that parallels how young black men fear catching a criminal case (see chapter 5). To understand more completely the role of the state in ameliorating and/or reproducing inequalities, child welfare is an area of state practice that must be examined.

The Child Welfare Population

The child welfare system deals mostly with cases of child neglect, and the families most likely to be involved in the system face numerous social disadvantages. They are almost exclusively poor and disproportionately families of color. According to national data from 2008, a large majority of reports, 79.1 percent, was found to be unsubstantiated; that is, the caseworker found no evidence of maltreatment. Among substantiated cases, neglect cases outnumbered abuse cases by roughly 3:1 (U.S. Department of Health and Human Services 2010, 25–26).[3] Studies have demonstrated that poor children form an overwhelming majority of those served by the child welfare system (Berrick et al. 2006; Roberts 2002). Data from 2005 and 2006, for example, showed that children from low socioeconomic status (SES) families are more likely to be neglected, with a rate of 16.1 per 1,000 children versus 2.2 per 1,000 in non-low SES families. In other words, the risk for poor children was more than seven times the risk for other children (Sedlak et al. 2010, 5–12). Nationally, in 2005, black children composed about 16 percent of the population of children under the age of eighteen but made up about 32 percent of the foster care population (Children's Defense Fund 2007).[4] Although surveys that ask about specific behaviors among parents find that rates of maltreatment do not seem to vary by race (Hill 2004, 2006), children of color are more likely to be labeled as maltreated by child welfare caseworkers and to be placed in foster care. Patterns of racial disproportionality exist at all steps of the child welfare process: reporting, case indication, removal, and neglect findings in court (Derezotes, Poertner, and Testa 2004; Hill 2004, 2006; Rivaux et al. 2008).

Statistics from New York City also highlight the extent to which child welfare cases and foster care placements are concentrated in poor communities of color. Black children are grossly overrepresented in the foster care population. In 2008, African American children accounted for 27 percent of the children under the age of eighteen in the city but comprised a staggering 57.1 percent of the foster care population. In contrast, 24 percent of the children under age eighteen in New York City were white, but white children comprised only 4 percent of the foster care population. Asian and Latino children were also underrepresented relative to their percentages in the under-eighteen population.[5] Child welfare cases and foster care placements are also highly concentrated in a few neighborhoods. The numbers of children placed from each Community District (or CD)[6] show that many of the children placed in foster care came from only a few CDs. The ten CDs with the most placements accounted for 42.2 percent of all children placed, while only 1.9 percent came from the ten CDs with the fewest placements. The CDs with the most placements are also those with large percentages of families of color and children and families living in poverty. These communities are plagued by other social problems: large percentages of unemployed adults, high infant mortality rates, low percentages of adults with more than a high school diploma, and high rates of incarceration as compared to the rest of the city.[7] In talking with parents it became clear that they were struggling to raise children despite poverty, crime, violence, housing problems, lack of childcare, and failing schools.

Although these patterns of child welfare involvement have been discussed at length, there is still debate about why they exist (Hill 2004, 2006). The fact that black children are more likely to live in poor families than white children might account for some of the reason black children are disproportionately involved with the child welfare system, but there is also evidence that race and racism play a role in decision-making practices. For example, Latino children, who are also more likely to be poor than white children, are not overrepresented in the child welfare system (Roberts 2002, 48). Roberts (2002) reviews several studies that show racial biases and argues that both views about "proper" family composition and negative stereotypes of black women play a role in decision making. For example, longstanding cultural stereotypes of black women as careless mothers and the pervasive idea that single mothers and those who rely on welfare are responsible for poverty and other social problems leads to a devaluation of the caregiving of black women. I found similar patterns in my research.

There is also evidence of a strong correlation between poverty and maltreatment (Berrick et al. 2006; Lindsey 1994; Pelton 1989; Waldfogel 2004). Some researchers posit stress as the link (Roberts 2002, 31), while others argue that poor families are simply more subject to reports by public services (Appell 1997; see Pelton 1989 who disagrees with this conclusion). Others argue that neglect and poverty are conflated, and conditions such as inadequate housing, lack of childcare, or an inability to get drug treatment are often labeled neglect (Krane and Davies 2000; Swift 1995). It is also clear that women are the main clients of the child welfare system while men are less often involved (Featherstone 2006; Scourfield 2003, 2006; Strega et al. 2008). In part, this reflects the fact that many families who come to the attention of the child welfare system are made up of single mothers and their children (Risley-Curtiss and Heffernan 2003). It is also the case, however, that women are more likely to be held responsible for child maltreatment, and researchers link this to the naturalization of motherhood in mainstream culture and in the psychology and child development literature (Turney 2000, 52; Strega et al. 2008, 706). Popular thought contends that mothers "naturally" put their children first at all times and that maternal care and love are necessary for a child's well-being and proper development (Turney 2000). These views lead to blaming child neglect primarily on mothers.

The poor women of color who are thus most likely to be investigated by child welfare and who are most vulnerable to the loss of their children already face numerous constraints in raising children and supporting their families. Most of the parents in my study were women of color living at or near the poverty line.[8] The low-wage, mostly part-time service jobs for which they were qualified did not provide enough income to adequately support themselves and their children. Such jobs had no benefits, such as sick leave, personal days, or health insurance, and arranging childcare with changing or inflexible schedules was difficult. Many of the women moved in and out of paid work as they dealt with the difficulties of finding childcare and other services. For example, schedule changes might make finding childcare impossible or taking time off for a sick child could mean losing a job completely. Other parents relied on government benefits that were subject to being cut off and had to deal with onerous bureaucratic requirements (endless requests for paperwork, long waits at offices, or errors that led to money being unavailable or suddenly reduced). They were also required to participate in work requirements without adequate provision for childcare.

Given the combined effect of class inequality and racially segregated housing, many parents dealt with crowded or dilapidated housing, and some regularly faced eviction and homelessness due to income loss or, in some cases, gentrification and increased rents. The mothers generally lived in unsafe neighborhoods where drugs and violence were common and where they were constantly worried about the safety and futures of their children. Drug treatment and other services were scarce, and many raised children with little financial support from fathers and other family members.

These parents have also dealt with personal problems and struggled to find help for them. Many have used illegal drugs, sometimes as a way to deal with traumas and other untreated mental health issues. Because they were vulnerable to testing and surveillance, they thus became involved in child welfare. Three mothers, Nicole, Rose, and Olivia, have mental disabilities or illnesses that have kept them from working, and they receive disability payments. Two mothers, Salina and Jasmine, were foster children themselves and have been involved with child welfare as adults. Three of the four men living in poverty have a criminal history that has hindered their ability to work and gain custody of their children. Two of their criminal histories were related to selling drugs, and one had a history related to gang activity as a teen. The combined effects of poverty, race, and gender created situations in which these parents faced barriers to caring for their children and were vulnerable to child welfare reports.

Even parents with college degrees and/or more stable jobs faced material constraints that left them vulnerable to child welfare involvement. A degree does not necessarily translate into a stable middle-class lifestyle for a woman of color, especially in New York City. The women I came to know in this category were all single mothers who did not have financial cushions. They became involved in child welfare after a period of living near the poverty line when they lost jobs or housing or became involved in drugs. In other cases, they relied on public social services (most prominently public hospitals) that reported them to ACS. The working-class parents I met were generally able to make ends meet, and some had benefits such as health insurance and were in unionized occupations. Their jobs were inflexible, however, and some could survive only by combining jobs or relying on food pantries or food stamps. They too were vulnerable to child welfare involvement if they were unable to find resources to deal with personal problems or if they lost jobs. They still tended to live in unsafe neighborhoods where social services were generally unavailable or not affordable.

All the parents I came to know lived lives shaped by profound inequalities that made them both vulnerable to child welfare involvement and more constrained in their ability to navigate the system. In addition, they were perceived as irresponsible and unfit mothers (and fathers) whose reproductive labor was of little value (Collins 1990; Mullings 1995; Roberts 1997; Williams 1995). The child welfare system itself, I argue, reinforces these perceptions and gives them legitimacy. The most important thing to know about my informants, however, is that they loved their children and wanted the best for them. They were hurt by being labeled neglectful and struggled to deal with the pain of losing custody. They wanted to be adequate providers and good role models and to provide stable and happy lives for their children. They fought hard to regain custody and to get through "the system" intact. They are more than a list of problems and a set of risks to their children, but they were rarely treated that way.

Regulating Poor Families

An important message of this book is that child welfare is at least as much about regulating poor families, and especially poor mothers, as it is about protecting children. Child welfare should be seen as one of the main arenas of state practice that contributes to the re-creation of stratified reproduction and of inequality more generally. Scholars have written much about how welfare, policing, and incarceration work in this way (see, for example, Johnson 2011; Mullings 2005; Wacquant 2012), and researchers must add child welfare to this picture. Daily practices in child welfare re-create inequalities through the particular ways in which mandated reporters, caseworkers, and family court personnel intervene, at least in urban areas, in the lives of those who are at the bottom of social hierarchies. These interventions parallel those of the criminal justice system: they subject parents (especially mothers) to surveillance and deal punitively with problems (such as domestic violence, poor housing, inability to deal with drug abuse and mental health issues, and so on) that have their roots in poverty, racism, and sexism.

Since the early nineteenth century, child welfare has drawn lines between those families who were thought to be able to comply with dominant social norms and properly socialize their children and those who were not. Although there has been a prevailing American belief that parents are solely and individually responsible for the care of their children, there has also been a feeling that children need to be protected. In part, they needed protection as future resources and citizens, but this protection was also necessary to ensure that they did not grow up to be poor, dangerous, or criminal (see chapter 2). Throughout its history, the child welfare system has been part of the "therapeutic state" (Polsky 1991) that has combined aspects of helping and policing. Daily practices have judged parents to be "fit" or "unfit" and have used the power of the state to remove children to the care of others and/or to enforce compliance with various forms of counseling to help unfit parents learn prevailing social norms. These interventions have always primarily targeted poor populations that were seen as dangerous (that is, either recent immigrants who were seen as not quite white or racial minorities) and are one way that stratified reproduction is enacted and maintained.

The modern child welfare system has continued to intervene mainly in poor families and in cases of neglect, even though it was designed primarily to encourage reporting of severe abuse so that it could be dealt with through reform of parents and/or foster care placement. The system, which combines policing/investigative and helping/supportive functions, is supposed to determine the truth of allegations and enforce decisions through the family court while it simultaneously provides services to prevent foster care placement and/or reunite families (see chapter 3). In the last several decades, however, the policing and surveillance aspects of the child welfare mandate have come to overshadow its helping mission (see chapter 5). Parents are likely to be individually blamed and to face child removal, even in cases that are closely tied to poverty, while the services they are expected to complete do little to address the complex problems that negatively affect child well-being. Instead, service plans, often "one-size-fits-all," focus on various forms of counseling and education that aim to make parental behavior more closely fit social norms.

Rather than finding support, parents experienced punitive treatment in many cases. One mother whose case involved her drug addiction stated, "They think they can punish you into getting sober." This change toward more punitive practice mirrors the overall shift in state practices that reflects the influence of ideologies championing small government, lower taxes, and personal responsibility. As others have pointed out, these ideologies have promoted a restructuring of the state (Clarke 2004), and changes in welfare and increasing incarceration evidence moves "toward the punitive regulation of racialised poverty" (Wacquant 2012, 67) created by global shifts in production (Gilmore 1999; Mullings 2003; Pettit 2012; Wacquant 2001). I see child welfare as an important aspect of this more general trend, an aspect in need of greater attention.

An Overwhelmed System

The public tends to see protecting children from severe abuse or severe and intentional neglect as the main role of the child welfare system (chapter 2), and, especially in large cities, there is enormous media-driven pressure to prevent *all* tragedies (see chapter 4). This focus often leads, most dramatically in the aftermath of a high-profile child death, to an overwhelmed system that is unable to adequately provide needed services, monitor all cases, and help families reunite with their children. This media-driven focus on preventing tragedy leads to a system in crisis that cannot adequately serve its dual mission: to support families and to keep children safe.[9] Instead, a narrow focus on safety leads to cautious decision making in which saving children from their parents rather than strengthening families becomes the default position. In addition, when child welfare agencies are left to deal with too many cases, stress and overwork for officials and inadequate services for families result. I found that caseworkers were severely overburdened, courts were bogged down with too many cases, and adequate time and information to make tough decisions was lacking (see chapter 4).

In addition to being overloaded, child welfare is severely under-resourced. Services are often hard to come by with long waiting lists and/or inconvenient locations and schedules. Too few caseworkers with adequate training are available to conduct thorough assessments of family needs. Staff attorneys, relatively poorly paid, lack necessary time to fight vigorously for all clients. Many courthouses are dilapidated and crowded, a general atmosphere that adds to the feeling of hopelessness. This overburdened and under-resourced system does not serve families well. Although everyone who worked in the system agreed that it was "in crisis" (I heard this phrase throughout my research from people who worked in different parts of the system) and that the crisis was longstanding, the political will necessary to correct these problems was largely absent. Various organizations raised alarms and wrote reports detailing the resources that would be needed (see, for example, Council on Children 2007), but there was little interest in finding these resources among city, state, and federal policy makers. This situation stems from the fact that over time the system has evolved mainly to deal with poor families of color who are seen as undeserving of support.

Dealing with the Effects of Inequality in the Lives of Children

The modern child welfare system is also based on an individualistic model of child maltreatment that places blame on the pathologies of parents and assumes these issues can be remedied through counseling and education (McConnell and Llewellyn 2005). In most of the cases described in this book, however, the problems reported to child welfare were about the problems facing poor mothers of color that they had inadequate resources to manage. Cases commonly involved illegal drug use, mental health issues, and domestic violence (see chapter 6), and the mother's inability to find the services she needed to overcome these issues was often the reason she came to be supervised by the family courts or lost her children to foster care (see chapter 7).

In general, the legal definition of neglect is applied in everyday casework and family court practice in a way that takes parental problems and risks to children out of their social context by ignoring their roots in structural inequalities (see chapter 6). To a great degree, parents are held to standards of proper family life and childcare that are extremely difficult, if not impossible, for working-class and poor parents to meet. These standards reflect middle-class norms, and meeting them requires access to resources such as money, time, flexible work schedules, health insurance, mental health and substance abuse treatment, and quality childcare—resources that are generally unavailable to poor parents of color. When parents cannot meet these standards or are not offered adequate assistance to meet them, they are labeled neglectful and risk losing custody of their children (chapter 6). In addition, parents are often judged almost solely on the basis of problems that are thought to present risk to children, like drug addiction and mental health issues. Such dismissive assessments seem related to the influence of stereotypes of unfit mothers of color, while more comprehensive evaluations of the overall care parents provided to children were rare. Rather than being seen as parents in need of support, these parents were seen through the lens of racialized stereotypes of unfit mothers and deadbeat dads, risks from which children needed to be protected.

In this context, and in many cases, the difference between retaining/regaining and losing custody came down to compliance. If caseworkers were convinced that parents were dealing with problems in a way that conformed to agency definitions of the problem, followed agency directives, and fit with agency timelines, then parents were able to avoid foster care or regain custody, but too often caseworkers did not acknowledge the very real barriers to compliance that parents faced (chapter 7). Many of these barriers resulted directly from poverty: lack of transportation, inflexible job schedules, lack of health insurance, lack of access to high-quality drug treatment, an inability to escape violence, and so on.

Although there are certainly parents who intentionally mistreat their children, most of the cases I witnessed involved issues of poverty or an inability to deal with problems due to a lack of resources. Caseworkers had access to few services that could deal with these complex issues, and parents, in turn, felt that their most pressing needs were not met by the services they were required to complete. In this context, child welfare becomes "a kind of triage, a battle-front hospital where casualties are sorted and only the most seriously wounded receive attention" (Lindsey 1994, 2). Services that address key issues such as lack of adequate housing, education, and jobs are extremely scarce. The lack of fit between the services available and the core problems in many families is related to the basic structure of child welfare and the assumptions it makes about child maltreatment. Instead of this misalignment, universal and comprehensive services to allow families to raise children safely are required so that child welfare can focus its limited resources on real abuse and severe and willful neglect (see also Lindsey 1994; Waldfogel 1998).

The Re-creation of Stratified Reproduction and Inequalities

In addition to dealing with the effects of large-scale inequalities in the lives of children, the child welfare system also plays a role in re-creating these very inequalities. I found that, in many ways, parents have very little power in their interactions with caseworkers, family court officials, and service providers. In general, parents are not treated as potential partners in the process of creating a safe environment for their children. Instead, they are viewed *only* as risks to children (a prime example of stratified reproduction). They have almost no ability to resist state intrusion into their lives, must reveal intimate details of their lives even when the details are unrelated to the allegations in their case, are often subtly forced to take drug tests, are unable to define their own needs and problems, and have practically no say in creating a service plan that meets their needs. In the end, this meant that many parents were required to complete services that did not address the root causes of family problems, and their lives did not always improve. In this context, parents' ability to comply with directives and service plans is often the decisive factor in whether they will retain custody of children or regain custody of children placed in foster care (see chapters 6 and 7).

Furthermore, although the family court is involved in child welfare cases (ideally) to ensure that the rights and needs of parents are balanced against the rights and needs of children and that state intervention only occurs when necessary, daily practices in family court do not adequately protect the rights of parents or ensure that "reasonable efforts" to prevent foster care and reunite families are made. In this way, the family court system re-creates a situation of stratified reproduction by legitimating evaluations of parental unfitness with little to no scrutiny. In many cases, child welfare authorities are not asked to justify their decisions either to place families under supervision or to place children in foster care, and failures to provide needed services are not remedied. A legal finding of neglect, which is practically guaranteed if a family ends up with a case in family court (see chapter 7), helps to reinforce and give legitimacy to the idea that poor families of color are broken and require state supervision. Some positive steps, however, are being taken to deal with these common failures to protect parents' rights, and this book ends with a brief discussion of them.

I also argue that the child welfare system plays a role in the re-creation of stratified reproduction and racialized, inner-city poverty. Decision-makers draw on various overtly color-blind, but nonetheless racialized, discourses in making decisions about neglect and child placement. These discourses paint mothers of color as irresponsible and unable to care for children adequately and fathers of color as either "deadbeat dads," who will not care for their children, or as criminal and violent and therefore unsuitable caretakers. When caseworkers use these discourses as a filter through which to understand parents, it can become easier to define them as neglectful and to make the decision to place their children in foster care. By continuing to define poor parents of color by what they lack and by not providing the services that might enable them to better care for their children, the idea that they are unfit is reinforced and reproduced.

The child welfare system also played a role in deepening the poverty some parents experienced or in making a more stable economic situation worse. This occurred, for example, when parents lost service-sector jobs if they needed too much time off for court appearances, visits, and service appointments. In other cases, parents lost housing when welfare cases were terminated due to an inability to make appointments and conduct job search activities. An inability to support their children was then sometimes used to define them as neglectful and undeserving of regaining custody. Because parents and children of color are disproportionately involved with child welfare, this particular form of increasing economic instability deepens racial inequality as well. Thus, child welfare is a key arena in which lines are drawn between parents whose reproductive work is valued and supported and those who are seen as unfit parents undeserving of assistance.

The Research Process

My research was carried out between October 2006 and November 2007 and included observations, a survey of parents, in-depth interviews and informal conversations with people involved in the child welfare system, and following the lives and cases of parents. I conducted observations in courtrooms,[10] parenting classes, and support groups. I chose these locations because they enabled me to see the broad range of cases child welfare deals with, to gather information about cases and how decisions are made, and to understand the common problems faced by parents in their daily lives while navigating the child welfare system. The Child Welfare Organizing Project allowed me to sit in their support groups, and my understanding of the system is informed by the general themes that arose in their conversations and my view of the range of cases and barriers with which parents must deal.[11] As time went on, I was able to talk with parents in support groups and parenting classes about their cases and to share with them what I had observed and learned through my research. I also volunteered to accompany parents to court, something commonly requested of parent advocates that they rarely had time to do.[12] My contacts with activists and parent advocates at one foster care agency were especially valuable in my research. They gave me their insights into "the system" and taught me what they knew. Their acceptance of me also made it easier to develop rapport with parents.

I met many parents whom I later interviewed in support groups and classes, and I also found a few parents willing to allow me to follow up with them and their cases. During my observations at court, I met attorneys and caseworkers to whom I talked informally and with whom I requested interviews. I conducted twenty-eight interviews with lawyers, judges, and caseworkers,[13] and twenty-four in-depth interviews with parents. I also conducted a brief survey of forty-two parents in parenting classes and followed the cases of several parents throughout the project (this included getting updates from them as well as attending conferences and court appearances).[14] Finally, I attended public forums, hearings, rallies, and meetings about the child welfare system in New York City. I attended conferences for lawyers and other professionals about issues in child welfare and kept up with news about the system in newspapers and other periodicals that cater to workers in the nonprofit sector and/or feature stories about child welfare. All of this material informs my analysis of the system and how it works on a daily basis.

Conclusion

All the parents in my study found that their efforts to parent well and adequately provide for their children were constrained by inadequate incomes, lack of affordable childcare, housing troubles, unsafe neighborhoods, and/or lack of social services to deal with personal problems. All of these factors must be understood as part of the larger context of how they became involved with child welfare and why they were considered neglectful. It is unfortunate that the current child welfare system cannot adequately deal with the complex realities of their lives with the available resources and under the constraints of current policies.

I argue that the child welfare system helps to reproduce the very racial, class, and gender inequalities and stereotypes that constrain these parents. In New York City and other large cities, the child welfare system deals almost exclusively with the problems of poor minority families, and it deals with them in a particularly punitive way, often through child removal. In contrast, white families are more likely to be able to deal with family problems by turning to "separate and less disruptive mechanisms," such as private counseling, therapy, and drug treatment (Roberts 2002, 10). This raises the question of whether child welfare would be as punitive if it dealt primarily with white families, and I am convinced that it would not. Families of color are subjected, through the child welfare system, to profound disruption of family life that increases insecurity for children (see also Roberts 2002, 2008).

The likelihood of being reported to child welfare authorities and losing custody of children also disrupts poor communities of color as a whole. It creates distrust of neighbors and service providers, which, in turn, often causes parents to be reluctant to seek help for problems such as drug use or domestic violence. High rates of child welfare involvement can also exacerbate the poverty already concentrated in these communities. In addition, disproportionately placing families of color under state supervision of their parenting perpetuates "stereotypes about Black people's incapacity to govern themselves and need for state supervision" (Roberts 2002, 237). The high rates of child welfare investigation and family disruption among poor people of color as compared to whites send a message that some groups of parents are unfit and that their children are better off in the state's custody, again reinforcing stereotypes about irresponsibility (Roberts 2002, 244). These community effects parallel those created by the high concentration of policing, arrests, and incarceration in these communities (Clear 2009; Goffman 2014; Mauer and Chesney-Lind 2002), and they must be added to our picture of how state practices reinforce and re-create inequalities.

My argument that child welfare helps to reproduce stratified reproduction and larger social inequalities is structural. The system's racialized, gendered, and classed effects cannot be blamed mainly on individual biases in decision making, although negative stereotypes of poor parents of color did unconsciously affect how parents were viewed and how their cases were handled. Instead, the failures in the system and its role in re-creating stratified reproduction largely stem from the aims and underlying assumptions at work in child welfare. These goals and assumptions condition day-to-day practice and policy, including what caseworkers and other decision-makers take into account, what they are able to see as relevant and irrelevant in making decisions, and the solutions they have at their disposal for dealing with complex family problems. There are institutional reasons why child welfare works as it does, and these are closely related to larger societal beliefs and policies about race, class, gender, family, poverty, and the care of children.

2

A History of Child Welfare in New York City

Before delving into how the child welfare system works on a daily basis, it is important to know the history of efforts to protect children from maltreatment. This context is necessary to both understand the structure of the modern child welfare system and explain why its inadequacies are a product of this structure. Moreover, the state policies that have accumulated over time still govern the system's workings and shape its daily practices; in fact, we still see traces of this history in the underlying assumptions of current policy and practice. Chapter 2 thus traces how definitions of maltreatment and efforts to protect children have changed in response to changing ideas of family, gender, and the role of the state while keeping in mind the important continuities in how the causes of child maltreatment are understood and linked to ideas about the causes of poverty and the behaviors of poor, urban populations.[1]

Child welfare institutions and policies are part of what Andrew Polsky terms the "therapeutic state," that is, the body of public practices and institutions that work to change the behaviors of populations who are unable or unwilling to comply with dominant social norms. Therapeutic states approach those at the bottom of social hierarchies with the main assumption:

> If they are to acquire the value structure that makes for self-sufficiency, healthy relationships, and positive self-esteem, they need expert help. Accordingly they become the clients of behavioral specialists, clinicians, and social workers—a group I refer to generically as social personnel. . . . Through instruction, counseling, and supervision, clients are assisted in overcoming their personal deficiencies and learning to bear the pressures placed upon them. Social personnel can maintain subsequent oversight to assure that clients have not slipped back into their former ways. (Polsky 1991, 3–4)

Although more privileged members of society might seek out the help of "social personnel" to deal with their problems, the character of this relationship is profoundly different when it involves people who are "marginal" and under the supervision of the state. State officials assume that poor and socially disadvantaged people require nothing less than "wholesale personal and family reconstruction" so they cannot choose when to begin and end their treatment. Furthermore, the coercive power of the state can then be used to punish them if they do not demonstrate change (Polsky 1991, 3–4).[2] To this day, child welfare is one realm in which the line between "fit" and "unfit" parents is drawn. The state expects those deemed unfit to engage in education and therapy to become responsible parents, and family courts enforce compliance.

Child welfare has long been targeted toward groups that were seen as dangerous and/or troublesome—especially the urban poor (European immigrants in the nineteenth and early twentieth centuries and poor people of color since then) and Native Americans (Briggs 2012). Although these institutions do aim to protect vulnerable children from the violence and neglect of adults, child welfare is also part of larger efforts to "regulate the poor" (Piven and Cloward 1993) and cannot be understood apart from intertwined ideas about poverty, gender, and race. In short, this system is a primary instrument in creating and re-creating a situation of stratified reproduction, and an analysis of child welfare history brings this into focus.

Poor families and children have been a target of intervention by private organizations and the state as "Americans have been torn between a *fear for* children and a *fear of* children" (Grossberg 2002, 3). The safety and lives of children have been of public concern because the public sees them as both public resources and future citizens. At the same time, a fear of poor children has been widespread, and many have believed that, if not given a proper upbringing, poor children would remain poor and drain resources, would become criminals, or would eventually mistreat their own children. Public concern with poor children has also coexisted with the idea, consistent across most of US history, that families should be private and the care of children the responsibility of individual parents (Pleck 1987). Thus, public intervention has been seen as suspect (Grossberg 2002). Through most of this history, discussion about policy and the role of the state or the larger community has revolved around individual parental culpability and "saving" children, most often by removing them from the care of their parents, rather than acknowledging the social-structural issues that impact children's well-being.

Here I follow several threads, all of which are also themes evidenced in my fieldwork. First, child welfare operates in the context of social inequalities and is profoundly shaped by ideas about the causes of these inequalities and about the behaviors of the poor and ethnic or racial minorities. Second, although policies and institutions often overtly focus on severe abuse and maltreatment, most of the cases dealt with on a daily basis are linked to poverty and its effects on family life and the well-being of children; often poverty is actually conflated with maltreatment. Third, inadequate resources for families and a lack of political will to deal with the roots of poverty, combined with ideas that parents are individually responsible for children, have led to child removal becoming a primary solution to family problems.

Nineteenth- and Early Twentieth-Century Child Welfare Institutions

Concerns about unprecedented levels of urban poverty, crime, unrest, and the influx of southern and eastern European immigrants drove early institutions and policies aimed at protecting children from maltreatment (Folks 1902; Katz 1996; Schneider and Deutsch 1941). There was increased anxiety among a rising middle class about the behavior of the "dangerous classes" (i.e., urban poor immigrant groups) who were thought to be criminal, vicious, indolent, and intemperate (Stansell 1990). At the same time, changing notions of children and childhood, specifically the idea that childhood is a separate and special part of life, took hold at this time, and society came to view children as dependent, innocent, and in need of protection (Ariès 1962; Zelizer 1985). These new ideas led to increasing concern about poor children and the long-term effects of an improper upbringing. For those worried about social problems among the working-classes, the poor, and recent immigrants, it also made sense to focus on children because they thought that these problems would be "perpetuated if the patterns of poverty were not broken among society's youngest members" (Lindenmeyer 1997, 10–11). For example, the writings of Charles Loring Brace, a prominent child saver, make clear that he was driven, in part, by the belief that only by taking poor children out of their families and the city would they be taught proper morals and behavior and saved from a life of poverty and crime (Ashby 1997; L. Gordon 1999; Katz 1996; Stansell 1990). In short, he felt he needed to work directly with children as their parents were beyond redemption (Ashby 1997; L. Gordon 1988, 1999; Pleck 1987).[3] Brace's views were common among middle-class reformers.

In the 1850s these concerns led to the creation, by private citizens and organizations, of special institutions for "dependent" children: orphan asylums. Some states also passed laws (New York's was passed in 1875) that removed dependent children from poorhouses (where they were previously housed along with adults) into asylums and allowed law enforcement officers to commit children, most of whom were recent Italian, Jewish, and Irish immigrants (Katz 1996; Schneider and Deutsch 1941). Commitments were generally permanent, and, until 1884, many asylums sent children to work as contract laborers in private homes in an effort to contain costs (Sobie 1987, 63–64). Private organizations, such as Brace's Children's Aid Society (CAS), founded in New York City in 1853, built lodging houses and other institutions (including schools). The CAS also began to suggest an "anti-institutional strategy of child rescue" (Katz 1996, 110). They placed some dependent children with families, often outside the city, and organized "Orphan Trains" to send children west (L. Gordon 1999). By the mid-1890s, the organization had placed at least 90,000 children (Katz 1996, 110).[4] Although Brace presented his work as saving "orphans," the majority of children placed had at least one parent, and many were simply poor and found on the streets in activities that contributed to their family income (Ashby 1997; L. Gordon 1999; Stansell 1990). The CAS was, in fact, criticized for patrolling slum areas to look for mistreated children and for pressuring parents into surrendering them. Many poor parents feared that their children would be taken

(L. Gordon 1999), and this fear of "catching a case" continues to exist in poor, inner-city neighborhoods today.

By the late nineteenth century, reformers became more concerned with the "cruelty" of poor and immigrant parents toward their children and blamed such cruelty for various urban problems (L. Gordon 1988). The New York Society for the Prevention of Cruelty to Children (NYSPCC) was founded in 1874 after the highly publicized case of Mary Ellen, a child who was malnourished, inadequately clothed, and beaten by her stepmother.[5] The creation of Societies for the Prevention of Cruelty to Children (SPCCs) and Humane Societies (which handled both animal and child cruelty) followed in many cities and small towns in the Northeast, mid-Atlantic, and Midwest (Pleck 1987). The SPCCs were instrumental in creating laws defining maltreatment and were authorized to investigate cases of parents reported for violating these laws. These organizations had the power to obtain warrants to enter homes, to arrest parents, and to bring children on the streets into court to ask that they be placed in orphan asylums (Pleck 1987). The SPCCs, the first organizations given the power by the state to remove children from the care of their parents, are the precursors of modern state-run child protective agencies.

The SPCCs had a broad view of "cruelty" that went beyond the kind of abuse suffered by Mary Ellen,[6] which included sending children out during "unreasonable hours" to beg or sell, employing children in "degrading, unlawful, or immoral callings," and neglecting them in terms of food, clothing, shelter, and care (Pleck 1987, 83). In other words, cruelty included the effects of poverty and the behaviors associated with poverty that were seen as problematic by the child savers. It was not just (or even mainly) about the physical abuse or willful neglect of children.[7] In fact, in examining the records of SPCCs in Philadelphia and Chicago, Elizabeth Pleck found that most cases involved various forms of neglect linked to poverty,[8] and SPCC officers were generally willing to overlook physical cruelty when parents were "otherwise temperate and industrious." In addition, much of the group's work focused on counseling families to follow middle-class patterns of a bread-winning father and caretaking mother (Pleck 1987, 81–84). This pattern of overt concern with severe abuse and neglect while day-to-day practices actually dealt with the effects of poverty on children's lives and attempted to enforce middle-class norms (with the threat of child removal as a "stick") runs through the history of child welfare up to the present.

In addition to the role they played in the control of poor, immigrant populations, the SPCCs were also used by poor families for their own ends. Families brought children to them to find a place for them in times of economic distress; women sought help from abuse at the hands of husbands; and reports to SPCCs were used as a way to settle disputes or as a weapon against family members and neighbors (Broder 2002). Gordon finds that the SPCCs did actually help women escape abusive husbands, and, in general, the presence of these agencies somewhat lessened patriarchal power (L. Gordon 1985). Poor women, however, experienced the SPCCs ambivalently; the women viewed the societies as sources of help but also commonly referred to them as "The Cruelty" (L. Gordon 1986; 1988) because women and children, of course, had the most to lose from SPCC intervention. As Linda Gordon notes, the most common outcome of agency action was not prosecution and jail sentences for men, but the removal of children (L. Gordon 1985, 219). This pattern is also apparent today: poor communities of color fear the intervention of child welfare and are critical of how the agency operates; at the same time, they sometimes turn to ACS for help in the absence of other options (see chapters 5 and 8).

Progressive Era (1900–1935) reforms, reflecting changing views of poverty (Ehrenreich 1985; Polsky 1991) and the idea that only the state was able to address the complex problems of modern society (Ehrenreich 1985; Kunzel 1993; Willrich 2003), created a bigger role for the state in child welfare. Reformers enlisted state power in child-saving efforts because they believed it would make their work more legitimate and thus more accepted by the poor and because the state had the power to force families to submit to therapeutic interventions and comply in a way that private philanthropists could not (Polsky 1991). As in earlier periods, child removal was often a solution to the problems faced by poor families. In contrast to earlier periods, however, children were more often placed in private foster homes with the help of separate courts for children (Platt 1977; Ryerson 1978, 3; Sobie 2003). New laws regulated the placement of children and allowed state agencies to inspect and close foster homes deemed unsuitable (Schneider and Deutsch 1941). These laws and the institution of the family court remain important today and have changed only partially from their origins. Some states also created mother's pensions to support women (mainly widows) who were raising children alone. Part of the argument for creating these pensions was that women living alone needed support so that their children would not have to be removed from their home "for poverty alone" (Pelton 1989, 10). This link between antipoverty policy and child welfare practice also remains important today.

Partially reflecting an increased role for women in reform efforts and a larger societal shift toward valuing a mother's nurturing and seeing it as essential to the proper upbringing of children (Mason 1994), the focus of child-saving organizations shifted to neglect, which was thought of as a failure of mothering, rather than cruelty. Emerging definitions of neglect tended to conflate it with poverty and reflected the class-based expectations of a proper home environment held by middle-class philanthropists. For example, the Massachusetts SPCC list of "elements and factors" in their cases included many elements reflecting moral concerns (drinking, illegitimacy, divorce, women living alone, sexual activity among girls), parental characteristics (insanity or "feeble-mindedness"), as well as physical neglect and delinquency (L. Gordon 1988, 77). Many of the definitions of physical neglect included assumptions about a proper upbringing and home environment that "were not only inaccessible to, but unimaginable by, turn-of-the-century agency clients" (L. Gordon 1988, 121). Children playing in the streets, children under twelve minding their siblings, and children contributing to the household through their own work all qualified as physical neglect. Although these were the realities of poor family life at the time (L. Gordon 1988), they were labeled neglect and blamed on individual mothers. In some cases Gordon examined, it seemed that the children were in danger from abuse, but the worker was focused on convincing the parents to marry (L. Gordon 1988, 134)!

As an example of how the conflation of poverty with neglect worked in practice, Gordon cites the case of a single father during Prohibition who was reported by neighbors because his children were not supervised, were running in the street, and were inadequately clothed and fed. Although he received money from public welfare, he complained that it did not come regularly and that he still did not have enough money for food. The MSPCC pressured him to get rid of his housekeeper, who was supposed to care for the children, because neighbors said she was unreliable and drank. He became angry with caseworkers, but complied. Despite hiring several other women, the children were still not supervised. The neglect allegations made by the MSPCC were "inadequate food, inadequate child care, and a father's hostile response to agency workers" (L. Gordon 1988, 122). Here it is clear that the father's poverty was the cause of the problem, and his attitude toward caseworkers was faulted as well. This case is eerily similar to cases I encountered in my fieldwork (see chapter 7 and the case of a Haitian immigrant father in particular).

Thus, as Gordon demonstrates, the regulation of poor life and the upholding of middle-class notions of morality were at least as important as child maltreatment to the SPCCs. Despite the belief that poverty alone should not lead to family break-up, emerging ideas of child neglect allowed for the conflation of neglect with poverty and did not provide guidance for deciding parental culpability (L. Gordon 1988, chap. 5). This situation is still, to an extent, present today. Despite decades of social work practice and research, definitions of neglect, as they are used in practice, remain murky and continue to allow for the conflation of poverty with neglect (see chapter 6).

The Great Depression to the 1960s: Shifting Demographics in Child Welfare

This period showed little change in the overall structure of the child welfare system, although the state did expand its role in small ways. In New York City, most cases of child maltreatment were brought to the courts by the SPCC, which was the only agency solely responsible for investigating reports until 1962 (Polier 1974; Sobie 1987). The Bureau of Child Welfare (BCW) was created in 1940 to determine eligibility for Aid to Dependent Children (ADC, created by the federal government in 1935), to find placement for children who were removed from "unsuitable" homes, and to supervise the payment of ADC funds to private agencies for the care of children who were removed. Placements were almost always with private, religious institutions that were subsidized by tax money. Although the BCW was authorized to investigate maltreatment, they rarely did so and usually referred cases of suspected maltreatment to the SPCC. Temporary shelters for children who were awaiting placement with a foster family, initially created and run by the SPCC, were taken over by the city in 1945, and the city did come to run a small number of foster homes and adoption assistance agencies during the mid-twentieth century (Kahn 1961).

The demographics of the poor population did profoundly change from being largely European immigrant to African American and Puerto Rican. Members of both groups were often displaced farmers or farm laborers fleeing unemployment (Drake 1945; Freeman 2000; Rodriguez 1989; Tolnay

2003). African Americans also moved from the South to northern cities to escape Jim Crow laws and violence. Except for a few years during World War II, they faced a situation of chronic unemployment or underemployment in the lowest rungs of the occupational ladder (Freeman 2000, chap. 11; Tolnay 2003). They were confined to racially segregated neighborhoods in the least desirable areas of the city with dilapidated housing (Drake 1945; Freeman 2000, chap. 11; Tolnay 2003). In response to these stresses, the rate of family break-up among African American migrants increased (Gutman 1976), but networks of extended kin and friends allowed for the care of children and the pooling of resources (Stack 1974). Although eligibility rules for the newly created ADC program were less restrictive in northern cities (Piven and Cloward 1993), poverty and discrimination led many Black families to become involved with the child welfare system. In contrast, despite often being more economically disadvantaged than many African Americans (Freeman 2000, chap. 11), the percentage of Puerto Rican children involved with child welfare was far less than that of African American children. This shift is reflected in Judge Justine Wise Polier's account of the cases that came before her in July and August of 1938, the first report I found that recorded the race/ethnicity of the children: 47.2 percent were white, 43.4 percent black, and 9.4 percent Puerto Rican. As in the past, most of these children were poor: 64 percent came from families on some kind of public assistance, and 6.5 percent came from families with no discernible income (Polier 1974, 113).

Polier describes the inadequacies of the system, especially for black children who faced blatant discrimination. She complained, quite forcefully, about agencies that were allowed to make their own eligibility rules and could reject whichever children they chose while many children remained in institutions with few efforts to place them in individual homes or to work toward their return home. Few agencies would accept "negro" children,[9] and thus many judges hesitated to find them neglected and in need of placement. They remained in "improper home situations until behavior difficulties appear[ed]," and then they had to be placed in institutions for delinquent children which were more often public and accepted all children (Polier 1974, 240–241). If neglected black children *were* removed from their homes, they were likely to remain in severely overcrowded "temporary shelters" for months or even years in some cases (Polier 1974, 245; see also Rosner and Markowitz 1997).[10] Alternatively, judges labeled them delinquent to allow placement in New York State–run training schools

(Rosner and Markowitz 1997, 1846).[11] This situation did not change substantially until the 1980s when a class-action lawsuit against the agencies, *Wilder v. Bernstein*, was finally settled.[12] By this time, however, minority children made up an overwhelming percentage of the child welfare caseload (as they did during my research). Inadequate resources and race- and class-biased practices still, in the second decade of the twenty-first century, mean that these children are not served in the ways that they deserve.

1960s and 1970s: The Creation of Modern State Child Protection

> The unfortunate turn federal legislation took in child protection in the 1970s was to make it into an arm of the police with primary investigative and removal powers. A great opportunity was lost to transform child welfare into a program that served the needs of vulnerable families. (Guggenheim 2005, 211–212)

For a variety of reasons—the centrality of the medical profession in "rediscovering" and defining maltreatment, an increasingly conservative political climate, and the racial politics surrounding discussions of poverty—the state system created at this time focused narrowly on simply reporting individual cases of abuse and neglect. Rather than becoming a mechanism to serve the needs of families, the system was tied even more firmly to state structures of policing, investigative and law enforcement functions even more strongly overshadowed helping functions, and child removal remained the main solution to family problems.

With the increasing use of x-ray technology in the 1950s, pediatricians and radiologists started to document repeated injuries in children, and Dr. C. Harry Kempe's coining of the term "the battered child syndrome" brought attention to the problem. This "syndrome," a set of symptoms (that is, injuries and their psychological effects), was associated with the "disease" of inadequate parenting (Pleck 1987, 171). This language implied that parents who beat their children were sick and deserved help and treatment rather than criminal prosecution (Nelson 1984). The necessary intervention to cure the disease was protection of the child in foster care while the parents completed therapy and parenting training (Pleck 1987, 170). Dr. Kempe also argued that, if presented with a choice between parents' right to custody and a child's safety, the bias should favor safety. Since doctors were often reluctant to report injuries that seemed deliberately inflicted, laws requiring reporting were needed.[13] The term, and the fact that it came from the medical profession, went a long way toward focusing attention on child abuse and bringing it to the attention of federal and state governments (Nelson 1984).

Those who pushed for a government response to the problem of child abuse argued that it could happen in any class group. This made proposals for government involvement in families seem warranted and removed child maltreatment from an association with poverty policy, which, by the 1960s had again become politically unpopular. As a result of these developments, between 1963 and 1967 every state passed a bill requiring certain professionals to report child abuse and set up "hotlines" or other methods to allow anyone to report suspected cases (Pleck 1987, 169–173). That "no other piece of modern social legislation has been so quickly adopted by all the states" (Pleck 1987, 173) reflects the level of public concern about severe child abuse and the fact that that the proposed solution seemed relatively simple and low-cost (Nelson 1984). Most states, however, were not prepared for the flood of calls they received after the passage of mandated reporting laws;[14] thus, child protective services had to be expanded across the country, often with inadequate budgets. In addition, little thought was given to dealing with the numbers of children placed in foster care. Almost as quickly as the mandated reporting system was created, it was viewed as in crisis. There was a flood of reports, and scholars and observers became concerned that reports were too often made needlessly while necessary reports were still not made often enough. (Besharov and Laumann 1996; Hutchinson 1993; Lukens 2007). This situation persists today.

Changes in federal poverty policy, Aid to Families with Dependent Children (or AFDC, the name was changed from Aid to Children, or ADC, in 1962), also greatly impacted child welfare during this period. In 1961, the secretary of the U.S. Department of Health, Education, and Welfare, Dr. Arthur Flemming, informed states that they could still create their own rules regarding "suitable homes" to which aid would be given, but that they could no longer use the mother's conduct to deny funding to the child. Under the "Flemming Rule," which was made law by later amendments to the Social Security Act, states were required to report neglectful families to the courts and provide services "to address parents' inability to properly provide childcare" (Lawrence-Webb 1997). If the child was removed from the home, then money that would have gone to the family would be used to pay for foster care (Frame 1999; Hacsi 1995).

In many states, caseworkers who were responsible for determining AFDC eligibility were not qualified to provide help in situations of maltreatment. Therefore, if abuse or neglect was suspected, many removed the children from the home (Lawrence-Webb 1997).[15] The Flemming Rule thus "placed welfare mothers' parenting under greater scrutiny while a bridge to child protection was established through foster care. If mothers were deemed 'unfit' even after social workers provided services, federal monies could be withdrawn from the mother but were still available to the child through foster placement" (Frame 1999, 729). After this change, the numbers of children in foster care overall (Hacsi 1995) and the percentages of Black children (Billingsley and Giovannoni 1972; Roberts 2002) increased dramatically.

The first federal law regarding child maltreatment, The Child Abuse Prevention and Treatment Act (CAPTA), was passed in 1973 in an attempt to deal with the issues created by mandated reporting and the increasing numbers of children in foster care that resulted from increasing reports and enforcing the Flemming Rule. Walter Mondale, chairman of the recently created Senate Subcommittee on Children, proposed the legislation after a failed attempt to pass a comprehensive bill to fund social services for all children.[16] He then switched tactics and worked to secure federal funding for child abuse prevention. The hearings leading up to the bill were dominated by testimony about severe child abuse and by a medicalized view of the "epidemic" of child abuse and the need to stop the "cycle of violence" before the victimized child grew up to become criminal or violent himself (Pleck 1987, 177). This narrow, medicalized view and individualized focus allowed both liberal and conservative legislators to support CAPTA.

Under CAPTA, states were required to meet federal guidelines for reporting, investigating, and providing treatment for child abuse and neglect in order to qualify for federal funding. The law authorized state agencies to remove endangered children from their homes for three days during which time they had to bring the case to court to file for custody to keep the child out of the home (Ashby 1997, 135–137). Funds were also made available for child abuse prevention, but these could only be used in cases in which the child would have been eligible for AFDC (Shireman

2003), a policy that again shows the link between poverty and maltreatment. This policy both devised a role for the family courts and institutionalized funding priorities for foster care over prevention and family services that still persist today. Little thought was given to foster care itself and what to do after children were removed—an oversight that caused profound problems in later years.

Despite the fact that the modern system was created out of concern with severe abuse, poor children were still those most often removed from their homes, usually for neglect, which was still poorly defined. During this time, the regulation of poor families through child welfare shifted more directly to the state and was focused increasingly on families of color. The politics surrounding race and tackling poverty, now largely imagined to be a problem of inner-city Black populations, largely shaped efforts to deal with a growing foster care population in the following decades.

1970s and 1980s: Crisis and Reform

The 1970s and 1980s saw important reforms in child welfare that attempted to deal with a foster care population continually growing from the combined effects of the Flemming Rule, mandated reporting, and increasing inequalities (Pelton 1989; Tobis 1989): efforts to fund foster care prevention and a "permanency planning" movement (Pelton 1989).[17] The mid-1970s brought an economic downturn as well as, in New York City and other large cities, deindustrialization (Bluestone and Harrison 1982) and the growth of a two-tiered service economy. These trends greatly exacerbated inequalities and increased poverty and homelessness (Mollenkopf and Castells 1991). The growth of the informal economy in poor neighborhoods sometimes took the form of illegal drug selling, which created more violence both within communities (gangs and domestic violence) and in the form of state-sanctioned violence like the war on drugs and the growing incarceration of poor and minority people (Bourgois 2003; Mullings 2003; Sharff 1998; Wacquant 2001, 2008). These economic and social changes were accompanied by the rise of rhetoric that not only blamed the poor for their own poverty but also charged that providing money to impoverished families was itself a cause of poverty because it created intergenerational dependency and irresponsible mothers (Williams 1995).

These societal changes led to a greater need for family services, but policy efforts sought to contain costs and limited money for prevention programs while continuing to fund foster care. The permanency planning movement within child welfare, driven by concerns with an increasing foster care population and the newly documented harms to children from placement, also influenced policy changes at both the state and federal levels. Influenced by the controversial theory that children needed a secure and permanent connection to a "psychological parent" (Goldstein, Freud, and Solnit 1973), permanency planning was an effort to ensure that children would not experience long periods in foster care and multiple moves from foster home to foster home.[18] Such limited time in foster care was to be accomplished by planning for a permanent arrangement (either return home or adoption) quickly and by reviewing the cases of children in foster care periodically to ensure this occurred. The movement did not, by and large, focus on preventing foster care placement in the first place but rather on dealing with the large numbers of children who were placed (Pelton 1989, 79–80). Federal and state laws, however, did attempt to mandate foster care prevention efforts, mainly in an effort to control costs.

In New York State, the Child Welfare Reform Act of 1979 provided funding for preventive services, required agencies to offer them before foster care placement, and mandated that the state develop standards for assessing whether foster care was necessary and for promoting permanency.[19] It attempted to control costs by placing a ceiling on foster care funding and by denying reimbursement to agencies that did not create standards, violated standards, or failed to implement permanency planning (Sobie 1987; Tobis 1989). At the federal level, the Adoption Assistance and Child Welfare Act, which used the New York State law as a model (Tobis 1989), was passed in 1980. It similarly aimed to prevent foster care placement when possible and promoted adoption if reunification was not feasible. The law made continued federal funding for foster care contingent upon a state plan to reduce the numbers of children in care for more than two years, a written case plan for each child, and six-month reviews of their placements. The legislation created more federal funding for preventive programs, but such funding remained inadequate and much smaller than foster care funding (Pelton 1989; Reich 2005; Roberts 2002; Wexler 1995).[20] These funding priorities are the same today. The act also required that agencies make "reasonable efforts" to prevent foster care placement and promote family reunification. Finally, the law stipulated that, before foster care placement, a judge must determine that reasonable efforts have been made and that leaving the child at home would be "contrary to the welfare" of the child (Reich 2005; Shireman 2003). These policies remain the basis of foster care practice and form the legal framework that continues to govern family court.

These policies did create a short-term dip in the numbers of children placed in foster care (Pelton 1989; Reich 2005; Roberts 2002; Wexler 1995), but the population increased again in the mid-1980s. Although this change was commonly attributed to the crack cocaine "epidemic" (see, for example, Reich 2005, 43), the causes are more complex than this.[21] I want to examine this period in some detail because the views that shaped how crack cocaine was dealt with are still largely present thirty years later. These views also influenced the creation of the most significant piece of child welfare legislation that shapes the system in its current form. Here it is important to question both why child welfare responded as it did and how this was related to an increasingly conservative political climate. In this climate politicians took a "get tough" stance on crime, especially drug-related crime, and policy makers and the public tended to blame the poor, especially poor women of color, for their own poverty and for various social problems. In this context, parents who used illegal drugs, especially poor women of color who used crack cocaine, were demonized and dealt with through either the criminal justice system or child removal. In fact, this pattern of dealing with drug cases is still largely unchanged and represented in my research (see chapters 5 and 6).

I want to be clear that the drug trade, which became a more important part of the informal economy of inner-city communities in the mid-1980s, *did* have deleterious effects on these communities. Violence escalated (Mullings 2003), and, since crack cocaine also was also one of the first drugs to pull in large numbers of women, children were affected (Humphries 1993). My critique of how officials dealt with crack cocaine is not meant to deny these negative effects. Nevertheless, it is necessary to highlight the fact that child welfare officials dealt with the problem in a largely punitive manner by either removing children from their homes or by initiating criminal and civil prosecution. Increased provision of drug treatment, preventive services to the family, and concerted efforts to avoid placement were not the solutions government agencies tried (Gomez 1997; Humphries 1993; Ortiz and Briggs 2003; Roberts 1991, 1997; Zerai and

Banks 2002). A panic about drug abuse among poor women of color and its effects created a climate in which removals to foster care seemed the only solution; exploring and funding alternatives lost traction. Hospitals began to institute drug-testing programs that almost exclusively affected poor women and women of color,[22] and many women lost children immediately after birth if they tested positive. When the foster care system was unable to handle the children removed, the capacity of the system and its funding were increased (Ortiz and Briggs 2003, 47).

In New York City, the child welfare system was overwhelmed. Beginning in late 1985 a bed crisis emerged in which caseworkers had a very difficult time finding homes for children who then spent long periods in offices and hospitals awaiting placement. The situation was largely due to a declining number of foster care beds, but the press attributed the crisis to crack cocaine (Tobis 1989).[23] My informants who worked in the system during that time described a flood of cases and an inability to keep up. Even those who weren't working in the system at the time often referred to the crack epidemic. Despite evidence that the negative effects of crack were grossly exaggerated, caseworkers and attorneys still treated mothers who used drugs in a similar fashion and argued that drug use, especially crack, was almost automatically harmful. Some in family court were still in panic about crack cocaine use and believed in its supposedly hyperaddictive properties, severe harm to unborn children, and extremely detrimental effects on women's ability to care for their children. These beliefs persisted despite the fact that research has shown them to be false (Humphries 1993; Reinarman and Levine 1997; Zerai and Banks 2002). I discovered the persistent misinformation during a conversation with an ACS attorney about drug cases: I mentioned that the evidence shows that children born positive for crack do not suffer the widespread, long-term ill effects that were reported at the beginning of the "crack epidemic" in the late 1980s; he looked at me as if I were completely crazy, argued this could not be true, and reiterated that crack was extremely harmful to children.

During this period of increased fiscal and social conservatism, then, attempts at reform fell short as prevention and reunification efforts were underfunded and as poor mothers of color were increasingly dealt with punitively. The following decades saw an even sharper move away from supportive services as poverty and child welfare policies were reformed again, largely justified by negative stereotypes of poor, black mothers.

1990s to the Present: The Adoption and Safe Families Act

In the context of a strong political right and the hegemony of neoliberal ideas, the welfare and child welfare systems were further reformed. Proposals to "end welfare as we know it" drew on conservative ideas that welfare itself was a cause of poverty and argued that stricter work requirements and time limits were necessary (Waldfogel 2004). Some media and political accounts explicitly linked welfare to child abuse and neglect by Latina and African American mothers. This connection reinforced the perception that welfare was utilized mainly by women of color who were "immoral, deviant, dysfunctional—and solely responsible for every physical and behavioral problem of their children" (Williams 1995, 1191–1192). These images underpinned calls by some conservatives to end welfare benefits to unwed mothers and to use the money to house their children in orphanages or foster care instead (Ortiz and Briggs 2003; Williams 1995).[24] The detrimental effects of poverty itself on child well-being and the well-documented problems that children in foster care often developed were not well publicized.

In this climate Congress passed the Adoption and Safe Families Act (ASFA). The legislation made important changes to federal child welfare policy and, like welfare reform, placed limits on the amount of help to which poor families would be entitled. In fact, most provisions of ASFA were originally part of the Personal Responsibility and Work Opportunity Reconciliation Act of 1996, or welfare reform (Ortiz and Briggs 2003). As one of the bill's few opponents, Rep. Patsy Mink, commented during debate around AFSA: "First you take their money away. Then you force them into desperate conditions of poverty. Then you deem them unfit to raise their children . . . and place [the children] in foster homes. Then after 18 months you put the children up for adoption. Whose family values do we stand for?" Concerns that the child welfare system was another way the government was spending too much on the undeserving poor also drove support for ASFA. Conservatives pointed to the sheer growth of the child welfare system as well as to an increase in kinship foster care which "stirred enormous public anger about the possibility for relatives of 'bad' parents boarding their children simply to obtain extra money from the state."[25] Data that showed a particular type of family preservation service was less effective than originally thought also raised questions about family preservation services more generally (McGowan and Walsh 2000, 13–14).

ASFA overtly addressed the concerns that "efforts to reunite children with their birth families have favored parental rights over a child's safety and need for stability in care" (Stein 2000, 587) and that children were spending too long in foster care. Lawmakers gained much support for the law by pointing to a small number of horror stories that represent the small numbers of cases involving serious abuse or death of children at the hands of their parents. In many of these accounts, "the implication [was] that lives were lost because social workers were attending too much to family preservation and reunification" (Stein 2000, 587). Thus, under AFSA, the "key principle" governing decisions about child placement is that "the child's health and safety shall be the paramount concern,"[26] and reasonable efforts can be denied completely in some circumstances.[27] The law also limited the time families could receive reunification and prevention services and focused on the problem of long foster care stays through a quicker route to adoption. Termination of parental rights must be initiated for a child who has been in foster care for fifteen of the last twenty-two months, except in certain circumstances,[28] and permanency planning must begin immediately. Permanency hearings are to be held within twelve months of the child's removal from the home, and states are supposed to encourage concurrent planning: caseworkers simultaneously plan for the child to return home and to be adopted. The act also provided assistance and financial incentives to increase the number of adoptions and provided tax breaks for families who adopt special needs or hard-to-place children.[29] The act did not, however, completely abandon either family preservation or the idea that reasonable efforts were required. It reauthorized family preservation and support services (that is, money to provide services to parents in an effort to avoid placing the child in foster care) and added some funding for *time-limited* family reunification services including counseling, substance abuse treatment, mental health services, temporary childcare, and transportation to and from any services. The list indicates that the law continues to see parents' individual problems as the causes of child maltreatment, despite evidence of the connection between poverty and child neglect, and placing time limits assumes parents will not change unless they are forced to.

Although this law is laudable in its attempts to deal with profound problems in child welfare, it does not address the systemic reasons for long foster care stays: court delays, lack of services, and lack of clarity about what reasonable efforts are and how they should be made (Moye and Rinker 2002; Stein 2003). It also doesn't necessarily create permanency for children because there is no guarantee that adoptive homes will be found when children are freed for adoption (Guggenheim 1996). Moreover, the law is problematic for the poor parents of color who are the main clients of child welfare. In large part because these parents are poor women of color, the state assumes them to be irresponsible and in need of strict rules to force them to take responsibility. This law, like welfare reform, took an approach that blamed individuals for family problems that are closely related to poverty, which is, in turn, closely related to gender and race inequalities. In the absence of better and more comprehensive services, these families often cannot deal with these problems on a strict timeline. In my mind, the more productive way to address the concern with children spending too much time in foster care is to reduce the number of placements in the first place by limiting the use of foster care to only the worst cases of abuse and severe and willful neglect (see also Guggenheim 2005). The savings from this approach could then be used to more adequately fund universal services to deal with the long-term problems faced by poor families of color, whether they are involved with child welfare or not.[30]

These national trends were likewise reflected in New York City reforms. In 1996, in response to the high-profile death of a child "known to the system" and to a lawsuit,[31] Mayor Rudolph Giuliani restructured CWA and renamed it the Administration for Children's Services (ACS). The new commissioner created a comprehensive reform plan that "all but equated child protection with child removal" (Bernstein 2001, 437). It stated that "any ambiguity regarding the safety of the child will be resolved in favor of removing the child from harm's way" and that only when families demonstrated that "their homes are safe and secure" would children be returned to their parents (Bernstein 2001, 437). Child welfare cases that stemmed from poverty were increasingly handled as crimes: "Poor mothers were led away in handcuffs because they had left a child unattended while trying to buy milk at the grocery store, or because a child had wandered away during a family eviction" (Bernstein 2001, 438). This change in agency policy thus came down hardest on poor mothers for matters related to poverty. This shift was in keeping with other aspects of the Giuliani administration, which emphasized a punitive tough-on-crime approach.[32] Aspects of this attitude were still evident during my research, conducted in the aftermath of a high-profile case of a death of another child "known to the system" (see chapter 4).

Conclusion

Although the child welfare system has long purported to be about protecting children from the worst forms of harm at the hands of their parents, it has always affected poor families far more often than other families, it has always mainly dealt with cases of neglect that are difficult to separate from poverty, and it has always been closely related to, and intertwined with, ideas and policies about poverty, its causes, and its solutions. Furthermore, child removal has been the intervention more often made in child welfare cases, despite a persistent belief that parents' rights to their children are important and should be protected and despite rhetoric since at least 1909 that children should not be removed from their families only due to poverty. In general, we spend more money to support children living away from their parents than we do on the essential services that would help families improve the material conditions of their lives and enable them to raise their children safely. Definitions of neglect have tended to blur the lines between the willful denying of care from children and the inability to provide for them adequately. At the same time, moral concerns about family and maternal behavior have been central to child welfare practices, and the state has dealt punitively with family issues that often stem from conditions of poverty. Although this aspect of American policy and practice has been guided by a genuine concern for children, it is also a piece of how poor and nonwhite families and populations have been regulated. As the child welfare system has come to deal almost exclusively with the problems of poor families of color, it has become harsher and more punitive. As the focus has explicitly narrowed to child protection, the system has often focused on policing these families and on providing foster care services rather than on providing the help that struggling parents need.

The current child welfare system begins with two main underlying assumptions that are fundamentally tied to this history: (1) child maltreatment has individual, as opposed to social-structural, causes; and (2) services should focus narrowly on protecting children, caring for them when they cannot be at home, and reforming parents so that they stop pathological behaviors. These assumptions are fundamental to how this system creates and re-creates stratified reproduction.

As Jane Waldfogel writes, "to the extent that parents are seen as perpetrators, it is assumed that they are part of the problem, not part of the solution." Furthermore, as in a criminal investigation, the state assumes that parents will not cooperate without the threat or use of state authority in the form of court-ordered services or child removal (1998, 69). Thus, child welfare more closely resembles policing than assisting (Lukens 2007). The initial investigative focus leaves parents with very little power in dealing with caseworkers (see chapter 7 and Reich 2005) and sets up an adversarial situation because, in many cases, parents are aware that the information being collected by caseworkers might become evidence in court. The tension created also makes accepting help from child welfare officials difficult for many parents, which often slows the process of reunification (see chapter 5).

The prominent model of child abuse implicit in this orientation is that it is mainly a problem of "parental pathology/dysfunction or incompetence" (McConnell and Llewellyn 2005, 555) that can be cured by helping parents overcome their pathologies (Erickson 2000; McConnell and Llewellyn 2005). The model assumes that the rights and needs of children are opposed to the rights and needs of adults and should be the main criteria in decision making (Anglin 2002; Collings and Davies 2008; Golden 1997; Guggenheim 2005; Kline 1992). The view that child welfare is dealing with competing rights and needs and is primarily investigative accounts for the increasing role of the family court. This is, of course, a profoundly inadequate model. Research has consistently found that child protection cases involve families dealing with poverty, social isolation, disability, addiction, and other similar issues and that parents generally lack the means, both in terms of material resources and social support, to deal with stressful situations and their personal problems (McConnell and Llewellyn 2005, 554). In many cases, helping the parent with resources can help create a stronger and safer family for children.

Second, child welfare services remain, both by necessity and by design, narrowly focused. As Martin Guggenheim asserts, "ours is a culture struggling over how to help innocent children but not to support their 'undeserving' parents" (2005, 196). Given the pervasive American belief that individual parents bear sole responsibility for the care of children, the system takes a "residual approach" and only becomes involved when the family is already in crisis and a child's needs are not being met (Lindsey 1994, 2). When this approach is coupled with an understanding of child maltreatment that is individual rather than social, "the rules of child welfare insist that all systemic explanations for deficiencies in marginal families' capacities to raise children safely at home are out of bounds for consideration or discussion. We enter child welfare within well-defined limits of what is up for discussion. If families need certain basic goods such as income support, better housing, child care assistance, respite care, or the like, they are, for all practical purposes, outside the field" (Guggenheim 2006, 835). This view is closely related to the fact that the majority of families involved with child welfare are poor and disproportionately African American and Native American. In the larger context of declining support for poor families of color, funding for foster care prevention and family reunification services is limited, especially as compared to funding for foster care itself (Guggenheim 2005, 189). In the end, "when parental deviance is the foremost explanatory factor, child protection authorities are more likely to 'see' children in need of removal rather than families in need of support" (McConnell and Llewellyn 2005, 561). Because the public generally sees these families as dysfunctional and these mothers as irresponsible, this view is easier to maintain.

3

The Life of a Child Welfare Case

In chapter 3, I describe the ideal process of a child welfare case from the initial report to the eventual reunification of the family or termination of parental rights. Very few cases follow all the guidelines, and the process is rarely smooth. I discuss the normal delays, missed steps, mistakes, and detours later. Readers who are familiar with the system can move to chapter 4.

A child welfare case begins when a call is made to the State Central Register of Child Abuse and Neglect (SCR). Anyone can make a call and can choose to remain anonymous, but mandated reporters have an obligation to call if, while doing their jobs, they have reasonable cause to suspect a child is being maltreated or might be harmed by their parent or caretaker. The list of professionals with this obligation is lengthy and includes all medical and mental health professionals, social workers, substance abuse counselors, school officials, child care workers, law enforcement officials, and researchers on some federal grants. Mandated reporters are immune from liability regarding a report if they act in good faith, which is presumed to be the case if they report within the context of their job. At the same time, failure to report is a criminal offense that can leave individuals civilly liable and at risk of losing their jobs. Materials posted on New York

State's website for mandated reporters expressly encourage professionals to report if they have *any* suspicions that a child is being maltreated.

The SCR operator asks the caller to describe the suspicions and/or what has been seen. If the operator decides to accept the report, it is sent to the local child protective office. Operators screen calls differently, and some operators give more scrutiny to reports than others.[1] The report that the operator generates has the basic information about the family given to the SCR by the caller—the number of children, their approximate ages, their names, the parents'/caretakers' names—a list of all prior reports and whether they were indicated (that is, the caseworker found evidence of maltreatment) or unfounded (that is, no evidence was found), and a narrative containing the allegations as given by the caller. If the caller was a mandated reporter, their name and contact info is listed, and this information is listed for other callers unless they opt to remain anonymous. The report is then sent electronically to the Administration for Children's Services (ACS) Field Office that is responsible for the area of the city in which the family lives. At the field office, the case is given to a unit appropriate for both the kind of case and the geographic area in which the family lives. The report goes to a supervisor who assigns it to a caseworker, either to one who is well suited to handle the case, to one who has dealt with the family in the past, or to the one who is next in the rotation.[2]

Once a caseworker is assigned, within twenty-four hours she must go to the home and attempt physically to see the children and speak with the parents. In conducting her investigation she takes multiple steps: interviews all members of the household (this includes parents and others "legally responsible" for a child); collects basic demographic information; gets a list of all caretakers; and obtains information about the children's doctors, therapists, medications they take, any special needs, and a list of teachers and schools. Caseworkers are also supposed to speak to doctors, school officials, and any other collaterals who are warranted to get their assessments of the child and information about whether medical and educational needs are being met. Caseworkers might also request that parents take a drug test and often ask about parents' own medical or mental health needs/providers if allegations (past or present) involved drug or mental health issues. During the investigation stage it is important to note that caseworkers, who hold more power in these interactions, can legally only *request* a drug test, but parents realize that failing to comply with requests can mean a loss of custody (see chapter 7). Parental ability to refuse is thus very limited.

Within seven days, the caseworker must complete a safety assessment of the home. This assessment includes items such as the presence of smoke detectors and window guards, adequate sleeping arrangements, cleanliness of the home, availability of adequate food supplies and clean clothing, working condition of utilities and bathrooms, and absence of fire hazards. This checklist is used to determine the basic level of safety in the home, and caseworkers must deal with any safety issues immediately.

Within thirty days the caseworker will also complete a risk assessment that evaluates various factors, such as the number of prior reports, inadequate housing, limited financial resources, alcohol or drug abuse, domestic violence, and so on, all of which are thought to be able to predict those children who are more likely to be maltreated in the future.[3] The caseworker notes the presence or absence of these factors, and a computer generates a risk score. Cases that are high or very high risk should be kept open for services, and cases can be classified at this level of risk even if the initial allegations in the case are not found to be true. These assessments should be used to classify which cases warrant services because it is not possible to provide services to all families. Ideally, risk assessment should help determine when foster care placement is warranted, but caseworkers did not discuss assessments, except as paperwork to be completed, and they seem to play very little if any role in decision making. If services seem warranted, then usually another caseworker (either from another branch of ACS or at another agency) conducts a more comprehensive assessment of what is needed.

Caseworkers have sixty days to make a determination about the allegations in the case. If there is credible evidence of maltreatment, then the case is marked indicated; if not, the case is marked unfounded or unsubstantiated. This determination, made in consultation with supervisors, must be approved by them. Supervisors can ask the caseworker to gather more information, to double-check things, to ask questions in a different way, or even to change their decisions.

If the case is unfounded, then it is generally closed, but services may be offered. If a case is indicated, the caseworker can take several steps. In order, corresponding to the level of risk from low to high, she can: (1) close the case,[4] (2) offer services and close the case, (3) keep the case open to monitor that the services are done (usually telling the parent that if he or she does not engage in services the caseworker will either bring the parent to court or take the child to foster care), (4) go to court to ask that services and/or behaviors be mandated, (5) go to court to ask for a removal, or (6) remove the child on an emergency basis. Most cases that result in removal are done on an emergency basis; I almost never saw caseworkers come to court first.[5] Sometimes, family conferences are held to ensure a parent is in services, arrange for a court order of protection to keep a caretaker away from a child, and/or arrange for the child to be cared for outside the home by a relative or family friend, either by informal agreement or through a formal foster care arrangement.[6]

If foster care or court intervention is the plan for the family, then an attorney is generally consulted (one is assigned to each field office) to make sure that the basic legal criteria for abuse or neglect exist before the caseworker seeks these interventions. If a child is removed on an emergency basis, the caseworker has two options: she must either get the parent to sign a form that gives consent to place the child temporarily in foster care and then bring the case to court within three business days, or, if the parent refuses to sign or is not present, then she must go to court within twenty-four hours.[7] The family court is responsible for weighing the evidence of harm to decide whether state intervention is warranted, and this determination structures how cases are handled from the beginning. The stated goal is to remove children from their parents' custody only in circumstances of harm or severe risk, and this goal is supposed to be accomplished by balancing parents' right to raise their children with childrens' right to safety (see chapter 6; Bailie 1998; Guggenheim 2007).

Once the investigation is completed or the court is involved, the case moves to a different caseworker. If the child remains with the parents, the case goes to an intensive foster care prevention program such as the Family Preservation Program (FPP) within ACS or to a similar program at a foster care prevention agency (see below). If the family is under supervision by the family court, it goes to a Family Support Unit at ACS. If the child is in foster care, a foster care agency is given the case. There are numerous foster care and preventive agencies around the city. Although they are formally private, nonprofit agencies with their own policies and procedures, they might more properly be called "quasi-governmental" because not only does a large portion (and in the case of newer and small agencies practically all) of their budgets come from the state and city but also their practices are bound by government regulations. They are contracted by ACS, and, if they lose these contracts, they will most likely close (or be incorporated into another agency) due to lack of funds and clients. Most of these agencies deal almost exclusively with families that are referred to them by ACS or mandated to participate in their programs by ACS or the family court.

Prevention programs are supposed to provide intensive services during a short period of time in an effort to avoid foster care placement. Caseworkers are supposed to have small caseloads so that they can visit the family often, make referrals, closely follow up with services, and keep tabs on the children's safety (Gelles 2000; Lindsey, Martin, and Doh 2002; Roberts 2002). These programs assume that families are in a temporary crisis, which can be solved mainly through having a caseworker readily available to them. Often, however, not enough of these intervention programs are available, caseworkers are not able to spend most of their time with parents, and the services for which parents need referrals are not available. Most important, this short-term, individualistic approach, which has a tendency to focus on counseling and home visits, cannot solve the complex problems such as dangerous neighborhoods, lack of jobs, substance abuse, and poverty that plague many of these families (Roberts 2002, 137–139). I also found that this kind of intensive casework often served as another level of surveillance rather than genuine help because preventive caseworkers were told to report problems to ACS immediately rather than attempt to solve the problem (see chapter 5).

When cases are transferred to agencies outside of ACS for foster care prevention or foster care services, efforts are made to connect families with agencies near their homes and to place children with either family members or in their neighborhoods. In many cases, however, children are placed in other neighborhoods or boroughs, and some parents are unable to find services and agencies near them, given long waiting lists. Such inaccessibility of required programming can make it difficult for parents to comply with caseworkers' mandates to avoid foster care placement and can make reunification difficult (see chapter 7).

If the family court is involved, then the legal process begins with the attorneys for ACS filing a petition. This process begins every morning when caseworkers discuss their cases briefly with a supervising attorney who asks for general information about the case and checks the evidence the caseworker has collected to see if the allegations fit the legal definition of neglect. If the attorney is neither satisfied that there is a cause of action nor sure of proceeding, then he or she can either send the caseworker to get more information or defer the case to be filed later. If the attorneys decide to file the case, they then discuss what relief they will be seeking from the judge. There are three choices: (1) Parole the child to the parent, which means the child stays in the home and the process of obtaining court-ordered supervision of the home begins. Court-ordered supervision means that the parent has to comply with certain conditions in order to retain custody (for example, enrolling in particular services, allowing caseworkers to come to the home to monitor the family, enforcing an order of protection to keep a boyfriend or father away from the mother and the children, not using drugs). (2) Parole the child to a relative, which means the child is removed from the home, placed with a relative who will not be a foster parent, and the home is unsupervised by a foster care agency. (3) Remand the child, which means placing him or her in foster care, either with a relative or in a foster home. The court can issue orders of protection in any case. The casework side of the agency, ideally, has the main responsibility for deciding which option they want, but the attorneys do have some input and can advise the caseworkers about whether the judge is likely to approve what they are seeking. The caseworkers, however, have not always decided what they believe is going on in the home and what intervention is warranted. In addition, some cases are brought to court precisely to substantially involve another set of decision makers (see chapter 4).

After the first step is decided, the case is assigned to an attorney. The lawyers are divided into teams of several attorneys who have intake on a particular day of the week, and team leaders assign cases. Once the case is assigned, the attorney talks to the caseworker to get more detailed information to use in drafting the petition. The petition is a legal document that explains why the child is neglected or abused, who is responsible for the maltreatment, why the child was removed or should be removed from the home (if applicable), and the reasonable efforts made to prevent the removal. Petitions are drafted with legal aims in mind—that is, proving and winning a case. When the petition is drafted, it is checked by a supervisor and then filed with the court clerk. Copies of all the petitions filed that day are then taken to the offices of the Legal Aid Society whose attorneys are assigned as law guardians for the child. Given that parents' and children's needs and rights are assumed to be in conflict, the law guardian is in court to advocate for the child's best interests. The law guardians similarly work in teams whose members get cases on particular days of the week. Each judge also takes cases on a particular day, and the judge on intake that day automatically receives the case, unless the family is or was before another judge; the case then might go to the judge of initial family contact.

Because there are a relatively few attorneys who handle these cases and, more important, given the way cases are assigned, sets of lawyers get to know one another quite well, might have several cases together, and are often in front of the same judges. According to the lawyers, this makes things go more smoothly because they can be in contact and get to know how the others work. I, however, found it also heightens the many parents' feeling that everyone is against them, that all sides are working together, and that they have no advocates in court (see chapter 7).

In the afternoon, the second part of the intake process begins when the attorneys assigned to the case and the parents, if they are present, are brought in for an initial hearing with the judge. The parents are asked about their income (judges vary on how detailed this questioning is). The vast majority of the time (I estimate at least 95 percent of the cases), the parents are eligible for assigned counsel, which means they make no more than 125 percent of the poverty line. If eligible, an attorney is assigned to them. Court-appointed attorneys are members of the 18B Panel and are often referred to as 18Bs.[8] The 18B panel is a set of independent lawyers who have been accepted to the panel by virtue of having expertise in family law, and they are paid by the state rather than their clients. Recently, new institutional providers, the Bronx Defenders, the Center for Family Representation, and the Brooklyn Family Defense Project, were given contracts to represent parents in child protective cases; these groups of lawyers, social workers, and parent advocates work together to represent and help parents,[9] and, if it is their day to get cases, one of the group's lawyers is assigned.

In the initial hearing, the judge reviews the petition, and the ACS attorney asks the judge to approve the relief the agency wants. The judge decides whether the allegations warrant the intervention sought. If she finds that the child is at risk in the home and needs protection, she then orders court supervision or the placement of the child in foster care. In general, these hearings are very short, usually ten to fifteen minutes. It is rare for the petition and the evidence for reasonable efforts to be examined, and there is generally no questioning of ACS and their plans for the family (see chapters 4 and 7). The legal standard for finding that a child should be placed in foster care is that he/she would be in imminent danger or at imminent risk if allowed to remain in the home so removal would be in his/her best interests. The judge must also rule on whether the agency made reasonable efforts to prevent the removal or if these should not be required due to the severity of the case or its emergency nature (such as if a child was in extreme danger or a parent was, for example, arrested and not available as a caretaker).

If parents are present, they might be given the opportunity to request, through the lawyer, that the judge have a full hearing about the case, which will require ACS to prove that their child would be at imminent risk. If ACS cannot, their child will be returned. Referred to as a 1028 hearing, this happens very rarely (see chapter 7). More commonly parents are able to request that their child be placed with a relative or family friend, but this only happens if the foster care agency decides that the chosen individual is suitable and the home is appropriate.[10] If parents are not present, they are at a disadvantage in that they will not have the opportunity to provide information that might change the outcome of the initial hearing. Also, if the children involved are older (at least age eleven or twelve, but this varies between law guardians), and they are present at court (which is rare), they can speak with their law guardian and tell her what they would like to happen. If the children say that they wish to remain at home, for example, their lawyer can advocate for this and possibly sway the judge. In my experience, the law guardian's advocacy generally carries more weight than what a parent asks for; if older children are present, they have a good chance of having their first choice honored (for example, either staying home or going to foster care).

After this initial hearing, the case proceeds as a legal matter in which the ACS attorney tries to prove the allegations and the parents' attorneys (ideally) defend them. The law guardian is there to represent the child's interests, but this advocacy varies by the age of the child. Generally a series of court conferences and appearances not only makes sure everyone has been properly served with court documents but also works out issues regarding visitation, explores "kinship resources" (i.e., family members who are willing to be foster parents), talks about what services the parent will be doing, and so forth. Eventually in a fact-finding hearing the judge decides on the truth of the allegations in the petition. Alternatively, there can be a settlement of the case so that a finding can be made without a trial. It is very common for cases to go on for *a year or more* before a fact-finding is held or a settlement reached, and settlements are far more common than fact-findings (see chapter 7). After the fact-finding or settlement, if there is sufficient evidence against the parents, a finding of abuse or neglect is entered against them, which stays on their record until the youngest child is twenty-eight years old. This finding bars the parent from many jobs, including many of those that are commonly held by poor women of color (home health aide, daycare worker, jobs at schools). It is extremely rare for a parent to win a fact-finding hearing or to end involvement with family court without a neglect finding (see chapter 7).

After a finding is made, a dispositional hearing is held. This is the first time parents can actually be ordered to complete services, but they are generally told they must do so from the beginning because getting more visits and unsupervised visits with their child are usually conditional on participating in services. For these reasons, many parents have done some or all of the services required of them by the time the dispositional hearing is held. At this time a plan is made about when a child in foster care might return home, how long the family will remain under ACS supervision after the child returns home, or how long supervision will continue if the child was never removed.

As these hearings dealing with the facts of the case proceed, a parallel process of judicial oversight of how the foster care agency is doing its job and/or of monitoring the parents and their services also occurs. This is the second important role of the family court. It is thought and hoped that judges will be impartial parties who can hold agencies and ACS accountable for following laws about reasonable efforts. Judges, however, cannot always closely scrutinize agencies due to crowded court calendars and lack of information, and it is rare for judges to refuse to find that agencies made reasonable efforts. Thus, meaningful oversight is, practically speaking, extremely limited (see chapters 4 and 7).

In terms of reasonable efforts, the judge should check to see that visitation is occurring (if the child is in foster care), that services are being offered and proper referrals made, and that conferences are being held. The judge asks the law guardian how the child is doing, and the parent is monitored and asked if he or she is attending visits and services. These issues are dealt with for at least a few minutes at all court appearances (most appearances are short, maybe ten to fifteen minutes) and take up far more time in family court than does scrutiny of the particular facts in the case or of the plans ACS has for a family (see chapters 4 and 7).

If the children are in foster care, after eight months and then every six months thereafter, a permanency hearing should be held. The purpose of these hearings, which are required by federal and state laws, is ideally to ensure that permanency planning is occurring so that children are not left to linger in foster care. A comprehensive report about the child and the case is supposed to be prepared and circulated to all parties two weeks prior to the hearing so that it can be read and the parent can prepare evidence if he or she disagrees with the report. During the permanency hearing the judge makes two crucial findings. First, she approves a permanency goal for the children—that is, what the planned permanent arrangement (as opposed to foster care) is for the child. Usually this goal is either return-to-parent, adoption, or a concurrent goal of both of these.[11] She must also decide whether the agency has been making reasonable efforts toward the goal. A finding that reasonable efforts have been made is necessary in order for the state and city to be reimbursed for foster care costs through federal funds.

While all of this is going on in court, another process is at work in the foster care agency, which is responsible for several tasks: (1) finding and monitoring the foster home (including monthly visits to the home and ensuring the child's needs are met there); (2) creating and coordinating a service plan for the family and ensuring the parent completes the required services; (3) monitoring and coordinating visits between the child and the parents/siblings/other family members; and (4) creating a permanency plan for the children (i.e., planning for the child to go home, be adopted, or for some other permanent arrangement). Caseworkers attempt to make changes in the parents' behavior and monitor parents to decide if and when they are ready for the return of their children.

Throughout the case a series of conferences is held at the foster care agency to discuss and monitor the case. The first conference is supposed to be held within seventy-two hours of the child's placement in foster care to ensure that everyone is clear about why the child was removed, that parents have the opportunity to suggest family members with whom the child could be placed (often the child is placed in an already certified foster home until family members are found and checked out), and that parents agree to a service plan so that they can begin their services as soon as possible. There is also supposed to be a discussion of family strengths and weaknesses so that this assessment can inform the service plan. After the seventy-two-hour conference, additional conferences should be held after the first thirty days and then after ninety days. Following this initial period, a service plan review is held every six months to monitor services.[12] Every parent with a child in foster care is given a list of compulsory services (their service plan), and the caseworker is responsible for making referrals for these services.

In addition to the service plan, the foster care agency is responsible for coordinating visits. In the vast majority of cases, visits are supervised at the beginning of a case and generally occur for an hour or two once or twice a week at the foster care agency (the specific number of hours per week is discussed in family court). As the child's time in foster care progresses, the number and length of visits is usually increased, and the level of supervision is decreased. The progression is usually from a few hours of supervised time to a few hours of unsupervised time, to "day visits" (the parent can pick the child up in the morning and bring them back in the late afternoon), to "overnights," and, eventually, to entire weekends.[13]

As the foster care caseworkers prepare to allow the child to visit the parent outside the agency, and especially when it is time to have overnight visits, caseworkers must visit the parent's home to assess it and ensure that the parent has all the proper provisions for the child. They look for basic safety items such as outlet covers and cabinet locks for younger children, as well as window guards, smoke detectors, and a lack of fire hazards and clutter. Caseworkers ensure that there is adequate room for each child, which means there must be separate spaces for boys and girls, no more than a couple of children in the same room, and separate beds for each child. They check that there is enough clothing, food, and other supplies. Finally, they check that everyone living in the home is safe—that is, there are no parents or caretakers with orders of protection against them and no adults with criminal records or child welfare histories, for example. If the parent does not have an adequate apartment, overnight and weekend visits generally do not occur.

Family reunification occurs if parents complete their service plans and caseworkers decide that parents have made the required changes in their lives. In addition, parents must demonstrate that they have adequate housing and income for their children. Significantly, they are held to a higher standard in this regard than they were at the investigation stage (see chapters 7 and 8). An inability to complete services, to behave properly, and to secure adequate means to care for their children are common barriers that delay reunification (see also Reich 2005).

Under ASFA, any child who has been in foster care for fifteen out of the last twenty-two months should be freed for adoption unless it is proven that it would not be in the child's best interests to do so. Freeing a child for adoption entails a legal procedure in which parental rights (for the legal parents)[14] are terminated so that the child can be adopted. This process starts when lawyers hired by the foster care agency file a petition in court to terminate the parent's rights on the basis of either abandonment or permanent neglect.[15] Abandonment, legally, is a situation in which there has been no contact between the parent and child, or the parent and the foster care agency or ACS, for six consecutive months. It must be proven that the parent did not visit the child, send any gifts or means of support (money, clothing, food), ask about the child at ACS or the foster care agency, show up for any conferences, or return any phone calls or letters. Permanent neglect means that, for a period of twelve consecutive months or for fifteen out of the previous twenty-two months, the parents "failed . . . substantially and continuously and repeatedly to maintain contact with or plan for the future of the child" (New York State Social Services Law Section 384-B) although able to and despite the agency's efforts to help them remain in contact and create a plan. In general, proving permanent neglect means showing that the parent has not completed required services, missed many visits, or does not have adequate means to provide for the child. Past severe abuse of a child or previous terminations are also taken into account, as set out in ASFA.

The child welfare system in New York City is complex, with several different agencies involved, and the process occurs on both social work and legal levels. There is ideally a process of reforming the parents through services and of caring for the child while this rehabilitation is occurring. At the same time, and again ideally, proceedings establishing and protecting legal rights and judicial oversight of service provision take place. On one level, this is a single system, in that there is, at least in theory, coordination among these various parts and shared overriding goals, namely to protect children while helping families and respecting parents' legal rights. Although these goals seem easily reconcilable, I show in the rest of book, especially chapters 5 and 7, the extent to which these goals conflict and the potential reconciliation of the tensions between them.

The complexity of this system makes it difficult for many parents to navigate, particularly because dealing with the requirements of a case is practically a full-time job. Parents are judged, in large part, on their ability to comply with the system's demands while the common barriers they face are not always considered (see chapter 7). The various requirements of a case and the variety of agencies and officials involved also means that there are ample opportunities for things to slow down and cases to get stuck, especially when the system becomes overwhelmed with large numbers of cases.

4

Fear and a System in Crisis

> Protection is a major concern of all components of the Family Court and child welfare system. But in reality, the protection of the system itself frequently overshadows the protection of children. (Lansner 2007, 639)

As the child welfare system has narrowed to a concern with child protection, it has received more public attention and has had to deal with a dramatically increasing number of reports. Child welfare agencies have come under scrutiny and attack as accounts of children "known to the system" who were killed or severely injured by their parents are periodically discussed in the media. When these scandals hit, agencies' practices are scrutinized, the death is blamed on caseworkers, and a surge of reports and child removals often follows (Anglin 2002; Besharov and Laumann 1996; Hutchinson 1993; Parton 2006; Parton, Thorpe, and Wattam 1997; Waldfogel 1998).[1] Child welfare agencies are under increased pressure to handle the flood of cases and ensure that they protect all children but do not interfere too much, a trend that has led to several changes: a focus on risk assessment, which also helps to target interventions in a climate of limited resources; a reliance on the courts as way to ensure, at least formally, that officials are acting properly and all rights are respected; and, often, cautious decision making (that is, more reporting, more supervision of parents, and more removals) (Anglin 2002; Gillingham 2006; Parton 1999; Parton, Thorpe, and Wattam 1997; Waldfogel 1998).

The Nixzmary Brown Case

As I was first proposing this project, I was handed a clipping from the *New York Times* with the headline: "Placements in Foster Care Are at Lowest Since Mid-1980s" (Santos 2005). This "historic change" was reported to be the outcome of a concerted effort by ACS to offer more services to preserve families and avoid foster care. Although the article noted that some experts worried this left too many children in harm's way, overall the tone was positive. A few months later, in January 2006, news of Nixzmary Brown's death broke, and it was immediately linked to what was then seen as a mistaken focus on family preservation.

Before her brutal death at the hands of her stepfather, Nixzmary's family was "known to the system," and at least two reports had been made by her school for excessive absences and injuries. An investigation of the case found that neither report was investigated thoroughly, inconsistent explanations for the injuries were apparently accepted without question, and a follow-up visit to the family was not completed until a month after the second report. By this time, she was already dead. In contrast to the limited coverage generally given to the other similar deaths that happen every year, this case was widely covered and discussed, in part because of the brutality with which she was treated and eventually killed by her stepfather as well as her mother's alleged failure to protect her. The vast majority of the press coverage blamed the girl's death on ACS's failure to adequately investigate the case and argued that caseworkers should have been able to prevent it. The mayor, the ACS commissioner, and the City Council speaker all vowed, almost immediately, to review the case and other similar deaths to see what was done wrong. Much of the coverage placed the blame squarely on the shoulders of individual decision makers. Firings were called for (Kaufman, McIntire, and Santos 2006), while op-ed pieces asked if the agency was simply incompetent (*Daily News* 2005) and charged it with covering up its mistakes (Goodwin 2006). Blame was also placed on policies that supposedly favored family preservation over child protection: "Family preservation is a wonderful theory and a noble goal. . . . But not all families are equal. Some don't deserve the word 'family' at all. To call them that is a triumph of language over reality. And for the government to preserve a hell house that is dangerous to children is to turn a noble goal into an accomplice to murder" (Goodwin 2006). Although some coverage did point out the larger context of extremely high caseloads and insufficient time and staff to thoroughly investigate, the main message in the coverage was clear: bumbling caseworkers and family preservation policies were to blame for this child's death.

An investigation of this case and ten other fatalities of children known to the system found several troubling patterns in casework practices: conducting superficial investigations that did not follow mandated timelines, ignoring both previous reports and credible evidence of allegations, failing to recognize or reconcile inconsistent accounts of events and injuries, falsifying records, failing to use the family court to compel parents to cooperate with investigations, and supervising caseworkers inadequately (New York City, Department of Investigation 2007). ACS made various changes in the wake of the case: they disciplined or suspended the workers and supervisors involved, ordered reviews of all open cases, hired more caseworkers, created mechanisms for more cooperation between police and caseworkers in conducting investigations, and created a new system called ChildStat (modeled on former Mayor Giuliani's CompStat).[2] Childstat tracks data about investigations, uses scorecards to rate them, and requires weekly meetings in which ongoing cases are described to upper-level management who ask questions and give criticism and feedback. In talking to caseworkers and other officials during my fieldwork, however, several problems with the agency that might have accounted for the mistakes in the Nixzmary Brown case were still present. Caseworkers still did not receive much training in conducting investigations, they were generally overworked, and they had little time to conduct thorough investigations.

When I began fieldwork in October 2006, ACS officials were still dealing with the effects of the Nixzmary Brown case and felt that practices had changed noticeably. Overall, the caseworkers I talked to felt that decision making had become more cautious and noticed increased pressure to make the correct decision in all cases. Carl, an African American in his late twenties who had been a caseworker for five and a half years, commented: "I think since Nixzmary Brown died, a lot of people are, like, they see the littlest thing; they call it in without really doing some more investigation." He also stated, "So Nixzmary Brown happened, it was, like, 'Well, remove and ask questions later.' That was the mentality." He went on to say that "*everybody* got scared." Statistics show that, systemwide, decision-making practices did change:

- In 2006 the number of reports of child abuse/neglect increased by about 32 percent over the previous year (Kaufman 2006);
- The rate at which reports were indicated increased from 32.6 percent in 2005 to 36.6 percent in 2006 (White, Hurley, and Solow 2007);
- The average caseload per caseworker increased to 16.6 in 2006, up from 12.2 in 2005 (White, Hurley, and Solow 2007);
- Filings in family court more than doubled; increases ranged from 146 percent in Queens to 240 percent in Brooklyn (Council on Children 2007);
- Foster care placements increased by 53 percent in 2006 over 2005 (White, Hurley, and Solow 2007);
- The median length of time children spent in foster care increased 20 percent from 8.2 months in 2005 to 10.3 months in 2006. This was the first time such an increase had been recorded. (White, Hurley, and Solow 2007)

Fear, Stress, and Cautious Decision Making

Although incidents like the Nixzmary Brown case lead to both a heightened sense of the consequences of a bad decision and more cautious systemwide decision making, caseworkers *always* deal with the fear of having a tragedy on their caseload, and this affects their decision-making practices even though most caseworkers rarely, if ever, deal with such abuse. In carrying out their mandate to protect children, caseworkers face much uncertainty when making decisions about situations that are colored in multiple shades of gray, rather than in black and white. They rarely deal with clear-cut cases in which the facts unambiguously show that a child is in danger. Instead, most cases involve more subtle issues of neglect (see chapter 6 for what this means in practice). At the same time that caseworkers must assume that all parents and families are potentially dangerous, they also realize that they cannot be in homes constantly to monitor safety, nor can they simply remove all children from their homes. This situation creates important challenges for caseworkers and has led to an increased focus on risk assessment as a way to aid them in making decisions.

Risk Assessment and Fear

The social work literature on risk assessment in child welfare notes that risk assessment instruments are unreliable, with subjective measures that allow caseworkers to rate similar behaviors at different risk levels (Gambrill and Shlonsky 2000; Hughes and Rycus 2007; Leschied et al. 2003). Some studies have found that assessment instruments do not standardize decision making (Hughes and Rycus 2007; Kang and Poertner 2006; but see Sullivan et al. 2008, who found perceptions of risk did not vary between experienced and inexperienced caseworkers), and they are sometimes used to defend rather than to make decisions (Lyle and Graham 2000). Some researchers have even argued that risk assessment itself can be as much about protecting child welfare agencies as protecting children (Goddard et al. 1999; Rzepnicki and Johnson 2005). Despite these problems, risk assessment instruments are part of child welfare practice, but recall from chapter 3 that caseworkers did not report they used these assessments to make decisions.

Some caseworkers talked about the fear of having a tragedy on their caseloads, mainly because they truly care about protecting children but also because they fear possible media scrutiny and job loss. The high-stakes nature of their work creates enormous pressure and stress. Barbara, an African American in her forties who worked as a CPS in Harlem for more than ten years prior to the Nixzmary Brown case (she worked in an office that does community outreach at the time of our interview) explained:

> I mean, we do dream about our cases. We do, we dream about them. There's been many times I have turned over in my sleep, and like, "Oh my God, I gotta see this woman," or "Oh my God, I gotta do this paper," you know what I mean? Just being on your mind too much, and just, you know, and it's like a Russian roulette, 'cause you know, you don't know when a kid is gonna die,

> you don't know, you know, you coulda just seen them, and the mother coulda killed them the minute you left, but it's gonna be your fault. You will have to answer to the board on what did you do or didn't do, and today it's even worse.

The fear of tragedies also leads to more cautious decision making. Carl's story illustrates this point poignantly. The mother in this case had never actually harmed her children, but, given her mental health issues, she seemed unable to adequately care for them, which lead to their removal. Carl later decided to reunify the family because she was compliant with all her services and seemed to be behaving normally. A few days before getting the reunification plan approved by the court, however, Carl got a call from a local hospital saying that the mother was in the burn unit.

> After I hung up the phone, I started to cry because I was saying to myself, "Had we put these children with her, it'd be a totally different story." And I felt bad and I was, like, saying to myself, "Oh, God." And the lawyers were saying, "Well, at least we didn't put the children back with her because if we had put the children back with her, we could've had two children dead." . . . And that was the thing. She burnt herself, she set the apartment on fire and she burnt herself so severely that both of her arms had to be completely amputated. And I mean, I just felt grateful that we didn't place the kids with her. After that, that was when I had a change of heart like I think what we do is the best. And I've always looked at it as we're doing what's in the best interest of the children, no matter what it is.

This story illustrates one reality of doing child protective work—tragedies happen, and they are not predictable. Thus, caseworkers must deal with fear of the worst-case scenario, which can lead to more cautious decisions. In the context of our larger conversation, it is clear that "what we do" is a reference to removing children, and this experience made Carl think differently about that. He came to see removals as necessary actions taken in children's best interests rather than occurrences to be avoided whenever possible.

Fear and Family Court Practices

Fear of a tragedy also extends to practices in family court. One 18B attorney, Bob, a white man in his fifties, described it as practicing "*New York Post* Law":

> Certainly they wouldn't tell you for attribution, but if you were to ask my colleagues what . . . motivates judges, okay, they will tell you quite frankly that we practice *New York Post* law, and what that means basically is that no judge wants us to let a kid go home and see his name in the tabloids the next day that a kid got killed or maimed badly because of a decision he or she made. And it's always safer to, you know [remove a child or leave them in foster care], and that's what you're . . . up against [as an 18B attorney].

Marcus, a white ACS attorney in his thirties, felt that the change in how they were dealing with cases after the Nixzmary Brown incident was actually against the stated mission of ACS:

> MARCUS: It seems like they've moved away from the mission statement just out of a sense of fear, and there have been a lot of repercussions of that. Then on top of that, just with the number of new cases coming in, called in to the State Central Register, it just seems like another frustrating thing is just the high caseloads and workloads.
>
> TINA: What kinds of changes do you see after Nixzmary Brown? . . . So if you could tell me more about what they tell you the mission is and how you think they get away from it.
>
> MARCUS: Okay. Well, I feel like there were four main principles that they imparted to us. One is children are safe. Children's developmental needs are met. Families are strengthened, and permanency is achieved. And I feel like after the Nixzmary thing, there was a whole lot of emphasis on the safety aspect, but some of the others haven't been focused as much. And I don't know if it's 'cause people . . . I mean, no one wants to be responsible for something happening. So the way decisions are made are only toward safety and not necessarily toward strengthening the family. And then it feels like, it feels like some of those things are an afterthought. It's like we file a case so that there's a, so that it's in court. And then the responsibility is off us.

These attorneys suggest that the agency is acting in the interests of ensuring safety above all else in an effort to guard against criticism that they are not doing all they can to protect children. Marcus also emphasizes that some ACS caseworkers bring cases to court to have another set of decision makers involved and another party to absorb any future blame. Rather than balancing safety and service-provision, decision makers focus on deflecting blame.

Although this dynamic was more pronounced after Nixzmary Brown, it always exists in family court practice. The process of deciding whether to file a case in court and what family intervention to request is complex; multiple people (lawyers, caseworkers, and supervisors) play a role in making the decision and, at times, simply try to avoid making any decision. Not all situations that might fit the legal definition of neglect must or will be filed in family court, and the child protective staff, in consultation with the legal staff, has discretion about whether to file cases. Ideally, determinations about what is going on in the home and the level of risk to the child should be made before bringing a case to family court, but it seemed to me that cases were sometimes brought to court primarily to involve another set of decision makers. This practice was described by attorneys, judges, and caseworkers, at times, as simply a "CYA" (Cover Your Ass) move. When I observed one courtroom in Brooklyn, for example, the judge pointed out a couple of cases she felt were in this category that should not have been filed. It is significant that she did not dismiss them.

Marcus also hinted at the reasons he thought these kinds of filings were being made:

> I guess it depends on the situation, but it feels like in some of those cases, they're more toward *punitive* or more toward thinking they *won't be held responsible* if the case comes to court. Where if, you know, if it's deferred, especially if the manager defers it from legal, you know, they are at some risk, I suppose, [if something bad happened later they could be blamed], because the caseworker side will say, "Well we sent it there because we thought it should be filed, they convinced us not to," or whatever, "and we didn't." But it seems like it goes both ways because sometimes the cases are only brought to cover, or they perceive it as, *covering themselves*, by bringing the case and they don't particularly, they're not strong one way or the other whether it's deferred or not, it's just "at least we sent it to legal to decide." [emphasis added]

Marcus hesitates and does not say directly that these cases should not be filed; however, he feels that some cases are questionable—filed to be punitive or to protect the agency from the criticism that they did not do everything they could. In other cases, child protective staff come to court to involve another set of decision makers so that blame can be shared or deflected in the event of a problem.

A couple of the caseworkers I interviewed had a similar assessment of why the decision is made to file a case. They felt that managers would push them to file (which takes up an entire day) when it was not necessary. For example, Carl stated:

> But I think the three managers that I've had, only one manager was, like, "Seek legal," or "Go get a legal," *every* case. If we disagreed on whether a case should be indicated or not, "Get a legal." It's like . . . and we'd go get a legal and the legal department would take a look, say, "Okay. Your manager needs to make a decision on this case." Once again, it's on the manager. The manager's saying, "Okay. Well, we need to go to talk to her [the attorney's] manager." So then you go to talk to her manager and her manager's, like, "We hired you as a manager to make decisions like this. Make a decision."

Filing large numbers of cases in an effort to protect the agency affected the families that were involved with child welfare before the Nixzmary Brown case as well as those caught up in the system afterward. As Marcus stated: "So those cases are all here, and they take up the calendar. And then I think even the kids who may have been closer to final discharge at some point, I think everything slowed down with that because people are taking a second and third look to make sure everything's right." Another ACS attorney, Katherine, a woman of Middle Eastern descent in her thirties, put it this way: "But the agency really, really sort of buckled down on their idea of returning children from that point forward because nobody wanted their names in the newspaper."

Although many attorneys directly linked the filing of marginal cases and more cautious decision making to the Nixzmary Brown case, Sandra, an 18B attorney and white woman in her forties, felt that, in general and at all times, making the decision that a child is at imminent risk says more about efforts to protect ACS than it does about the actual risk to a child:

> I don't think the decision on imminent risk really is about the risk to the child in most cases. I think it's about the risk to the system. I think, you know, ACS doesn't want another Nixzmary, the judges don't want to appear on the front page of the *Daily News*, and so imminent risk has taken on—it's like everybody's *hiding* behind it, and that it doesn't mean, here in New York County, what it means in Syracuse County [outside York City, upstate]. In Syracuse County, I think it really does mean, "We're only gonna take your child away if

> we find you standing over the child with a bloody knife" or, you know, "we go to your house and there's no food at all in the house, and the children are hungry." Here, it means, "If your house is dirty . . ."

It is important to note that Sandra is also pointing to a difference between cases upstate, in counties that are whiter and less poor, and cases in New York City. It is not simply a matter of more caution in child welfare in general, but the differences in how state structures are involved in the lives of different racial and class groups; that is, state agencies are more involved in a more punitive way for those who are disadvantaged by structures of race, class, and gender. This issue is at the crux of my entire discussion.

Fear in Initial Hearings

In my observations at family court, I saw this cautious decision making in practice. It was very rare for the judge or the law guardian to oppose or to raise questions about ACS requests. It was also rare for these officials to ask the ACS caseworker exactly what efforts she had made to prevent the removal. On only a couple of occasions did I see the judge hold a full-blown hearing by carefully questioning ACS, studying the steps already taken, and considering the agency's proposed solutions. Most of the time judges deferred to ACS in terms of assessing risk and authorized their proposed solution with very little, if any, questioning or scrutiny. Law guardians rarely asked for full-blown hearings either, although they are charged with ensuring that the children's needs and interests are protected, and this would presumably include avoiding unnecessary removals (see Guggenheim 2006 for a discussion of why law guardians tend to focus on the potential harms faced by children at the hands of their parents and not on the potential harms from removals). The practice of having a *pro forma* hearing at this stage is so ingrained that attorneys from the Bronx Defenders, who take an explicitly social justice perspective and vowed, in the words of one of their social workers, to "really litigate these cases," told me that, when they attempted to force questioning and scrutiny at these hearings, they were heckled by fellow attorneys.

This situation is, in part, due to overloaded court calendars, which leave little time for full hearings. It is also related to the *New York Post* law phenomenon and to the fact that judges, appointed by the mayor, are reluctant to go against another city agency (see also Lansner 2007). These factors create a situation in which judges have little incentive to challenge ACS when they seek to intervene in families and more incentive to *avoid* doing so. In addition, the fact that most parents' attorneys are relatively poorly paid and overworked means that they do not always have the time or interest to fight vigorously against these interventions.

I observed the initial hearing in a total of sixty cases, and in only thirteen of these (22 percent) were any questions raised about what ACS requested. Most of the questions involved where the child would be placed and not if the intervention was warranted. In only five cases (8 percent) did the judge order something other than what ACS had requested. In one of these cases, the judge deferred making a decision about sending a baby born with a positive drug test to foster care without exploring a mother-child inpatient drug program, but the baby remained in the hospital and not in the mother's care.[3] Although the judge did question ACS, this was still a "safe" decision. In another two cases, ACS wanted to parole the children to their parents, and the judge ordered that they be placed in foster care instead. Although caseworkers who had met the family and assessed the situation felt that the children were safe in the home, court officials decided that this was too risky and ordered removals. ACS officials did not object to the judge's decision, which was safer than their own decisions. In only two cases (or 3 percent) did the judge find that a removal was unwarranted.

Fear, Race, and Class

The parents I talked to were acutely aware that caseworkers were afraid of failing to remove a child from a dangerous situation and therefore were likely to treat them as if they were a potentially grave danger to their child. In attending weekly support groups at the Child Welfare Organizing Project (CWOP), the idea that parents are treated as if they are all the worst child abusers was a common theme. The parent organizers' sophisticated analysis of where this attitude came from highlighted the roles of race, class, and the media. When I first attended one of their meetings, they still had press coverage of the Nixzmary Brown case tacked to the wall along with comments presenting their analysis. They posted the *New York Post*'s front-page story about the case with a picture of the child's stepfather that took up most of the page with the huge headline: "MONSTER: Evil, Ugly, Face of Sadistic Stepdad from Hell." Next to this there was a comment: "This is what sells papers." There was also a story from an e-mail about the mayor of Bridgeport, Connecticut, who was forced to admit to a cocaine habit he kept secret for years that came out as a result of a federal drug investigation. The federal prosecutor almost immediately apologized for letting the information get out and asked a federal judge to seal the records. The e-mail, which was sent to parent advocates, pointed out that the mayor used cocaine while he was in office and that he was also a father. The message highlighted the mayor's public statements that he wanted to deal with the situation privately and commented that the parents investigated by ACS probably want the same thing but are never given the chance. The comment next to the story and e-mail stated: "Stories like this are seldom told."

The implication of juxtaposing these two stories and their captions is that a double standard exists with regard to how personal problems such as drug abuse are handled. If you are wealthy, white, and powerful, like the mayor, you are able to hide your problem and ask people to let you deal with it privately. It is highly unlikely that anyone will call an agency like ACS (see chapter 5) or attempt to keep you away from your children, much less place them in foster care (see chapter 6). But if you do not have these class and race privileges, then you do not have that choice. Your problems are more likely to come to the attention of ACS who will not let you deal with them yourself as you see fit; instead, your children are likely to go into foster care. Sensationalized stories that demonize some parents fuel the public's desire for agencies to get tougher on child abusers and protect children rather than "misguidedly" attempt to leave them in their homes. The people who are likely to be caught up in this tough approach are neither wealthy nor white; most often, they are poor people of color in the neighborhoods in which ACS involvement is already most concentrated—people who are already seen as irresponsible and undeserving of help. Many of the parents in this study felt they were targeted because of their race and class and treated harshly, especially if they had the misfortune to be investigated by ACS in the aftermath of a high-profile tragedy. At the same time, many of them did admit that they had problems and needed help for them (especially in the cases of drug addiction), but, instead of being helped, the parents often felt they were only being punished. In this way, then, the child welfare system is one example of relations of stratified reproduction.

An Overwhelmed System

As discussed in chapter 2, mandated reporting laws have led to an expanding number of reports while budgets have remained inadequate (Besharov and Laumann 1996; Hutchinson 1993; Lukens 2007). This situation has led to constant discussions of child welfare as a system in crisis (Lindsey 1994; Parton, Thorpe, and Wattam 1997; Waldfogel 1998). During my fieldwork it was hard to escape the feeling that the system was indeed in crisis with high caseloads, unmanageable workloads, extremely long delays, and families who were not getting the assistance they needed.

Caseloads

When I spoke with caseworkers, between twelve and twenty-four months after the Nixzmary Brown case, caseloads ranged from seven to thirty-two, and most workers managed between fifteen and twenty cases.[4] Official statistics on the average caseload of child protective workers reflect the sharp increase in cases that my informants reported. Many of the caseworkers with whom I spoke told me that they believe these are inaccurate statistics that do not adequately reflect the stress, pressure, and overwork they face. Some went so far as to say that the agency actually lies about caseloads. Meredith, an African American woman in her mid-twenties who had been a CPS for seventeen months and who is, in her own words, a "bubbly" person, described the stress:

> We don't get paid for what we do. We really do work 24/7. . . . He says, the commissioner says, twelve to fifteen cases. That is a lie because only during the summer may we have twelve to fifteen cases. During the school year, you could have anywhere from fifteen to twenty, and the help that you're supposed to be getting from your supervisors . . . it's not help. It's barking down on you, and it's not just me. I'm just saying what I've noticed. Barking down on you like, "Why hasn't this get done? What hasn't this get done?" So on and so, and I'm just like, "Wait a minute. How am I supposed to get this done? I have this case due, and I have that case due, and this case takes precedence over that case because mom said this, and blah, blah, blah, blah, blah." And with all the things that we have to do and get them done by a certain deadline, we don't have the time to do it. That's why the work piles up because, at the end of the day, the caseworker is just saying, "Fuck it."

Most caseworkers, like Meredith, told me they found their caseloads unmanageable. Each case has a rigid timeline to be followed and requirements that are demanding and time-consuming (see chapter 3): paperwork; multiple visits with children and parents; collateral contacts to be made; and family court obligations including preparing reports, being present when hearings are held, and filing new cases, which is an all-day process. I asked Zadie, an African American woman in her twenties who had been at the agency for about two years, if her caseload of around eighteen was manageable:

> No, but you do what you have to do. It's not really manageable. What is hard is trying to see families on a bi-weekly visit and then to have to do court reports, to speak to collaterals, and then to do notes and documentation and then still getting other cases, and then if you get a high-risk case that really may have problems or may concern you, you have to really focus on that case because, in worry of, you know, the children or anything like that, so. To me it's not manageable. . . . I've had cases where I've had probably three or four that needed to be, that were overdue. And I got in a new case, and I couldn't even really actually address those three or four cases that needed to be closed because I had to work on this new case, run around, go see the doc, speak to the therapist, do this, make visits, try to find this out, find that out . . .

Most of the caseworkers I spoke with shared Zadie's view. They felt overworked and unable to keep up with all their work, to investigate thoroughly, and to make the best decisions possible. Nevertheless, caseworkers are judged by how well they complete concrete steps on their cases—the steps that are necessary to close the case and move on. The focus often shifted to the performance of these steps, not to the adequacy of the decisions made.

Caseloads at family court were similarly high and difficult to manage. ACS attorneys reported anywhere from 90 to 150 cases, with the lowest number in Queens and the highest in Brooklyn. The caseload numbers I found are consistent with what has been reported by Child Welfare Watch and the New York City Public Advocate, who further note that the American Bar Association recommends that attorneys representing child welfare agencies should have caseloads of no more than fifty (Feldman 2005; Office of the Public Advocate for the City of New York 2006). Here, the count refers to cases, but a case is likely to have multiple children and can become quite complicated. Each case requires regularly scheduled hearings and conferences (every week or two for the first several months of the case and a minimum of every six months later, but usually more often), preparation for settlements or trials, and keeping up with how the agencies handle either foster care prevention or permanency planning for the children who have been placed, which can mean following up with multiple caseworkers. All the ACS attorneys I spoke with found the work overwhelming and spent time during evenings and weekends just to keep their head above water. They felt they could neither adequately keep up with their work nor be prepared for their court appearances much of the time. Katherine described her job:

> It's kind of like you run in, you end up meeting with your client three seconds before you're running into court, asking them if they have reports, asking them if everything is okay and what's going on and running in and handing in a report and just sort of like keeping your fingers crossed that everybody's done what they've supposed to have done. That people are cooperating, the kids are getting the services they need, the parents are in services, that we've actually made referrals to services, or if the kids are home that we're actually visiting the homes to make sure that everything is okay. . . . I don't have the time to call a worker a day, much less a week, before a case comes up in court to ask them what's been going on and if everything is okay and if there are any issues. So every time I walk into court it's sort of a prayer.

Caseloads made it impossible, in other words, to check that families were actually being served, despite this being a primary function of family court.

Law Guardians reported caseloads of 140 to 295 clients (i.e., children).[5] This is consistent with what the Legal Aid Society reports as an average caseload of between 200 and 300 clients in 2006, up from 150 to 200 clients in 2005 (Council on Children 2007). They also reported having a hard time managing their cases. Michelle told me: "I mean it's very difficult to manage. It's hard, I mean, a big part of the job is seeing the clients and getting an update from the client, and seeing what the client wants. If you're trying to do that like maybe even every six months, it's like kinda a struggle sometimes." Judges reported having six to nine hundred open docket numbers, but they complained this did not fully capture their workload because counts do not reflect the numbers of hearings and conferences involved in a case, especially since 2006 legislation requiring permanency hearings every six months rather than the previous annual hearings (see also Council on Children 2007). Judges usually had about fifteen cases on their calendar on any given day and often held hearings, especially on intake days, well past 5 P.M.

Parents' attorneys, because they are technically private attorneys and have control over whether they will take a case, were less likely to report high caseloads,[6] but they felt pressure to accept all cases offered because judges will not go forward unless the parent is represented. In addition, the relatively low per-hour rate of $75 means that many of these attorneys take on large numbers of cases.[7] Despite all this, one Family Court judge told me she often has to seek out attorneys to take on parents' cases and often has to beg, cajole, or even threaten. I saw this happen one day in her courtroom when court officers were unable to find attorneys for two cases. She called in one of the 18B panel coordinators to enlist her help and told her that if no one came forward she would draw names out of a hat and assign the cases to them.

Foster care agency caseloads average twenty to twenty-two, which is about twice that recommended as an ideal caseload by a New York State Office of Child and Family Services study (Council on Children 2007). ACS attorneys regularly complained that these caseworkers did not have enough time to provide services adequately, monitor the foster home including regular home visits, and deliver all needed documentation to the court. The other service providers who work with child welfare clients are also underfunded and understaffed. Caseworkers and parents alike complained about long waiting lists for services such as domestic violence shelters and counseling, drug treatment, mental health counseling, and parenting classes. In addition, not all caseworkers are equally knowledgeable about available services, nor do they have the time to learn about them, given their large caseloads and high turnover.[8] Thus, sometimes they had trouble making referrals, even when they fully intended to do so.

Consequences of High Caseloads

The facts that court calendars are extremely crowded and that everyone has high caseloads have serious consequences for both the people who work in child welfare and the families who are involved with it. Family court is both hectic and glacially slow. Attorneys tend to almost literally run from place to place and rarely have time to prepare for their cases. It is frequently difficult for judges to hold hearings when they are unable to get all the necessary people in the room. At the same time, for caseworkers and families, family court is mainly about waiting. Hearings are generally scheduled as an "A.M. call" or a "P.M. call" (i.e., the case will be heard either before or after the lunch break). An A.M. call means getting to court usually around 7:30 or 8 A.M. to allow time for long waits to go through security and more waiting until possibly noon or being asked to come back after lunch. After waiting for hours, the case might be adjourned if a report is incomplete or someone is not present, or you might have a ten-minute hearing and find that nothing has changed. This situation is common and extremely frustrating for parents. Court generally means missing entire days of work, absences that put parents at risk for losing their jobs and, as a result, having a much harder time regaining custody when they cannot show a means to provide for their children (see chapter 8). Not only do parents often feel their time is wasted, but any issues that needed to be resolved, such as getting visits with their child or securing needed services, are not addressed.

ACS attorneys and law guardians described simply not being able to devote enough time to each case in order to do everything that needs to be done and thus having to make "triage" decisions about what to prepare for and what not to. For example, I observed many 18B attorneys who spoke to their clients only a minute or two before each court appearance, and almost all the parents I interviewed reported that their lawyer did not explain what was to happen in the case, much less prepare what they would be arguing for or how to defend them and push for what they needed. Consider one example: I attended what was to be a fact-finding hearing with two parents. The lawyer approached us about five minutes before the hearing was scheduled to begin and asked the parent what he wanted his defense to be. He then turned to me (I had never met him and was only in court to observe) and said, "What are you going to be testifying to?" It was quite clear to both the parents and me that he had not prepared a case. This lack of preparedness, on all sides in court, leads to multiple adjournments and prolongs cases, which, in turn, delays reunification if the child is in foster care. It also means that too often neither are parents defended nor is information adequately presented on their behalf.

The rushed atmosphere and lack of time means that parents are rarely given explanations of what is happening in their case. For example, one day while waiting with a parent in a very small waiting room in the Bronx, I overheard a father trying to ask his lawyer for an explanation of what had just happened in court. She explained, tersely and while trying to walk away, that the children were coming home but ACS would be supervising him. He continued to ask questions about what, precisely, this would mean and told her he didn't want anyone in his house telling him what to do. Rather than addressing his concerns, she snapped, "It's the best you can hope for" and walked away. Practically all of the parents I talked with experienced similar treatment and had an extremely limited understanding of the process and what it meant for their families.

Many parents expressed frustration that things were not explained and told me they felt their lawyer was doing nothing to help their case. Many complained that their phones calls were not returned and that their lawyers did not take the time to talk to them, meet with them, or provide explanations. This left many unsure about what was happening. Ramel, a young African American father with four children, described his experience:

> RAMEL: We go in there, and it's like the only thing they ask us is . . .
>
> TINA: Your name and relationship to the child?
>
> RAMEL: Yeah, name and relationship to child . . . and after that, I don't understand nothing. [laughs] I don't understand anything else, and the lawyer never explains anything to me. *Never.*
>
> TINA: Have you had any time to really sit down and talk with her? It's a her, the lawyer? Or you kind of see her five minutes before?
>
> RAMEL: Only that one time. And when I went to court the last time, I approached her, she said "Okay, yeah, the file's on the inside." But she never came back out to discuss anything with me about the case. *Never* came back out. And next thing you know, we've been called.

Another mother, Irene, a Latina with a working-class job and five children, felt that attorneys make certain assumptions about their clients which lead them to feel that explaining the process is not necessary: "He's not helpful. Like they don't, they already used to like; I don't want say parents that are ignorant, but most of the parents that come in there are minority, you know. And not much of an education, and no jobs. They on welfare, social security, or whatever, you know. And they [lawyers] don't think that, you know, maybe this parent might come in with a brain, you know and, know a little bit about the system." I agree with Irene that parents are looked down upon because they are poor and minority, and lawyers often assume they are unable to understand both the system and when they are being inadequately served (see also chapter 7).

Some parents understood that not being informed about their rights and the process in family court put them at a disadvantage. Nathan, an African American father in his fifties and a parent advocate, explained: "You know . . . that survival book [a publication of CWOP]? I used to come in and get those and give it to 'em so they can learn about the laws, different terminologies in the courts. And you know, things like that. You know, 'cause you gotta be well prepared when you go into a Family Court or they eat you up. They eat you up and you never get your kids back." Here, he acknowledges that parents must understand the process so that they can ensure their rights are respected and evaluate if they are getting adequate representation. If parents are not knowledgeable (and most were not), then the process of family court and regaining custody becomes much more difficult.

High caseloads also contribute to the huge delays that are endemic to family court (Council on Children 2007; Guggenheim and Gottlieb 2005; Lansner 2007; Office of the Public Advocate for the City of New York 2002, 2006). During my observations, I noted when the next hearing was scheduled and how many dates the parties had to try before finding a date and time at which everyone would be available. If the next court appearance needed a short amount of time (ten to fifteen minutes), then it was generally possible to schedule a hearing within a couple of weeks, but even that was often difficult when a time could not be agreed upon. If more time was needed, then appearances were generally scheduled for anywhere from three to, more commonly, six months later. During these months, in most cases, nothing changed—either the child remained in foster care and caseworkers did not increase visitation, or regular supervision of the family continued. It was an everyday practice to schedule full fact-finding hearings over the course of a few months in order to find enough time. It is also normal for cases to go on and children to be in foster care for a year or more before a hearing is held to determine if the allegations were true or to reach a settlement agreement. These delays almost always mean that children remain in foster care.

Consider another example: I witnessed a termination of parental rights fact-finding hearing in October 2006. The initial termination petition was filed in September 2004 and was still not completed. During this time another child was born to the mother (the baby tested positive for drugs).

That child's case was completed—the mother was not visiting the child or engaged in any services so it was dispensed with quickly—and a termination petition was filed for her. The delays meant the other children were not freed for adoption. In part, this case was drawn out when the foster care agency needed time to find the fathers and give them notice of the proceedings, but there were two six- to seven-month-long adjournments due to scheduling problems. On the day I saw the case, it was adjourned yet again, this time for four months, because the attorneys who filed the termination petition had not provided needed records to the other attorneys. This phenomenon is a common, and often unacknowledged, reason for lengthy foster care stays (Guggenheim 2005; Stein 2003). Katherine, an ACS attorney, pointed out that these delays are contrary to the stated goal of ACS practice. When I asked her what she thinks the goal of ACS and her work within it should be, Katherine stated: "I think in my mind is reunification. That's the way that the law is written. The point is for reunification of the family. It's not taking kids away from parents and never giving them back. But we don't move fast enough, and cases linger. Cases are before courts for years. Three, four, five. I mean I have cases that I started with [she has been in the job for five and a half years]. So I mean, that's, I think that's sort of telling."

Another concrete way that the court and high caseloads delay reunification is that permanency hearings in which the judge approves the goal for the children are very often adjourned more than once. When the hearings do occur, they are often *pro forma* as there is no time for a full hearing. Several judges complained to me that the permanency report, which provides the information the judge needs in order to approve the goal and ensure that the steps toward it are being taken, is done at the last minute, if at all. This means that the different parties have not read it when they go into the courtroom, and the parent is not given a chance to respond, correct any problems, or raise anything with which they disagree. Another judge told me that she frequently finds the reports contain "stale" information so she is unsure about what is currently going on in the case. And yet, most of the time little discussion takes place, and the judge hears no evidence but the report.

Also troubling was the way that parents' attorneys often disregarded the importance of a hearing for a parent and attempted to delay it so that it would better fit with their own schedules. For example, I observed the following on a day in which a 1028 hearing was scheduled. The mother had been in court when the child was placed in foster care and the hearing was scheduled at that time, but the father had not been present; on this day he was in the courtroom and also wanted the hearing.[9] A lawyer was found to assign to him, but he refused to have the hearing for his client, which is not unreasonable as he had just met the father and had no time to prepare. The mother's attorney suggested postponing the hearing until the following week and left to get permission for this from her client. A few minutes later she came back and reported that the mother would not wait for the hearing, at which point the two attorneys discussed how unreasonable she was being. Of course, from their points of view, waiting would have given them more time to prepare and might have allowed them to make a better case that the child would not be in danger in the home. The attorneys, however, neither seemed to remember that this hearing, from the mother's point of view, was an attempt to get her child back in her care nor did they understand why she might be unwilling to wait.

Brandon, an 18B attorney of Indian descent, was candid in his interview about having this kind of attitude (i.e., getting caught up in the routine nature of what is happening rather than seeing the impact these decisions and delays have on families) and where it comes from. I asked him how often parents are told to come to court when a case is first filed and what the consequences are if they are not present. He explained that if they are there on the first day, he can push for a detailed hearing and attempt to either stop the process of having the child placed in foster care or begin the process of having them returned if they had been removed on an emergency basis, *that day*. If, however, the parents are not present, they will not be assigned a lawyer, and the process proceeds without them; in this case, they will be told to come to court generally a week later to get a lawyer and only then will the lawyer be able to do anything to intervene. By this time, the parents will be held to the higher standards usually required to regain custody of a child in foster care, and the entire process is far more difficult (see chapter 8). If at this time the parent wants to argue that the child should go home, the lawyer can still ask for a 1028 hearing, but it will not happen immediately and will instead occur within the following three days. Brandon commented:

> It doesn't seem like a big difference. Like, oh what's the big deal between one and three days? And I don't have any kids, but I gotta figure, you know, having your kids taken away from you for one day or two days, not knowing when

> and if you're ever gonna get 'em back and, you know, these people know. In the communities they live in, this is a routine thing that goes on and they know how long it can take to get their kids back.... It's a major deal, and I think the people, even the lawyers and me included, you probably get to the point that you get so immune to stuff.... And you end up thinking that way because this is what just happens. Routine. And three days to me is nothing. Three days to them is probably like a big thing.

These attitudes, which are related to the crushing workloads faced by those who work in family court, often lead to situations where simply getting through the day becomes the focus rather than advocating for parents' interests.

Judges were also frustrated by delays and caseworkers who did not complete necessary tasks. One judge told me that she felt that things were going less well since the Nixzmary Brown case and the new permanency law. She said they used to strive for "best practices" and now often do not even do "better practices." She has found that many caseworkers are neither coming to court with the required reports nor making the proper referrals, and she added that ACS attorneys complain about these things to her off the record. Because the caseworkers are technically the ACS attorneys' clients, they are under pressure not to state these complaints publicly, and many ACS attorneys will fight against a judge making a specific order for services because it leaves the agency open to fines if the order is not carried out. This judge told me she has threatened to subpoena the caseworkers' supervisors to testify about what they have been doing if things do not go smoothly. Another judge told me she finds she has to threaten to hold agencies in contempt of court for not doing their jobs. I never witnessed a judge actually holding an agency in contempt, although I saw many of them threaten to do so. Judges employed other common tactics: they raised their voices at caseworkers, ordered them out of the courtroom for a few minutes or a few days to take care of something, or both. Although judges do have some power to enforce reasonable efforts requirements, such power is often limited to informal means such as threats. Again, this situation means that families do not always get the services they need, reunification can be delayed, and the court is ineffective in holding agencies accountable.

This example illustrates this problem: I witnessed a court appearance in which a child (along with his four siblings) had been removed from his mother, in part because he had a serious mental health issue that caseworkers felt she was not addressing. The child was placed in a pediatric psychiatry ward, and the judge asked the caseworker and the ACS attorney about his diagnosis. When they could not tell her, she angrily ordered them to find out this information and return the following week. When they returned they still did not have information about the child and admitted that neither the caseworker nor the law guardian had visited the child. The judge told them, sharply, to "get a diagnosis and visit this child" since he isn't "just a number on a piece of paper." The mother complained that she was also not allowed to visit her son. At this point, it had been ten days since the child, who was only ten years old, was put in the hospital, and no one had visited him or checked on his diagnosis and treatment. In another case, this same judge, in a conference, asked what services the mother had been referred to. The caseworker began to say that they were having a meeting in a few days to come up with a plan. The judge cut her off and snapped (almost yelled), "Refer her to drug treatment. Just *do it*." These are clear examples of the ways in which this system serves the needs of neither children nor their parents.

Attorneys who work in family court told me they have noticed that referrals for services required of parents are often not made in a timely fashion and attributed this delay to caseworkers' workload. As one law guardian, Michelle, put it: "I can't imagine, as a parent, like trying to get referrals from a caseworker. I mean I can't even get in touch with half of them for simple information." It is important to note that, despite the fact that attorneys and judges had these experiences with caseworkers not offering services, when parents or their attorneys complained in court, usually they were either told to take responsibility or were not believed (see also chapter 7).

Parents agreed that a lack of referrals was a problem:

SALINA: They [caseworkers] don't do their job. Damn it. [Laughter] That's how I see them.

TINA: What do you mean by that?

SALINA: They just don't do they job. Everything that they supposed to do they don't do. Regardless with the services or whatever it is, if I don't go in *the office* to ask, you know, "What is it you need me to do, what is it you have to tell me?" I won't get a letter in the mail, nobody won't tell me until it's too late. So that's why I make it my business to go at least two or three times a week to the agency and see the worker. . . . And she [the caseworker] be like "Oh, I got others cases. I'm too busy." All right, then, but how do you expect

> for me to do all this stuff if you're not notifying me? So that's why I make it my business to do it . . .'cause if you sit here and wait on them there'll be nothing done.

Parents frequently experienced caseworkers who did not keep in touch with them, did not ensure that they knew what they had to do, and did not make needed referrals. Thus, many parents had to resort to constant follow-up. For many, this follow-up was difficult or impossible if agencies were far from their homes or workplaces or if they didn't have phones (see chapters 7 and 8).

During my observations in support groups and parenting classes, discussions about needed services and caseworkers who did not make referrals were common. I was asked on numerous occasions if I knew where a parent could get a mental health evaluation or a parenting class, and I began gathering information about possibilities that I could pass along. Parenting classes in particular, which are required of practically every parent who is under ACS supervision, are often hard to find. One parent advocate at CWOP said that parents call almost daily to ask about available parenting classes, and she is frustrated that she only has a few places to send them. Often, parents are told that a class is ongoing, so it will be several weeks or months before another will be starting. I offered to compile a list of classes and found that most were offered at foster care agencies. Although they would sometimes accept clients from other agencies, often there was either not enough room, or the agency wanted to reserve spots for its own clients. Even if there were slots, parents would run into the problem of having to wait for the next class. Again, parents were not given needed help, even when it was required by caseworkers (see also chapter 7).

Despite these problems, judges rarely refuse to find that an agency has made reasonable efforts. Occasionally, however, they do delay making a finding in order to give the agency time to correct any problems. One judge I spoke with told me that she is fairly certain the agencies would not be reimbursed for a least some of the cost of foster care since many hearings are held late, in violation of both state and federal law. In general, then, permanency hearings did not seem to serve their purpose in ensuring that the foster care agencies were taking the necessary steps toward reunification or another permanent plan for the child. Parents were not always getting the services and visits to which they were entitled, and children were left in foster care longer. The court, however, did not remedy the situation.

Foster care agency caseworkers' high caseloads are especially problematic given the variety of tasks for which they are responsible: monitoring the child's placement, working with the parent so that the child can be returned, supervising visitation, and planning for the child to have a permanent family if reunification fails. These all take time and require weighing various interests (those of the child, the parent, and the foster parent). Caseworkers should focus on permanency planning, which can often mean concurrent planning. In other words, caseworkers are encouraged to evaluate cases to see which are unlikely to result in reunification and then plan for this contingency at the same time that they plan for reunification. Although permanency is a necessary goal (everyone in the child welfare field agrees that having children in foster care for years is a problem and plans must be made to avoid it), balancing these various aspects of a case and the different interests involved is difficult. High caseloads leave little time to do the careful planning required, caseworkers are not always adequately trained, and high turnover means that, over time, multiple caseworkers are likely involved in a case, making continuity in planning hard to achieve. Pressures toward concurrent planning often lead caseworkers to deemphasize reunification plans, which can lead to service-plan delays and to a situation in which parents are, essentially, written off and not given needed help. This is especially likely given that caseworkers are prone to comparing parents and foster parents when thinking about what is best for the child (whom they tend to see as their ultimate client). Foster parents are assumed to be safe and have more resources than the average parent; they are thus likely to be seen as providing better homes for children (see also Gerstenzang and Freundlich 2005). This is another clear example of stratified reproduction.

This situation led many parents in my study to complain that their foster care agency caseworkers focused more on the child and the foster home than on their family. Joan described it very simply: "The worker's only going to do so much because they're not there to work for you, they're there to work for the child." Another mother, Claudia, stated: "And, you know, even though I wanted the focus to be about me and my family, what I found is that the focus was about the administration, and the foster care administration, and the foster mother. Nothing was really 100 percent about my family and what's going on with my family." In Claudia's case, she was not given help in dealing with her teen son's anger and violence toward her, and he was not taken to counseling by the foster mother. When she brought this up to the foster care agency worker, the worker told her that she could not tell the foster mother how to run her household. Claudia felt that this directly impacted the length of time it took for her child to come home and the fact that he was only home for a few weeks before there was another angry altercation and he ran away (see also chapter 8).

Conclusion

The child welfare system is overwhelmed and becomes even more so when a slew of reports and removals follow a high-profile tragedy. Large caseloads only add to the stress created by public expectations that child protective services should prevent all tragedies. Caseworkers, judges, and attorneys are all under pressure to make "safe" decisions, and this leads to more cautious decision making: more cases marked substantiated, more families taken to family court, and more children removed to foster care. The resulting high caseloads and crowded court calendars are not only unmanageable for staff, but they also often harm families and make it difficult for caseworkers and other officials to fully investigate cases, give each family adequate attention, and offer each case adequate oversight. When everyone is overwhelmed it is more difficult for parents to get the services to which they are entitled and which are required for reunification; likewise, judges find it difficult to order agencies to provide those required services. Most troubling is that the delays that too often exist in family court are an important, and preventable, reason why many children experience long stays in foster care.

The tendency for the public to focus on the horrible abuse of a relatively few children sets up a situation in which is it easy to think in terms of parents versus their children. This is especially easy to do when poor families of color are mainly involved, families that are already demonized in many ways. Often, in this way of thinking, the solution to the problem of child maltreatment is foster care rather than services for parents. Because services are not always readily available, this choice can seem logical or even necessary. I do not argue that all parents can be helped to care for their children properly, nor do I argue that cases of abuse should be ignored. Cases like Nixzmary Brown's are horrible and immediate. Rather, I argue that the larger context needs to be better known: most children are neglected, not abused, and general social conditions such as poverty, racism, unemployment, poor housing, lack of medical care, and underperforming schools are also dangerous and harmful to children.

To adopt a medical metaphor, maltreatment of children is less like an acute infection (as it was portrayed in the 1970s) and more like a chronic condition that has both individual and environmental causes. The system is geared toward preventing serious cases of abuse, while the interventions often made in families involve making decisions with a narrow view of child safety as the paramount criteria so that the agency is not blamed for future tragedies. This focus makes it difficult to provide services to families in an effort to strengthen them and improve the lives of children. After removal, it is still too often difficult for parents to get what they need in order to regain custody. This situation is tolerated because it mainly impacts poor families of color who are already, in many ways, blamed for their problems and seen as undeserving of help. In this climate, the child welfare system deals with families in a punitive fashion, with removals and court supervision, while services are inadequately provided and cases are allowed to drag on.

5

Policing versus Helping in Child Welfare

In the last few decades, with the rise of particularly harsh depictions of the "undeserving poor" (Katz 1996), which are profoundly shaped by ideas about race and gender, the balance between helping and policing in child welfare has changed (see chapter 2). As the state has shifted resources away from social provisioning and adopted more punitive measures, poor families of color are finding it more and more difficult to get the help they need while they are subject to both increased scrutiny of their parenting and greater risk of losing children to foster care. As in other state bureaucracies, welfare and criminal justice especially, some families are more subject to this scrutiny and to "catching a case" than others. Poor families and families of color are more likely than other groups to be reported to ACS, a pattern that is not unique to New York City. At least part of the reason for this disparity lies in the level of surveillance to which they are subject, surveillance that most middle-class and many white families can avoid (Appell 1997; Roberts 2002). When coupled with the stereotypes of unfit mothers of color and deadbeat fathers of color that influence how poor parents are judged, surveillance helps to account for the race and class makeup of the population involved with child welfare in New York City.

For example, most cases in which women are tested for drugs while giving birth involve poor women of color (Siegel 1997). In New York City, a positive test most often results in an ACS report, which very often can mean removal of the child. Despite the fact that drug use crosses racial and class lines (Zerai and Banks 2002), poor women of color are thus more likely to be caught and are much more vulnerable to having their children removed. This is a prime example of how "rather than surveillance indicating a rationalized and distributed imposition on individual privacy . . . surveillance is often applied selectively and with varying intensities according to one's social address" (Monahan 2006; see also Campbell 2006; Eubanks 2006; Gilliom 2001; Lyon 2002). Not only are poor families of color more subject to reports and more likely to face a loss of child custody, the service plans with which they are expected to comply offer little in the way of needed help; instead, the plans attempt to instill proper attitudes and test to see which parents are committed and "together" enough to regain custody. In these ways, the child welfare system serves to create and re-create relations of stratified reproduction. It draws lines between fit and unfit parents, while not providing adequate services to support parenting among its clients.

Surveillance and Child Welfare Reports: Race, Class, and Gender Patterns

Poor families of color are often reported to ACS by the public agencies they rely on to meet their health, mental health, and educational needs (see also Campbell 2004). According to caseworkers, particular schools, hospitals, and doctors call in reports more often than others. One supervisor in particular was quite clear that there is bias in who is reported, and she told me, as an example, about a particular emergency room doctor who "has issues" (her polite way of referring to racism) and makes calls frequently. When a child is absent (which can equal educational neglect and can therefore warrant a report), private schools will first call the parent to find out if there was a reasonable explanation; in contrast, public schools, especially in poor and minority neighborhoods, will automatically call in a report when a certain number of absences occur. This difference is illustrated by Carrie's (a law guardian and former ACS caseworker) story:

CARRIE: It's kind of confusing to me that some schools have never heard of ACS. I actually went to a school once, a public school.

TINA: Really? Where was it?

CARRIE: I was in, it was in Rego Park, which is a very middle-class, very mixed-race, ethnicity, whatever. It's actually, I used to live in Rego Park. . . . I went into the school, they didn't really understand what I was. I had to explain to the principal, "You know that mandated reported training you go to?" "Yes," "If you were to call in a case, I would be the person who'd come." "Oh, okay."

In listening to parents' stories of how they were first reported to ACS, it became clear that their interactions with public hospitals, public schools, social service agencies, foster care preventive agencies, and the police placed them in situations in which their lives could be examined by mandated reporters who in turn reported them. Poor families of color are more likely to be in contact with these agencies and officials than are white middle- and upper-class families who, for example, are not likely to be in contact with the police and can purchase the services they need rather than rely on public services. In addition, poor parents of color are more likely to be judged harshly for their problems or less likely to be given the benefit of the doubt when questions about parenting and child safety arise. Joan's story is a prime example and, when compared to the case of a wealthier family I saw in family court, illustrates the kind of surveillance poor women of color are under, surveillance that white, middle- and upper-class families are able, in general, to avoid.

Joan is an African American mother in her forties with a history of crack cocaine addiction. Years before I met her, Joan's older children were placed in foster care and were later adopted by her aunt. When we spoke, it had been almost a year since her youngest child was removed from her care after she had a relapse. She was living with her daughter's father at the time in a building owned by his mother, and he was the main caretaker for the child while Joan worked full-time as a nurse's assistant to support the family. Joan became depressed after the death of her best friend, attempted suicide, and was psychiatrically hospitalized. "Because it was a city hospital," she said, they gave her a drug test, which was positive. ACS was called, and the caseworker sent a foster care prevention agency to work with her. They helped her find an in-patient treatment program, but there was a delay in enrolling. Joan had no health insurance to pay for it as she had lost her union insurance when she was fired after her drug use was reported, and her Medicaid was not yet active. Although she could not enroll fully in a program accepted by ACS, she did go to an out-patient treatment group until her insurance was activated. Since she was planning to go into an in-patient program as soon as she could, the preventive agency was going to close her case and allow her to retain custody of her daughter. Joan felt that things were fine at that point.

A few days before her case was to be closed, however, a report that her partner was sexually abusing their daughter was made anonymously. This was quickly shown to be false, but during the investigation the ACS case-worker asked Joan to take a drug test, which she failed, so the caseworker looked into Joan's police record and found she had been arrested after a physical fight with her partner, something that she had not told case-workers. Because of her history, her arrest, and the delay in entering an in-patient program, the ACS caseworker decided to remove her child, despite feeling the child was well cared for. Because Joan used a public hospital to get mental health treatment, she was tested for drugs, which set off a chain of events that eventually led to the removal of her child when she could not pay for drug treatment due to her job loss, and when a caseworker searched police records electronically and found she had been arrested.

Joan's case is in direct contrast to the only case of a wealthy, white family involved with ACS that I observed during my fieldwork. This family was reported to ACS by a police officer who claimed to have seen the father act abusively toward his daughter in a public park. The initial allegation was found to be false during a 1028 hearing, and the children were quickly returned to the family. During the course of the investigation, however, the mother's severe depression and drug history, which had never been reported to ACS by anyone, came to light. The father admitted to the ACS caseworker that his wife's psychiatrist told him not to leave her alone with the children because it was not safe, and one of the children reported to his law guardian that his favorite thing to do with his mother was to spend time with her in bed, which was taken as evidence of her severe depression. Despite all this, the law guardian told me she was in favor of leaving the children home because the mother would be getting good psychiatric care. The ACS caseworkers not only accepted the father's promises that he would not leave her alone with the children but also knew this care was possible, given his severance from a Wall Street job and his ability to hire childcare. In similar cases I came across involving poor families of color, this serious mental health issue led to the children's placement in foster care.[1] This wealthy family's case was completely dropped after only a few months, and the parents were no longer subject to mandated services or monitoring by ACS caseworkers. In this case, the parents were able to purchase mental health and drug treatment for the mother privately, and these providers never called ACS, even though they clearly felt she might present a danger to her children. Because the father had the resources to pay for high-quality treatment for his wife and to be home full-time to ensure she did not endanger the children, their children were left in their custody. In addition, the couple was able to hire a private attorney who fought vigorously for them.[2]

The race and class differences between these two families meant they were subject to different levels of surveillance and different assumptions about their ability to adequately care for their children. In Joan's case, public institutions subjected her to drug testing and reported her to ACS. After she was reported, a foster care prevention agency was sent to her home to continue to monitor her drug use, and ACS continued to follow her case, putting the agency in a position to eventually learn of her arrest. The wealthier mother, in contrast, was able to get treatment from a private doctor, and her drug problems and severe depression were not reported. No agency followed up on her treatment or ensured that the father stayed home to protect the children. The wealthy couple was trusted to continue to ensure their children's safety because of the material resources to which they had access. In contrast, Joan's inability to get treatment, her arrest, and her ACS history cast doubt upon her ability to care for her child. These two cases highlight the role of class and race differences in structuring not only which families are reported to ACS but also which families are able to retain custody of their children.

Catching a Case

In general, I found that various helping institutions and poor communities themselves are drawn into surveillance through mandated reporting laws and a familiarity with the system. This situation made some parents reluctant to seek help or interact with others for fear of ACS reports (see also chapter 8). A social worker at a child welfare conference I attended reported that she has found there is a fairly widespread fear of "catching a case," especially immediately following the Nixzmary Brown case (Roberts, Hill, and

Pitchal 2006), and this phrase was used in support groups I attended as well. The social worker talked about one of her clients and explained that the idea of "catching a case" conveys "the experience of how this family was thinking about this in terms of a contagion, in terms of a virus, in terms of something that was being spread, and how it affected her relationship with every service provider that she had been involved with" (Roberts, Hill, and Pitchal 2006, 8). Fear that one might "catch a case" caused many parents to be cautious and reluctant to divulge problems when talking to neighbors and service providers, even if it meant forgoing needed help.

Many parents were reported to ACS by agencies whose purpose is to provide help and services to families: public schools, social services agencies, and foster care prevention agencies. Some parents even experienced calls to ACS, made with little evidence of maltreatment, that were later used to threaten or force them to comply with expert's directions (giving medication to children, attending therapy, taking children out of school). For example, in Maria's case (she is a Latina in her early thirties with four children who receives public assistance), her son was acting up in school (she describes him as hyper), and his teacher, rather than attempting to discipline him, would either send him immediately to the principal or call and tell Maria that she had to pick him up or the teacher would call ACS. Maria had to rush to the school on almost a daily basis to pick him up. He was rarely allowed to remain in class enough to learn, and she would then have to ensure he was cared for.

School officials, rather than working to educate her son and deal with his behavior problems so that he could learn, threatened her with calls to ACS so that Maria would take him out of school and the school would not have to deal with him. They had no evidence she was mistreating him, but the teacher used ACS as a way to force Maria to deal with her son's problems. Rather than providing for his education, both Maria and her son were punished—Maria was constantly fearful of a report and had to make continual trips to school, and her son was denied his education. Maria was eventually able to get the board of education to pay for her son to go to a private school, and she no longer had to deal with threats of an ACS report. She reported the new teacher was working with her on his behavior issues, and he was learning a lot more.

Foster care prevention agencies become, in many cases, a source of reports that actually lead to removals, although their overt aim is to prevent foster care placement. These agencies provide services that are meant to support families, including frequent caseworker visits or homemakers to help out several hours a week, but the provision of these services also places mandated reporters in a position to carefully watch a family and its parenting practices. Preventive agencies make it clear to caseworkers that they must call in a report if they have any concerns for the child's safety or they can lose their jobs. There seems to be little leeway for agency caseworkers to decide what situations are genuinely unsafe for children and therefore require reporting to ACS. These practices lead some mothers to resist having a preventive agency assigned to them because the mothers saw those caseworkers as not providing help, but simply providing ACS with another method of surveillance.

For example, Trisha, an African American mother in her thirties, informed her preventive caseworker that she began using crack cocaine again, and her caseworker attempted to avoid making a report to ACS. Instead, she encouraged Trisha to continue treatment and resist using again. She thought that Trisha could safely retain custody while dealing with her addiction and apparently recognized that relapses are common. An ACS official, however, eventually received a copy of Trisha's positive drug test and removed all the children. The preventive caseworker was fired for not making the report. Rather than helping to prevent foster care placement by providing services and support, the prevention agency was expected to act as surveillance by watching for possible continued drug use or maltreatment, events that required immediate reporting under agency policy. Trisha's relapse was seen, by ACS officials, as an automatic risk to her child that had to be dealt with by foster care placement rather than as an ongoing problem for which Trisha needed help and support so that placement could be avoided.

Some mothers I spoke with, however, did feel that their preventive agencies provided them with important help and were pleased with the services they received. Interestingly, in these cases the preventive agency caseworker was either replaced or fired because he or she was perceived as too close to the family. This led officials at either the agency or ACS to question the caseworker's judgment and maintain that he or she should have reported what was going on in the home rather than continuing to help the family. Irene, a Latina mother of five in her forties, for example, told me that her preventive agency worker came with her to court to argue on her behalf against a court finding that she was neglectful. He was dismissed from her case at the request of an ACS attorney. These experiences with preventive agencies call into question their effectiveness. Rather than supporting families and avoiding foster care, they actually led to foster care placement. If these caseworkers are perceived as providing too much support to parents and not enough surveillance to protect children, then they are likely to be removed from cases. Here, again, the agency expects the caseworkers' surveillance roles to be paramount.

Not only are various helping agencies drawn into surveillance, sometimes to the detriment of their roles as service providers, but poor communities are drawn in as well. Because ACS reports are common in poor neighborhoods around New York City (see chapter 1 for statistics), many people are familiar with ACS and the possible consequences of an investigation. In these neighborhoods ACS reports are used as weapons in disputes among families and neighbors or by batterers against their former partners (Roberts 2002; Roberts, Hill, and Pitchal 2006, 8; Voices of Women Organizing Project 2008). In contrast, I heard no stories of ACS reports being used to get back at people in middle-class and wealthier neighborhoods where reports in general are rare. One caseworker explained this phenomenon to me: "You do have cases where I'm the jilted ex-girlfriend, and I decided to hell with it. I know ACS will be in their life. I'm gonna call ACS just to fuck with them. It's happened. And unfortunately, we have to investigate and go out on every single case no matter what." This caseworker explained that people in many poor neighborhoods are familiar with ACS and aware of how the agency can become involved in people's lives. Thus, they understand that reports can be a way to "fuck with" people because an ACS report requires a caseworker to come to your home, look through your cabinets, refrigerator, and bedrooms, and question you and your children about intimate matters of family life. Parents are very aware that the result of such a visit can be the removal of their children. ACS is thus very often experienced as a negative and punitive agency rather than a positive one that might provide help. It is an effective weapon.

Maria, who has never lost custody of her children, nevertheless explained vividly how stressful and anxiety-provoking the investigation process is:

> But it's just to the point, like, now, still to now, my kids, if somebody knocks loud, it could be housing, it could be anything, they'd be, like, "Ma, ACS is at the door," my little ones 'cause they're, like, traumatized.... And I'm, like, now no one's allowed to even knock on my door. You have to whistle in order for me to know that it's someone that I know because I get paranoid, you know?

> . . . And then, like, and my kids' father calls me and argue, and they'd [her children] be, like, "Don't argue with him 'cause you know he's gonna call ACS." I'd be, like, "But, you know, what am I supposed to do? Stay quiet?" . . . It's like you can't live life the way, you know, you really want to, real calm and—because these people just come into your life, as I hear and, you know, and especially now after Nixzmary when they should have been doing something about it. But the way they come in and then they don't investigate. They just come and grab up your kids and all that, it's like—no, it's just, it traumatizes me. . . . Like, the other day, the door, they knocked real loud. It was my neighbor to let me know she was going down. And I'm, like, no, no. And I started screaming at my kids, "You see that loud knock and those rooms a mess? You see?"

This is a dramatic account of how reports can create tension, fear, and suspicion. The process of investigation itself causes anxiety and strains family and neighborhood relationships in the poor communities of color in which ACS is a constant presence. Thus, even reporting a family is an effective way to get back at or harm others, and the strain is detrimental to these communities as a whole (see chapter 8).

Not only is the investigative process stressful and painful, but reports can also make retaining custody of children difficult, even if reports are unfounded (i.e., the caseworker finds that there is no evidence of a problem). ACS policy is that caseworkers should take past unfounded reports into account when making determinations on new cases. I attended a public forum at which a deputy commissioner explained that agency policy is to assume that an unfounded case does not mean that no problem exists in the home; rather, it means simply that the caseworker could not find sufficient evidence. Under this way of thinking, a string of reports could indicate an ongoing problem, so caseworkers are to take them as evidence of a problem. This practice is understandable; sometimes caseworkers do not investigate fully, and a series of reports could very well indicate a pattern. It also, however, ignores the ways reports are used in poor communities of color and the incentive for mandated reporters to be "better safe than sorry" and call in a report, even if they have little evidence that the child is in danger. Caseworkers were aware of this policy and told me that they found it often inappropriate.

Nathan, a father whose children had been placed in foster care and who has been working as a parent advocate since he regained custody several years ago, described the effects of this policy: "You not getting along with somebody, they call ACS. Only gotta do it a couple of times then they come, and they check somethin' and it's all right. But if they keep gettin' called, you got a case." In other words, a string of calls increases suspicion, making it more likely that the family will be required to cooperate with further home visits and services or that they will either be taken to family court or have their children removed. Simply having multiple reports called in can lead to increased monitoring and possible loss of custody.

Although this is not, by any means, a complete discussion of the issue of ACS reporting and why certain families are more likely to be reported than others, this description does highlight two pertinent issues. First, more reports are made about poor families of color in part because they are likely to rely almost exclusively on various public services for their basic needs—public schools, public hospitals and doctors who accept Medicaid, and public assistance—and these institutions are more likely to report than others. I did not come across any cases in which a report had been made by a pediatrician paid for by private insurance, a private school, or a public school in a wealthier neighborhood. This seems to indicate (along with the disparities between community districts that tend to fall along class and race lines) that such reports are rare.

Second, the form that surveillance takes in child welfare demonstrates how various private helping institutions become part of the state policing and control efforts that have come to prominence in recent decades. Many of the mothers I met experienced agencies as sources of potentially punitive surveillance rather than help and support. Instead of carefully assessing needs, providing assistance, and generally helping with social provisioning, these agencies too often engaged in policing, surveillance, and punishment. In addition, this surveillance system extends beyond state agencies and encompasses both private agencies and individual citizens. Reports can be made without consequences, and poor communities of color have become familiar with ACS because they are the subjects of a majority of reports. This creates a situation in which ACS reports are used to get back at others. That individuals use child welfare in this way demonstrates the extent to which the community sees it as a punitive system rather than a helping one.

The Caseworkers' Dual Role

A caseworker's official title is child protective specialist or CPS, and, as the title clearly signals, the caseworker's job is to protect children from abuse and neglect. Caseworkers investigate reports and assess the safety of the child's living situation and the risk they face of being harmed. Using their judgments about safety and risk, they decide what interventions to make in the family. The children are their ultimate clients, and their safety and well-being are paramount. Caseworkers must also follow the mandate that removals should occur only when a child is in immediate danger or at imminent risk of serious harm. According to state and federal law, reasonable efforts to prevent removals should be made except in these extreme circumstances. Thus, caseworkers must assess the needs of the family and help them access services that might mitigate risk and eliminate or ameliorate safety concerns, but they must do so in a context in which services are often difficult to find and resources are usually inadequate to provide help for all the families who need it. Service provision can be simple: caseworkers can instruct a parent to get an order of protection against an abuser, they can help them fill out an application for food stamps, or they can refer them to another service agency. It can also be more complex: they can listen to parents vent, counsel them about family problems, and field phone calls when further crises arise. Marilyn, a Latina woman who has been a caseworker for six and a half years, described her work to me: "Our job is to protect children. Okay? Parents are involved, and we are to stabilize *them* in order to protect our children. So our initiative is to service as much as possible. If all of that fails, then we have to do our job [i.e., remove the children from the home]. But we have to prove to the court, prior to removing a child, that we have exerted every possibility." Thus, caseworkers actually combine two roles—investigator and helper.

These two roles are inevitably in tension, and caseworkers described how this conflict sometimes leads to uncomfortable situations or to feeling that neither role was satisfactorily completed. Amy, a white woman in her forties who worked as a CPS for five and a half years, discussed the complexities of investigating while also telling people you are there to help them:

AMY: But then what was kind of hard for me sometimes is that the more information you got, you had to develop a relationship with them to get the information, and then this is the information that I'm using against you. So

> the agency wants you to go, and they call, they call us caseworkers, really they want you to be a social worker, but it's law enforcement that you're doing. I'm investigating this case as if I were a detective, trying to gather information for a case that I might file against them. That's law enforcement; that's not social work. And the agency, I feel, always had an issue with that, because they really wanted to say, like, "Oh, social workers like to help people, and we're gonna put in services and we're gonna." But initially, that's not my job. That's what sometimes it turns out to. Sometimes it makes you feel a little—
>
> TINA: Schizophrenic?
>
> AMY: Yeah, that, you know.

Amy describes a basic contradiction faced by all caseworkers: their role is to both help the client and to enforce the law. They are investigating, but they must also build rapport with their clients to get a clear sense of the family's needs in case the agency decides to provide services in the future. As Amy describes it, this dual position can be uncomfortable.

Caseworkers mainly attempted to deal with this uncomfortable situation in two ways. First, they attempted to make it clear to parents what their role is. Marilyn described what she says to parents:

> I do not lie to any of the clients. The minute I go in, you know, I tell them, "This is a report. These are allegations. It is up to you to show me different. If you can't prove to me that these allegations are not true, then this case can end up being indicated. It can end up being in court, and it can end up being a removal. It all depends on what you tell me. And I hope that you're truthful because I can assist you with services and anything else that you may need, from housing services, furniture, clothing, food." I explain all that to them. But I also tell them, you know, that I have to do my job. "And if your children are in imminent danger, and you are failing to protect your own children, I have to protect them from you and whoever else is around them."

Caseworkers are trained to approach parents in this way and to tell them that they must protect children and this could include removing them from the home. On one level, and for Marilyn, this is just a fact they tell parents in the spirit of being open with them about what might happen to the family and what the caseworker's role is.

Although caseworkers thought they were simply informing parents, the parents I talked to viewed this information about the potential for child removal as a threat. When caseworkers presented themselves as being there to possibly remove the child, some parents felt that the caseworker was hostile—automatically looking for the worst, acting judgmentally, and/or planning to remove their child rather than offering real help. Trisha described her interaction: "Yeah, they just treated me like, you know, I was a bad person. You know, 'You shouldn't be using drugs; you got kids, why are you using drugs?' And 'Listen, you don't do this, you're not gonna get your kids back.'" For Trisha, this approach signaled to her that the caseworker automatically thought she was a bad mother and was not there to help. Other parents said explicitly that they neither trusted their caseworker nor felt she liked them; they thought that the caseworker had it out for them and came with the intention of removing their child. Leslie, an African American mother in her forties, stated: "I don't know what her agenda was, but I don't think it was trying to help parents. I don't think it was trying to help in any way. Her agenda was, you know, she didn't like me, and it was obvious, so she took them away." A caseworker telling a parent that she has the power to remove children has the collateral effect, in many cases, of interfering with the process of building rapport, assessing needs, and providing services. Clients also experience the disclosure as unnecessarily judgmental and punitive.

The power to remove a child can also be used to get parents to cooperate and/or to accept or "engage in" services. One caseworker, Alicia, an African American woman in her thirties who has been a caseworker for nine years, commented to me that she explicitly tells parents what they need to do to avoid having their children removed and gives them a list and a deadline, generally the sixty days she has to complete her investigation. Caseworkers, unless they go to court to obtain a finding of neglect and then an order for services, which is a very lengthy process, have no actual power to force a parent to accept services. They can, however, point out that they have the power to remove children and that parents can avoid this by taking specific actions like getting services or cooperating fully. This is often an effective tactic in securing compliance. In this way, caseworkers are not offering help that may be accepted or refused, but they can force compliance by letting parents know that the alternative may be losing their children. When caseworkers' law enforcement and assistance roles are combined, providing help turns into a coercive process backed up by a threat of child removal.

The second way that caseworkers try to deal with this tension between their two roles is by emphasizing one side of their job over the other.

Many of them, however, felt that having to do both made it difficult to do either well. Carl, an African American who had been a caseworker for five years, emphasized the helping aspects of his work and talked about how the agency's emphasis on completing investigations in a short time period and then, if possible, closing the case to move on to the next investigation short-circuits his efforts to provide meaningful help:

> We come in, as an agency, and we're told we have sixty days to conduct an investigation. And in such a short, minimal amount of time, we can't really, we as workers feel, we can't really effectively do our job because I'm only seeing a family, you know, twice per month. So out of sixty days, I'm seeing this family four times. So what real value can I add and bring to the family if I only see you four times out of sixty days? And what issues am I really resolving in a sixty-day period that have manifested, let's say, you know, for a five-year period or a three-year period?

Notice that he refers to his job as helping families with their issues, but he feels he cannot do this given the time constraints of investigation. Later in the interview, when I asked what he would change about the agency, he again returned to the issue of how he can help families: "It's very difficult to address and service all the service needs in a family when you have time constraints. You know, sometimes families come around toward the end of the investigation, not necessarily their very first week. You have to engage them. You have to develop a rapport with them until they can trust you." Here he points out that getting parents to trust you so that they will accept services in a meaningful way that might lead to family change is time consuming, and he does not have the time to do it effectively.

Marilyn, however, takes the approach that she is an investigator, not a social worker: "I'm not a social worker. I'm an investigator. I don't go to the home to try to fix their problems. I go to the home to assess for safety and immediate danger and refer to stabilize the home." She still has a mandate to provide services when appropriate, so her tactic is to refer for services and, when possible, move the case to someone else for monitoring.[3] For Marilyn, then, her job is to investigate, and she attempts to have others provide services when it's possible to divide the workload.

Although caseworkers juggle these two roles in these ways and attempt to manage the conflict by being clear with parents about their roles,

Marilyn acknowledged that there is a tension between the two roles that does not disappear:

MARILYN: They [parents] still fear ACS because they feel that we're just about removing children. They're very skeptical when I tell them, "You know, if you comply with services, we can stabilize you. We can assist you with this." And it's not until they see that all these things are in place that they come to trust me. Understand? In the beginning, it's just like, "I'm not telling you much because you're going to betray me and remove my kid if I tell you this." So it's kinda hard to service a community that comes with that idea already.

TINA: Right. And plus, that's, in a way, the reality.

MARILYN: No, it isn't. It isn't the reality. Okay.

TINA: You don't think?

MARILYN: No, I don't because that's not the way I work. . . . I can't tell you how other people work, but that's the way we're trained to do this job. Like I told you, that case where FPP [Family Preservation Program] was there for *seventeen weeks* is a perfect example of what I'm telling you. And all the services that we put in for this family [before finally removing the children to foster care]. And all of that failed, so what else can I do? My hands are tied at that point. You know, but that's our job. It's very hard to do this job because how do you explain to someone that you're trying to help them when all they see is you as the enemy, and they never trust you?

Marilyn acknowledges that her clients treat her with suspicion and see her as an enemy because they realize she can remove their children. She argues that the clients have no reason not to trust her because she isn't simply a child snatcher; she does removals only as a last resort. Nevertheless, client suspicion makes service provision difficult.

Parents agreed that they could not trust caseworkers. They reported that they understood all too well that what they said to a caseworker could be used as proof they had neglected their children, so they did, indeed, keep information from them. In Joan's case (see chapter 3), she deliberately never told officials about her arrest, but it eventually played a decisive role in her child's removal:

And this report [the one alleging sexual abuse by her partner and the last before her child was removed] came in November. But when that new report came they went through the system somehow and found out I had got arrested

> because I didn't tell preventative services. I didn't tell nobody. I got arrested on a Sunday. I came home Monday night. *This is not something you're supposed to tell.* Certain things you tell them. I didn't know that they can go and find these things. I swear to God I didn't know that. [Emphasis added]

This example shows not only that parents know what can happen and are then strategic about what they tell caseworkers, but it also demonstrates the kind of surveillance parents are under, made possible by technology that allows caseworkers to access information that parents choose to withhold.

Other parents who were less savvy about child welfare reported feeling manipulated into divulging family problems by a caseworker who was offering help. The parents then were shocked and extremely angry and hurt when, rather than being offered help, their children were removed. Sandra, a white 18B attorney, told me several stories in which her client's children were placed in foster care only on the basis of their statements to caseworkers. Usually, these statements were made after caseworkers had encouraged them to answer questions honestly so that the caseworker could help them with family problems:

> SANDRA: The caseworker says, "We're here to help you." She's [the mother] a really nice woman. She thinks, "Oh, great. These people are here to help me." She admits that she smokes marijuana. Right? Into the case records it goes. Into family court we come, blah, blah, blah. . . . They get this other client to take a drug test.
>
> TINA: This case, were they filing to . . . get supervision and court-ordered services or were they trying to take those kids to foster care?
>
> SANDRA: They didn't take the kids, but what happened is because she smokes marijuana, they violated her, and now they want to take the kids away [i.e., they wanted to remove the kids because she violated a court order]. So, I mean, it all relates back to this initial thing. *What* is she doing telling people? Now, in the criminal justice system, you can't go in and say that to people. You have to tell them they have a right, so all these cases, a huge number of these cases are *made on statements* by the parent to the caseworker.

Sandra and other 18B attorneys complained that parents' rights were not protected and that the involvement of ACS and the courts sometimes made situations worse. Rather than receiving help for relatively minor issues, parents were pressured into admitting problems that were then used against them later to justify child removal.

Having caseworkers be both service providers and law enforcement (without the normal rules law enforcement must follow to protect individual rights) creates tensions for both caseworkers and parents. Combining these two roles creates an adversarial situation (Waldfogel 1998) in which service provision is extremely difficult, if not impossible. As in the cases I described, the law enforcement and surveillance aspect of the caseworkers' job becomes by far the most prominent, especially in a climate in which fear of a tragedy conditions much of agency policy and caseworker actions. If parents had more access to services outside of child welfare, they might be more willing and able to get needed help, but, too often, child welfare, which is feared in many ways, is a main way to access needed help (see chapter 8). Child welfare is thus a part of the larger shift in state practices away from social provisioning and toward more punitive social control and surveillance with all the negative outcomes that entails.

Help and Policing in Service Plans

Once parents have been deemed neglectful or risks to their children, caseworkers create service plans that should address the needs of the family and reduce the risks that children face. I found, however, that plans did not meet the complex needs of parents and families. Instead, they focused on education and counseling in an attempt to "resocialize parents to behave in ways that are seen as appropriately parental" (Reich 2005, 115). These plans also tended to expand "beyond child protection into every realm of mothers' lives in the name of making them good mothers" (Appell 1997, 579–580). In addition, I found that decision makers focused mainly on parents' attendance rather than on articulating what kinds of changes they wanted to see and how parents could demonstrate them. Completing a service plan became more about demonstrating commitment and showing that a parent has his or her life "together" enough to raise children than about addressing the core of family problems. Although poverty is often at the root of the problems these families face, and although lack of housing, jobs, and childcare are prominent reasons why children are not returned from foster care (see chapters 7 and 8), services to address these issues were generally handled toward the end of a case, if at all. Again, practices surrounding service provision signal that the main problems underlying child maltreatment are thought to be individual parental shortcomings or pathologies rather than systematic structural disadvantages.

Cookie-Cutter Plans

When I asked one family court judge what she thought was done well in the child welfare system and what could be improved, she replied: "I sometimes think that we could do a better job on the assessment and the service plan definition because those are very, very complicated issues. There seems to be kind of a stock menu of services that get recommended, so it would require probably a higher-credentialed person making assessments, but I think that would improve the outcomes that we have. It seems a little ad hoc sometimes what's being recommended and ordered." This complaint, that service plans are not thoughtful enough and individualized for each parent and family, was one I heard from judges, ACS attorneys, parents' attorneys, parents, and parent advocates. As one parent advocate told a support group I observed: "We are being asked to do things that waste our time and don't serve us or our families." Service plans contain a very standard list of services. Practically every parent will take a parenting class, and most will be required to go to counseling. Apart from that, parents will be sent to specific types of "programs" (drug treatment, domestic violence programs, and anger management programs). Very few variations are made to address the specific needs of the parent, and practically no services deal with poverty. The services offered clearly signal that individual pathology, rather than inequality, is seen as the root of family problems.

It is important to acknowledge that some parents did feel that they were getting the help they needed. The parents who battled addiction, in particular, told me that the experience of having their children taken away did act as a catalyst for them to become more serious about getting treatment and remaining sober. It also meant that they received more help. One father, Ramel, an African American who began using cocaine as a teenager and crack as a young adult (at the age of thirty-two, he had been using on and off for fourteen years) put it this way: "Because we was in a shelter, a family shelter together, which we got no real help. . . . And even if we took steps to do things ourselves, we still didn't get no help. . . . We're getting more help from these social workers now, and it's sad that we have to go through this." Many parents of color like Ramel had trouble finding help without becoming involved with child welfare and losing custody. Parents had different thoughts about this. Ramel talked about how he was happy, in one sense, that things happened this way:

> It hurts. I cried in front of the lawyer, I cried in front of a lot of people, because I mean, like I said, I *never*, ever went through this before. . . . I'm happy I'm going through this, though. Because it's an eye-opener, you know? It's an eye-opener. But I don't wanna ever go through this *ever* again. I wanna get through this and that's gonna be it. . . . My son is the cause of me getting my life together, and because this happened, it's not forcing me to get my life together, because I want it to stop. . . . And it's like you know how sometimes you need a motivation to get you going?

Having to go through the child welfare system, although painful, provided motivation and meant Ramel received more help. Simone, however, felt that losing custody of her children was detrimental to her staying sober: "They think that they can punish you into getting sober. And [what] they don't realize is by taking the children and giving you no reason to live that you get so depressed." In general, parents would have preferred to access help without the potential for child removal.

Parenting Skills Classes

Although concrete services are sometimes made available to parents going through child welfare (drug treatment, help in escaping domestic violence, and counseling), parents, and even caseworkers and attorneys, found the most common services, particularly parenting skills classes, less helpful. When I told attorneys that I was attending these classes (one ACS attorney quipped, "Oh, so you're under ACS supervision too now?") they always asked me what the classes were like and told me that they felt these classes did not help anything; the classes were just something the agency did, without considering whether the class was appropriate for all parents. Caseworkers, like Carl, had this opinion: "We hope it fixes it, but it doesn't. . . . Which, a parenting skill class is, the actual content of the classes is, it doesn't address anything. A parent that's going to parenting skill classes because they have a drug problem is totally different from a parent that's going to parenting skills classes because she had a case indicated for domestic violence or a case indicated for inadequate guardianship. And once again, each case is different and each parent is different. . . . And they don't cover that in thirteen weeks." Most parents reported that classes did not cover topics related to their specific situations or to their children's ages and needs and that they learned little in the way of concrete skills to make them better parents. Many, like Olivia, an African American mother who had her children removed because she could not afford a big enough apartment and refused to go into the shelter system, felt that they were unnecessary:

> TINA: What do you think about the parenting skill classes? Are they helpful to you?
>
> OLIVIA: No.
>
> TINA: Not at all?
>
> OLIVIA: I tell you no, because . . . I've been a mother since my daughter was [born and she] is sixteen years old. Never had a problem with ACS till this. . . . What can you tell me? I raised all my kids by myself. No man, nobody. Me. So what can they tell me? Not to yell at your kids? Not to talk to your kids this way? Oh, sit down and talk, and maybe they'll talk back? Me and my kids, all my kids have good communication. . . . You could have told me stuff that, when my kids was little. . . . So it just be wasting my time going there. But I'll go, because that's what the judge wants.

Olivia was also instructed to take a special needs class because one of her daughters had been diagnosed with ADHD. When I asked if it was helpful, she told me she only was taught two things: that she should not go to bed before her children and that she had to remember to always give them their medication. She commented that she found these "dumb, stupid things" that she already knew. For Olivia, she was comfortable as a mother and found these very vague and basic instructions a waste of time. Most importantly, going to a class was not going to help her find a decent apartment.

Most of the positive comments I heard from parents about parenting skills classes had to do with enjoying the class, being around other parents going through similar experiences, and having a group of people to whom they could vent (either about their case or about the difficulties of parenting). I only heard one mother, Irene, a Latina, talk about concrete things she learned in a parenting class that she put into practice with her own children.[4] When I met her, ACS was involved in her family a second time, and she was told to take another class. She said that she did not mind taking it but felt it was unnecessary in her current situation, which stemmed from her teen daughter's out-of-control behavior and mental illness:[5]

> Why do they [ACS officials] treat people with the same set of rules. . . . Like if your child gets taken away for domestic violence, and her child gets taken away for child abuse, they offer the same programs to these people. . . . "Go to parenting classes, you'll be a better parent for it." Who's supervising this, you know, you really are learning what it takes to be a parent, and that you're not gonna do it again? That was my issue with them. Like, why do you assume everybody that comes through here, *its presumed that they not fit parents*? You know, why couldn't it be, "Oh, she lost it for a minute. She was human." You know. "She's been through so many parenting classes. Why make her go through this again?"

Irene hits on the main reason parenting classes are offered to everyone: the agencies assume that the people who come through the system, who are primarily poor people of color, do not know how to parent and need instruction in very basic parenting skills, despite the specific problems each individual parent faces.

Although having everyone take a parenting class makes sense on the surface (presumably, if your children are in foster care it is because you are an inadequate parent in some way), many cases I observed were less about problematic parenting practices and more about either parental behavior problems—like drug abuse or mental health—or a lack of resources (see chapter 6). For example, I met one mother who was told she needed to take parenting again when she had a drug addiction relapse, and another who was told to take a class after her children missed the first week of school because she did not have money for shoes. Even excessive corporal punishment cases are not necessarily about the regular use of corporal punishment, which caseworkers see as a parenting failure. These reasons for being in contact with the child welfare system do not exempt parents from the presumption that they are generally unfit parents and need to be taught the basics of parenting.

Within a therapeutic state bureaucracy one might expect an agency to offer parenting skills classes: agencies start with the idea that family problems are caused by individual inadequacies and that either the caseworker or the system must help the parent overcome them. In addition, most parents involved in child welfare are women of color who, according to prevailing discourses around poverty and stereotypes of unfit black mothers (Gilens 2000; Goode and Maskovsky 2001; Neubeck and Cazenave 2001; Quadagno 1996; Roberts 1999; Williams 1995), are irresponsible, accountable for their own misfortunes, and thus in need of personal change to make them productive citizens and decent mothers. Agency officials do not see it as enough to deal with the problem, probably related to poverty and lack of resources that brought the family into contact with the child welfare agency in the first place. Instead, caseworkers require even broader changes in the mother's life and her parenting.

In only one case I witnessed where parents had children removed were those parents not required to take a parenting class. It is significant that this was also the only case I witnessed that involved a wealthy family, and one of the few that involved a white family (this case was introduced earlier in this chapter and contrasted with Joan's case). Despite the numerous problems uncovered in the family, which in the other cases I witnessed would have likely meant that the children would have remained in foster care, the children were returned home quickly, and the parents were asked to undertake almost no services. Their lawyers were able to quickly (in only a few weeks) negotiate for their case to be dismissed, and no one suggested that they take a parenting class; they were only required to get family counseling. These parents' ability to care for their children and be adequate, responsible parents, despite the problems in the home, was never questioned in the way it was for poor and minority families.

In observing parenting classes (which are run by foster care, preventive agencies, or by ACS itself), I noticed that classes were rather generic with a fairly standard list of topics: definition of abuse and neglect, child development, the necessity of communication, why corporal punishment is inappropriate and that privileges should be taken away instead, various safety issues (hot stoves, electrical outlets, child molestation), building self-esteem, how to talk to your children about sex, and drug and alcohol abuse prevention for children. Thus, parents who did not use corporal punishment would be told not to, and parents with teenagers would be told how to baby-proof a home and how babies develop. Everything was presented at the most basic and commonsense levels that, at times, I felt the material was actually insulting. Although parents rarely found these classes useful, they are still expected to comply with the directive.

One of the implicit goals of requiring a parenting class was to see which parents were willing, on the one hand, to comply with the directive and were able, on the other hand, to show up, on time, for anywhere from seven to fifteen weeks in a row. Two of the three parenting classes I attended had elaborate rules about attendance:[6] what was an "excused" and an "unexcused" absence; at what time no one else would be allowed in the classroom; how many times you could be late; and how many times you could be absent before you were dropped from the class. The detailed nature of these rules and the degree to which they were emphasized and were generally the *only* measures of what a parent had gotten out of a class led me to think that showing up consistently and on time was at least as important, if not more important, than what a parent learned. Apparently attendance was taken as a sign that the parents "had their life together" enough to care for a child and were sufficiently committed to them.

Expanding Requirements

It addition to standard service plans that are not tailored to individual needs and do not get at the root of parental problems, it is common practice for family court judges to approve service plans that end with "and any other reasonable referrals made by the agency." This phrase allows agencies to add services when they gain new information, but it also gives wide discretion to add components with little or no justification. Parents can be required to complete almost any service and have very little, if any, ability to question whether it is necessary or not. Although ideally attorneys should argue on a parent's behalf against unnecessary services, I found that they rarely did so while judges were generally unwilling to question the recommendations of the caseworker. If the caseworker finds it necessary, then the recommendation generally becomes a requirement. It was also common for parents to be asked to comply with new services close to the time they thought their child would be coming home. As one parent advocate and mother who has been through the system, Stephanie, described this problem: "You know you've got weekend visits going well, you know? So why can't you just discharge the kids? . . . But they're dangling this, these kinds of things: oh, you need one more, or you need to do this. . . . Then my question to the caseworker is, 'Well, why are you asking my client to do this and we're right at discharge? Isn't that something that we should have done before?'" This situation led many parents I spoke with to feel that they were being asked to hit a moving target as services that seemed unnecessary or unconnected to the initial allegations in the case were added as the case went on. It was also the case that sometimes, as cases dragged on and caseworkers left or were replaced, the original allegations in the case would be either unknown or overlooked (see chapter 4). All of these issues delayed reunification and meant that parents were often jumping through hoops rather than getting meaningful help with the problems that brought them in contact with child welfare in the first place.

It is significant that anger management and mental health evaluations and therapy were the two most commonly reported services that were added later and seemed unconnected to the problems that led to contact with ACS in the first place. Caseworkers were seemingly so concerned about parents' attitudes and general demeanors that these services were often thought necessary for the kind of broad transformation in attitude and behavior that would make them fit to regain custody.

Anger management classes were frequently required of parents even if the case did not seem to indicate an anger problem. For example, one father, Henry, an African American father in his twenties, was told he had to take an anger management class in part because of a police report and in part because of his attitude toward caseworkers. The police report claimed that he had used violence against the mother of his child, Salina, a Latina also in her twenties, but she later admitted that there had been no violence and that she had made the report out of anger after a fight. The caseworkers were not trying to get her to leave Henry for the safety of her children as they would have done had they believed that domestic violence was a problem. Nevertheless, the caseworkers made anger management a requirement, and Salina asserted that it was only a requirement because he was often angry with caseworkers who were not doing their jobs. I met several other parents who were sent to anger management after they had become angry with caseworkers whom they perceived as incompetent or lazy. In these cases, anger that was not directed at their children was taken as evidence that the parents presented risk to their children and thus their "anger problems" had to be fixed.

Many parents were also required to undergo mental health evaluations, even in cases that did not contain allegations of mental health issues. This occurs mainly because evaluations are needed to gain access to counseling, from which many caseworkers feel that all parents can benefit. This model fits with a therapeutic approach that holds that counseling is necessary to instill proper values and habits. In most cases Medicaid pays for counseling so, for clinics and practitioners to be reimbursed, the parent must first be evaluated and given a diagnosis that justifies counseling (much like health insurance might require a patient to show that a specialist is medically necessary). This sequence can produce a major, though unintended, issue: therapists gave many parents serious diagnoses that then became justifications for children remaining in foster care (see chapter 8 for more on this issue). Evaluations also provide another expert opinion on the parent's mental health and when reunification should occur. A therapist who works with families in East New York, Brooklyn, told me that she constantly receives calls from caseworkers who, in her view, want her to make the decision about reunification for them. She realizes, she said, that her opinion is valued because of her training and that she has a lot of power over the families she helps. For foster care agency caseworkers, who are fearful of making a bad decision, expert opinions like hers about whether a parent is responsible and safe are welcomed.

I also met several parents who were told to have additional evaluations after one from a clinic they found on their own was not accepted. For example, one couple, Emma and James, who are both white and from middle-class backgrounds, had evaluations from four professionals, but, because neither the foster care agency nor the family court accepted those evaluations, the parents were required to have yet another one through the court. In the parents' view, this was done because all the evaluations they were given were positive. The caseworkers explained that, if the couple found their own evaluator, he or she would not be talking to the caseworkers about their case and their history and therefore would not have a full picture. Emma's 18B attorney argued against the court evaluation requirement because, he told me, he has never seen a positive report, or a report without a serious diagnosis, come out of the family court evaluators. Several other attorneys also told me this (see also chapter 8).[7] In the end, the court evaluation was extremely negative, and it likely played a role in the agency's plans to terminate their parental rights. Many parents were given a more serious diagnosis in these evaluations, and this made it much more difficult to have their children returned.

These commonly added services are, again, about personal transformation in terms of attitude and responsibility. They seem to be attempts to create parents (and citizens) who are able to control themselves and are mentally stable enough to care for themselves and their children on their own. The underlying assumption of parental pathology, which is tied to the fact that the system disproportionately deals with poor families of color, clearly shapes service plans that do not get to the roots of family problems.

Conclusion

Part of the reason that poor families of color are disproportionately reported to child welfare authorities is that their lives and parenting are under scrutiny by the public institutions that they rely on—public schools and hospitals, doctors, mental health professionals, and so on. Often, child welfare reports are used as weapons—by neighbors in disputes, by abusive former partners, or by service providers that use the state to enforce compliance. Although the child welfare system is supposed to make reasonable efforts to prevent foster care placement and to reunify families when possible, the services offered to parents do not always provide the help parents need and rarely get at the root of their problems, which are related to race, class, and gender inequalities. Rather than supplying needed help, institutions scrutinize their parenting and are likely to deal with risks through child removal. When investigation dominates caseworker practice, service provision becomes difficult or impossible. Once parents are in the child welfare system, service plans tend to focus on modifying attitudes and behaviors seen as problematic. Although help for domestic violence and drug use are frequently provided, these were too often tied to punitive child removals. Other assistance parents' desperately needed—housing, meaningful education and jobs, and resources to overcome personal problems while caring for children—were scarce. Instead, parents were expected to change their behaviors and show the correct attitudes to convince caseworkers that they were acting "properly parental" (Reich 2005, 115 see also chapters 7 and 8). ACS was thus thought of as mainly a coercive and disruptive agency rather than a source of help (see chapter 8).

6

Defining Neglect and Risk Assessment in Practice

The legal definition of neglect is the basis of casework and family court practice.[1] A child is neglected if he or she has been impaired physically, mentally, or emotionally, or if he or she is in "imminent danger" of being impaired as a result of a parent or caretaker's failure to provide a "minimum degree of care." In other words, parents are not expected to do everything perfectly and provide the very best care possible, but they should be held to the standard of doing the minimum necessary to keep a child healthy and safe. Within the broad range of what could be considered neglect, caseworkers label most of their cases lack of adequate supervision or "inadequate guardianship," a catch-all term for problems such as failing to protect a child from a domestic violence situation or exposure to illegal drug use. The majority of cases caseworkers investigate include allegations that children do not have enough to eat or clean clothes, that they are not in school regularly, that the parent is using drugs or has experienced domestic violence, that they have been left at home alone or inadequately supervised, or that they are not getting adequate medical care. Illegal drug use, excessive corporal punishment, domestic violence, educational neglect, and mental health issues were the most common categories. In my conversations with caseworkers and family court personnel and in my observations in family court, it was clear that child welfare often deals with cases in which parents' behaviors are thought to almost automatically put their children at risk. Moreover, many of the issues faced by families in child welfare are closely tied to poverty, and the two issues were often hard to separate in practice.

Given the relatively vague definition of neglect, there is room for variation in how child welfare officials understand what constitutes neglect. Few clear-cut guidelines define adequate care so child welfare officials often use evaluations of parental responsibility and judgment (discussed in this chapter) and compliance (discussed in chapter 7) when making decisions about whether harm or risk should be classified as neglect. In making decisions about when neglect becomes serious enough to warrant services, family court supervision, or foster care, risk is a key concept. Because in many cases it is not readily apparent that the child has already been seriously harmed, views about what imminent danger or risk means are key to decision-making. The most common issues seen in child welfare cases, while they can be serious and detrimental to children, are not issues that unambiguously place children in immediate danger or at imminent risk of harm and therefore warrant immediate removal of the child from the situation.[2] In some situations the family might be helped to care for the children through services, as mandated by the legal requirement that reasonable efforts to prevent removals should be made. In most situations assessing the risk to the child is a murky matter, and not everyone will agree about the best course of action. The vagueness of the definition of neglect allows for variation in decision making and for ideas about proper parental responsibility and home lives to come into play. It also provides space for negative stereotypes of poor women and men of color to influence how parents are judged.

The Legal Definition of Neglect

Although the legal definition of neglect is relatively vague, it does include some specific examples of what a failure to exercise a minimum degree of care can mean: (1) not providing for basic needs (including food, shelter, clothing, medical care, and education) if the parent has the means to do so or has been offered means to do so, or (2) not providing adequate supervision or guardianship. The first category essentially requires caseworkers to differentiate between poverty and the willful neglect of children. This distinction is difficult to make, especially given the pervasive and longstanding belief that poverty is the result of individual irresponsibility. When poor people more generally are blamed for their own poverty, it becomes easy to blame them for poverty-related issues that put children at risk.

The second half of this explanation includes "excessive corporal punishment" (defined in practice as using an object to hit a child or leaving a mark or bruise in the course of punishment),[3] misusing drugs and alcohol, and "any other acts of a similarly serious nature requiring the aid of the court."[4] As attorneys explained it, the line between excessive corporal punishment and abuse is drawn based on the severity of the injury and is, more or less, as one put it, "a matter of common sense." For example, if a parent spanked a child and a mark was left, this could be filed as neglect. If the child was cut seriously, given a black eye, beaten severely, had bones broken, or was injured in any way that could cause long-term damage, it would be abuse. Other behaviors that would normally be filed as neglect can also be filed as abuse if they are severe enough. For example, a parent who did not provide adequate food, and the child was found to be severely malnourished, could be accused of abuse. During my experience in family court, I found that abuse cases are very rarely, if ever, filed in situations unless serious physical abuse or sexual abuse were involved.[5]

It is significant that alcohol and drugs are treated differently under the law and in child welfare practice. ACS attorneys said they could file a case if the parent were using any illegal drug, not participating in a rehabilitation program, or testing positive while in a program. The child protective side of the agency, however, could decide not to bring cases to family court if they felt the child was not in danger in the home. In my discussions with caseworkers, it seemed that cases are filed when the parent does not get into treatment and stop testing positive fairly quickly. Use of any illegal drug if the parent is not enrolled in a rehabilitation program is thus often automatically taken as placing children in danger. In contrast to this, the law specifies that, with alcohol, it must be shown that it was used "to the extent that he loses self-control of his actions."

This difference in the law reflects, I believe, the view that illegal drug use leads almost automatically to addiction (Reinarman and Levine 1997), and thus rehabilitation is needed. In addition, drug use is viewed as incompatible with parenting, especially mothering (Gomez 1997; Reich 2005), because it is seen as almost automatically creating a state in which a parent is unable to provide adequate guardianship and supervision or loses control of her actions and places her child in danger.[6] The legal definition does not take into account nuances about how much is used, when, and under what circumstances, although ACS caseworkers can take these factors into account when deciding whether to initially file a case. The law also reflects a widespread societal demonization of illegal drug use, especially use by poor and minority communities (Reinarman and Levine 1997).

Parents often questioned how the legal definition of neglect was applied, and a few attorneys agreed. ACS attorneys complained that caseworkers and their managers asked them to file, and they often did file, cases that fit the legal definition but did not seem to them to warrant court intervention. In talking about their cases, parents questioned how neglect was defined and felt that their parenting was judged on the basis of one behavior, or one moment in time, and not on the larger context of how they parented and the overall well-being of their children. Many felt that it was as if any drug use or corporal punishment made them unfit parents in the eyes of caseworkers, attorneys, and judges. Claudia, an African American mother of two, for example, told me that she feels ACS would do a better job if it kept in mind that every family and every situation is different and so the interventions cannot be identical: "And that will help you deliver the very best that you can deliver if you deal with that family and where they're at and what's going on with them, not just the incident. Because, for me, the incident tells you absolutely nothing, *nothing* about the family. It really doesn't . . . And one incident does not take away your ability to be a parent. . . . ACS is very judgmental, I think. And I don't know that you have to be judgmental in order to protect children." Here Claudia points out what I frequently observed: parents were often judged harshly on the basis of one part of their lives while the things they did well were ignored. I agree that this judgmental attitude was counterproductive in terms of helping families and protecting children.

Because drug cases are so common and bring up important issues surrounding the role of inequality and stratified reproduction in child welfare, I want to explore parent and attorney views on how drug use was handled.[7] Both attorneys and parents felt that labeling *any* use of illegal drugs neglect was an oversimplification and that it was not necessary to bring all cases of drug use to family court. Specifically, they discussed several factors that needed to be taken into account when deciding whether to authorize state intervention in the family: how often a parent used, what drug they used, where they used, and how they were able to function in the rest of their life and in caring for their child. An ACS attorney, Joshua, a white man in his fifties who has been an ACS for many years, explained:

JOSHUA: I find the definitions are really vague, troubling.

TINA: Definitions of?

JOSHUA: Of abuse or neglect. However, neglect as statutorily defined, to most parents who are charged with this are really puzzled because of the statutory definition, again, doesn't fit a common sense or lay definition of neglect because—okay, alcohol, you do the alcohol to the point you lose control of your actions, fine. *But drug use is what's puzzling because as the statute is written and read, any misuse of a controlled substance and not being successfully in program, is neglect.* . . . I mean, mere use . . . I mean you have do it on a case-by-case basis. If you're leaving your kids alone, going out at four in the morning to score, or do tricks so you can score, that is neglect. Going to a party once in a while and snorting a couple lines, you know, that's not necessarily. It depends. It should be dealt with. . . . I think there must be less people doing hard drugs because of a lot more marijuana cases filed, and I find that kind of ridiculous, I guess [emphasis added].

Joshua points to the overall demonization of illegal drug use and the need for a thorough evaluation of parenting in drug cases rather than the assumption that drug use and adequate parenting are always incompatible. Significantly, whereas use by middle-class and white families is often not brought to the attention of authorities or is dealt with through counseling, poor families who use are more likely to face losing custody of children (see chapters 4 and 5).

I asked Carrie, a white woman in her thirties (who had previously worked as caseworker and then as an ACS attorney), if it would have to be shown legally that drug use affected parenting. She replied: "Technically yes. What do we actually see? If a parent's using on a weekend, while their kid's being babysat by somebody else, like staying at grandma's, I would hope they wouldn't bring that case in. Will they? If it's heroin, yeah, they will; if it's crack cocaine, yeah, they probably will. If it's marijuana, they probably won't; if it's alcohol they pretty much can't *unless* the person *loses* control so that they do something *really* bad like assault a police officer." She reads the statute in the way Joshua explained and describes standard

ACS practice in filing cases that I also observed; that is, *use* of certain illegal drugs is equated with neglect.

In describing her drug case, Stephanie, an African American, middle-class mother in her early forties, specifically told me that she was a "functioning addict" who always kept a job (even while going through treatment when her child was in foster care), a stable residence, and was able to provide "a closetful of clothes" for her daughter. She thus questioned being characterized as neglectful. An African American father in his fifties, Nathan, who raised his children alone after they were removed from their mother for her drug use and was randomly drug tested, he estimated, for two years with no problems, had his children removed after one "dirty urine":

> And what happened was, to be honest about it, I had just got a new promotion in the Housing Authority. I worked for the city for thirty years. So it was a lot of pressure on the job, too, plus taking care of my five kids, and all these years they was testing me because of my kid's mother, and I wasn't using no drugs or nothin' like that. But eventually, with all this pressure, I had picked up some drugs. . . . [Later in the interview he explained going out to a club, getting drunk, and accepting cocaine and then being called the next day to give a urine sample]. I went down and they took a urine, and they took my kids. . . . They tested me for, was like two years. It was like two years or somethin' and I never had a dirty urine. So one dirty urine. They came to my house like SWAT.

In his account of his case, Nathan points out that a single slip-up, unconnected, in his mind, to his overall care of his children and not put in its larger context, was dealt with punitively. His comparison to SWAT policing tactics is also significant in its reference to the punitive nature of the intervention.

These arguments are not to discount the fact that there are cases in which drug addiction can lead to parents' inability to care for their children. A few mothers I spoke to *did* consider themselves addicted and described how it affected their children. Trisha, for example, told me she sometimes sold her food stamps to get drugs, and Joan told me she noticed that her daughter would act differently around her because she could tell her mother was "not herself." Therefore, the point is not that drug use is always compatible with parenthood and that it presents no problems for children; instead, the issue is that poor mothers of color are more vulnerable to the loss of their children and have fewer resources that enable them to get treatment. There is evidence that patterns of drug use vary by class, and wealthier women "tend to have a greater capacity for controlling their drug use or getting out of trouble if they don't" (Murphy and Rosenbaum 1997). They are also less likely to come in contact with the criminal justice system, another way that drug use is brought to the attention of child welfare authorities. In addition, it is *not* the case that any illegal drug use is completely incompatible with motherhood, but this is the assumption made in family court and in American culture more broadly, especially when dealing with poor women of color who are already often presumed to be irresponsible mothers. Both the law concerning illegal drug use and its application are tied to stereotypes of unfit poor parents of color and especially to the images of women who use crack cocaine that were prevalent during the height of the so-called crack epidemic (see chapter 2).

Types of Cases in Practice

The cases I observed in family court provide a snapshot of the issues that come to be labeled neglect in daily child welfare practice and those most likely to be deemed severe enough to require placement in foster care. In this discussion, I am only counting those cases in which the main allegations were clear. When classifying cases (see table 6.1), I labeled them with the most prominent allegation—reflecting either that the caseworker presented the case to the attorneys as "a drug case" (for example) or that the child protective staff or the ACS attorney discussed the allegation in more detail or in a way that signaled its primary importance. In general, I could clearly determine the main allegations.[8] If, however, the court discussion made clear both the initial allegation and the subsequent issues, then I classified the case by the initial allegation and noted the accompanying issue. In a few cases it was not clear what, if anything, might be called the "main allegation." Those cases in which multiple problems existed, or that involved issues that were unclear or difficult to classify, I placed in the "other" category. I put cases involving teen mothers into a separate category because, in most of those, the allegations differed significantly from the allegations made against adults. Because most of these teen mothers were still in foster care themselves, different issues were involved.

Table 6.1: Court Cases in Which Allegations/Issues Were Clear

Type of Case	Number
Illegal drug use	77
Excessive corporal punishment	29
Domestic violence	20
Educational neglect	14
Parents' mental health	13
Teen mothers	9
Alcohol	6
Medical neglect	4
Child left home alone	3
Parent arrested	3
Malnourished child	1
Abandonment	1
Other	13
Abuse	26
Parental Rights Termination	16
Total	234

Table 6.2: Children in Foster Care by Type of Case*

Type of Case	Number Observed	Percentage (%) in Foster Care
Parent arrested	3	100
Malnourished child	1	100
Abandonment	1	100
Illegal drug use	73	81
Child left home alone	3	67
Parents' mental health	11	64
Alcohol	6	50
Other	12	50
Excessive corporal punishment	25	36
Medical neglect	4	25
Domestic violence	18	22
Educational neglect	12	8

*NEGLECT cases in which allegations were clear and court appearance was observed.

In discussing how often the children in the case were placed in foster care (table 6.2), I am only presenting those cases in which the child's placement was discussed when I witnessed the case and those intake cases in which I was able to observe the initial hearing when the judge ruled on the child's placement. An analysis of the initial hearings where the judge authorizes ACS caseworkers' plans provides further information about when neglect was considered serious enough to warrant foster care placement (see table 6.3). The initial hearing in a case provides the clearest evidence of when neglect is deemed serious enough to warrant foster care placement because, in ongoing cases, it was not always clear whether the children had been removed for the initial allegation or for lack of compliance later in the case.

First, it is important to note that most cases involve neglect and not abuse. Only 11 percent of the cases observed involved abuse. Second, most cases classified as neglect have to do with problems faced by parents which are thought to place a child at risk: drug use, mental health, and domestic violence (together these made up almost half of all cases). In some of these cases, evidence was presented in court to show how the child had been harmed by these issues, but often the fact that these issues are thought, in and of themselves, to present a *risk* of harm was enough to warrant a neglect label. The question of whether parents' actual care of their children did not meet a "minimum degree of care" was rarely addressed, at least in court, although caseworkers can evaluate that issue during the investigation stage. It is also important to note that questions about why parents were or were not getting help for these issues were rarely addressed; instead, parents were simply considered neglectful and were therefore likely to have their children removed.

A full third of the cases involved drugs, and in a large majority of these the children were in foster care when I observed the case. These cases are so common that special family treatment courts have been created in each borough to deal exclusively with drug-related cases.[9] It was not apparent in every case what drug the parent was using, but, when it was clear, crack cocaine and marijuana were most common.[10] It was also generally not apparent what drug use actually meant in any given case. The designation "use" could range from parents who were addicted and their use was substantially impairing their lives and their children's well-being to parents who could have been labeled a functional addict to cases in which occasional or recreational use was discovered. In almost 56 percent of the drugs cases I saw it was not apparent that there was any other issue in the home;

the problem seemed to be that the mother and/or the father had either admitted to using, failed a drug test, or was not enrolled or participating in a drug program (in a couple of cases a parent was in a program but was still testing positive). In some cases there were other issues; most prominent among them were parents who were arrested and foster care placement was needed due to the parent's absence. In only a small number of cases was it clear how parental drug use had affected their functioning and parenting (living in dirty homes, leaving a child home alone, not taking a child to school or to a doctor, or leaving a child with a relative or neighbor for an extended period of time). Note that these conditions could also be related to poverty itself (e.g., lack of health insurance or child care).

In domestic violence cases (see Lee 2015 for more detail), a child who had either witnessed or been caught in the middle of domestic violence was considered neglected. In general, the father was named as respondent in these cases while the mother retained custody of the child with the strict condition that she end the relationship, involve the criminal justice system, and enforce an order of protection to keep the father away from the home and the children. If she failed to comply, then she generally lost custody.[11] In a few cases women were also named as respondents due to their own use of violence, positive drug tests, or failure to enforce orders of protection and end relationships. In only three cases was the mother also a respondent, and then the child was placed in foster care. The mother was hospitalized in one case, and arrested in another; in the third the agency claimed she

Table 6.3: Foster Care Removal by Type of Intake Case*

Issue	Number Observed	Percentage (%) Resulting in Removal
Mental health	4	100
Drugs	21	76
Teen mothers	4	50
Alcohol	2	50
Excessive corporal punishment	13	31
Domestic violence	9	11
Educational neglect	7	0
Home alone	1	0
Medical neglect	1	0

*INTAKE cases in which allegations were clear and court appearance was observed.

"refused" to enter a shelter (she maintained that no shelter would take her teen son). If a mother violates an order of protection or does not leave the situation (the reasons for not following these directives do not usually matter [see also Lee 2015]), the agency considers the child at a great deal of risk, and a removal is very likely. In mental health cases the standard for neglect was whether the parent was getting treatment for their mental health issue. Engaging in treatment was assumed to alleviate the risk the parent posed to the child. In a majority of cases the parent was not getting treatment, and the children were then placed in foster care.[12]

Thus, the main issues in a majority of child welfare cares are about parental problems that are defined as neglect when parents were not quickly dealing with them in the ways expected of them. Drug use and mental health issues are very likely to result in a removal because these issues are thought to present considerable risk to the children involved. Children are likely to remain in the home only if parents are able to access treatment quickly or if caseworkers or judges believe the other parent in the home will not allow the negligent parent to be alone with their children. Caseworkers often believe that parents with these problems cannot be expected to either care for children or deal with their problems without state involvement. In excessive corporal punishment cases, removals are also common, unless it is possible to bar the parent from unsupervised contact with the child.

In the other kinds of cases, the harm to the children was clearer, but these cases were less likely to result in foster care than drug and mental health cases: in corporal punishment cases the child has sustained an injury; in educational neglect cases the child has missed school; in "home alone cases" he or she has been left unsupervised; and in medical neglect cases the child is not receiving treatment. It was not always clear, however, that the incidents were indicative of a parents' "failure to exercise a minimum degree of care," as in cases involving teens, where it is difficult to determine that the parent had acted improperly. In medical neglect and home alone cases, it was not always clear whether the problem arose from a parents' willful neglect or from poverty.

Home alone cases present especially clear examples of how separating neglect from poverty is difficult. For example, the attorneys at the Bronx Defenders told me about a home alone case in which a mother had left her young children home when she was called in to work at her Work Experience Program job (WEP, a welfare-mandated work program) at the last minute and was told her benefits would be cut off if she did not come in.

She was not able to find childcare and choose to work rather than lose the needed income. When the children were found unsupervised, they were placed in foster care, and the mother was arrested. A *New York Times* article from the time of my research pointed out that many poor families leave children alone out of necessity (Foderaro 2008), and research shows this is a widespread problem among poor and working-class families (Douglas and Michaels 2004; Edin and Lein 1997; Hansen 2005; Michel 1998; Mullings and Wali 2001). Thus, a common problem faced by many families is redefined as individual neglectful behavior.

In day-to-day family court practice, then, the relatively broad definition of neglect can include cases that stem from parents' problems or from issues related to poverty. Issues such as drug use and mental health problems are assumed to almost automatically place a child at risk and are used to justify intervention, while the court too rarely questions what help the system might give to parents to overcome these issues that are deemed neglect and avoid foster care. The legal definition allows for much flexibility in how it is applied and individualizes family problems rather than seeing their structural causes. Cases that involve parents' problems (drugs, domestic violence, and mental health) are those most likely to be seen as presenting "imminent risk" to the children, even if the court does not question the care the parent was providing. Those cases in which harm to children is more apparent—children who have missed school, who were left unsupervised, or who were not given medical treatment—are those least likely to be considered high risk and result in a removal. The system sees parents' problems as presenting more risk to children than these concrete failures of care, which caseworkers are likely to handle through services rather than foster care.

It is also important to note that parents' arrests play a large role in foster care placements. When an arrest occurs, someone needs to care for the children, and the state seeks foster care for this reason; however, after the parent is released, he or she will not be able to automatically regain custody and will have to meet the higher standards necessary to get a child out of foster care (see chapter 8). In poor neighborhoods of color greater police presence and more arrests thus play a major role in patterns of placement in foster care and contribute to black children's disproportionate placement. In addition, the prevalence of arrests shows the extent to which the state criminalizes neglect cases involving corporal punishment or cases in which parents cannot provide adequate care due to poverty and lack of resources.

Decision Making and Risk Assessment

Variation in Decision Making

Decision making by caseworkers and family court officials centered closely on their perceptions of risk and parental behaviors that are thought to place children at risk. Although risk assessment instruments exist and are required in every case, caseworkers never mentioned them as directly playing a role in their decision making. Caseworkers described the information they tended to look for, and this seemed to correspond to *some* of the items on the list while others were not mentioned.[13] None of the caseworkers, however, talked about going through the list when conducting their investigations or using the scores generated to make a decision about how to intervene in the cases. I think that these instruments supply more documentation than assessment and provide, as others have argued, a way to justify decision making and protect the agency (Lyle and Graham 2000). For example, one caseworker told me that she has made a removal and then filled out the checklist. In addition, the checklists are completed on a computer so I doubt they are referred to when caseworkers are visiting homes and interviewing parents (caseworkers did not have laptops at the time of my research). Because I was unable to observe caseworkers doing their jobs, however, the lists might play more of a role than was apparent from interviews.

I did, however, find that caseworkers take the same set of factors into account when making decisions: the severity of the incident/issue/allegation, the age of the child, the history of prior reports and problems, and the parent's willingness to comply with caseworkers and with services (for compliance, see chapter 7). Judgments about severity are used to draw a line between a child who is in immediate danger or at very high risk of harm and therefore should be removed to foster care and a child who is at less risk of harm and services could be offered to diminish the risk. Caseworkers generally think that older children are at less risk—they can supervise themselves to an extent, they are assumed to be able to seek help if they are being injured, they are more independent and can make their own decisions, and so forth. Caseworkers also take prior reports as evidence that the situation is chronic and that attempts to change it through services will be unsuccessful. How individual caseworkers weighed these elements and where along the continuum they drew a line between low and high risk varied *considerably* (see below, and Rossi, Schuerman, and Budde 1999).

Despite variation, caseworkers almost automatically view some kinds of allegations as very severe and thus presenting an immediate safety issue that warrants the removal of the child from the situation: (1) having a serious, diagnosed mental illness and not taking medication; (2) giving birth for the second time to a baby who tests positive for drugs; (3) allowing a man into the home in violation of an order of protection when the children are present; and (4) using illegal drugs and not enrolling in a drug treatment program. Assessments in these situations can be (but are not always) very rigid. For example, Amy, a white caseworker in her forties with five and a half years of experience, told me a story in which children were removed from a mother with a very old order of protection when the caseworkers went to her home and found her former husband in her apartment (he was now quite old and in very ill health, and she was helping him fill out paperwork for Medicaid). The children were removed on an "emergency" basis even though he was clearly not violent and there had been no incidents for years, but they were returned shortly thereafter when it became clear the mother was no longer in a relationship with the man, who was practically never there and presented no risk.

Although the process of bringing cases to family court is supposed to allow for legal oversight of removal decisions, I found that neither the legal staff nor the judges questioned these decisions in any serious way (see chapter 7). In watching ACS attorneys talk to caseworkers when cases were filed, it was clear that the attorneys were trained to defer to caseworkers in assessments of risk. For example, one attorney told me that he tries to have "no ego" about these cases and avoids inserting his own opinion into the process. He explained that he doesn't see the homes or meet the families and thus is in no position to judge risk. Another attorney told me that she was not allowed to tell her client (i.e., the caseworker) what she wants in the case; instead, her role was to facilitate getting the outcome the caseworker decided upon. For the most part, if the caseworkers feel strongly about an intervention sought in a case, attorneys simply find a way to facilitate the judge's approval.

In cases where a removal had already been made, I never observed attorneys questioning its appropriateness, except informally. Instead, the attorneys simply wrote a petition with the information the caseworker had collected and explained why the removal had been made. In the few cases in which caseworkers were seeking approval to place a child in foster care prior to doing a removal, I sometimes saw attorneys describing the situation in ways that would best convince the judge rather than in the way that seemed most truthful (see chapter 7). In a couple of instances a caseworker was unwilling to allow a child to be cared for by a father or relative, despite lacking specific evidence against that person. Attorneys deferred to the caseworkers in these situations as well.

Attorneys did push caseworkers on how they conducted their investigations to clarify the evidence collected. They deferred cases when investigations were not complete, but this only occurred in cases that were deemed low enough risk to warrant court-ordered supervision rather than foster care placement, and it was rare even in those cases. I did witness a couple of cases in which the attorneys felt the caseworkers had not collected enough information but felt the case was high risk. In those cases the attorneys found ways to construct petitions that would still convince the judge to approve the relief they were seeking. In a couple of instances, they deferred cases in which a parent was voluntarily complying with services and thus it seemed unnecessary to file.

I also found that caseworkers and other decision makers can judge severity and compliance quite differently, and the risk assessment instruments did not seem to have standardized decision making to a great degree. In my conversations with caseworkers and in my observations of the process of filing cases in family court, it became clear that caseworkers are allowed a degree of discretion in their decision making about how to intervene in their cases. There does not seem to be a set of clear-cut criteria such that a particular indicated allegation or a particular event automatically leads to a certain intervention. Cases with very similar allegations can be handled quite differently by different caseworkers; different managers (who must approve all removal decisions) also have different ideas about whether a child should be in foster care. Moreover, caseworkers and managers disagree about their cases. Carl, an African American in his late twenties who had been caseworker for five and a half years, described the differing managerial styles:

> You'll have one manager that's quick to say, "Let's go remove." And then you'll have another manager saying, "Okay. Let's put services in first. Let's see, you know, let's do this." . . . You have managers that will push workers to go file in court quicker than other managers. You have some mangers that will make a case indicated based on little information whereas, if you took the same case scenario to another manager, they'll say, "Oh, we really don't have nothing here." Some managers tend to indicate cases because they want to cover themselves. "Oh, we did indicate it."

Even when they had access to the same information, the caseworkers, their managers, and attorneys differed greatly in their assessment of the level of risk in a case. For example, in one case a mother was depressed and had tested positive for cocaine. She was reported to ACS after missing appointments in her drug treatment program due, she said, to a lack of child care. The caseworker visited the home and found the home environment good and the children doing well. The caseworker was told to bring the case to court to ask the judge to require the mother to enter drug treatment again. The attorneys almost deferred the case because they felt there was not enough risk to warrant court intervention, but eventually child protective staff convinced the attorney to file and ask for court supervision. During the initial hearing, the law guardian asked for the child to be placed in foster care on the basis of prior reports on the mother. The judge agreed, despite testimony that questioned the veracity of the prior reports. Again, caseworkers, attorneys, and judges, with access to the same information about the case, came to very different conclusions.

Attorneys sometimes disagreed with caseworkers and informally questioned their assessment of risk either by asking caseworkers probing questions about their assessments, or, more commonly, when the caseworker left the room, they mentioned their disagreement to me. If caseworkers were able to articulate their reasons for assessing risk in the way they did, the attorney would defer to them. For example, in one case involving an emergency removal of children from a mother who was using drugs, the attorney told me that he felt the situation was not an emergency and that "more restraint" could have been shown by the caseworker. In another case, the caseworker could not clearly explain why the children could not be left with their father. The attorney asked numerous questions to try to clarify the issue but was unable to resolve the situation. When the caseworker stepped out of his office to call a supervisor, he turned to me and complained that he felt the caseworker had no reason to think the father was a danger, and he thought it made sense to leave the children with their father. He did not push the issue further with the caseworker, however, and wrote a petition alleging the father was a danger (including the caseworker's information that was either unconfirmed or probably false).

Most interesting about the petition-writing and intake process is the way in which the caseworkers, managers, and attorneys negotiated these discussions. It often seemed to me that all parties wanted the others to make the final decision because no one wanted to be held responsible for the outcome. Attorneys and caseworkers alike found this frustrating. Particularly telling was the number of times that attorneys asked me what I thought about a particular case and what I would do. They all understood that I was observing and conducting research; nonetheless they often wanted to know what I thought. Such frustration and hesitancy speak to the difficult decisions required, the lack of clear answers, and everyone's worry about making the correct decision.

Race and Class in Decision Making

Recognition of the fact that all cases and situations are different leads in part to the lack of clear-cut criteria for decision making. Families should receive individualized assessments and interventions that match their unique situations. The leeway that caseworkers and others have in making decisions, however, allows space for racial stereotypes to affect decision making and for problems associated with poverty to be recast as individual failures and labeled neglect. In looking closely at particular case examples, it becomes clear that not only is the decision-making process complicated but also several other factors are at work which only become more apparent when an ethnographic approach is taken (see also Reich 2005). Caseworkers and other decision makers rely on their intuition about cases and often judge parents by implicitly comparing their clients' lives and the lives of middle-class families. In closely reading comments from these decision makers about the parents with whom they come in contact, it is also apparent that various overtly color-blind but nonetheless racial discourses play a role in their decision making. Caseworkers sometimes assume that the women of color they see are irresponsible, unable to learn from past mistakes, and unwilling to put their children's safety above their own desires and sexual needs. In this way, it becomes easy for caseworkers to see them as unacceptable risks to their children rather than as struggling mothers. Although most caseworkers are also black and Latino, they draw, probably unconsciously, on larger stereotypes about poor, black mothers, and these preconceptions affect how the caseworkers see their clients and understand their lives. Moreover, caseworkers, as middle-class professionals, are likely to judge parents using middle-class parenting standards.

In discussing cases with caseworkers and observing hearings in family court, I felt that caseworkers, attorneys, and judges all relied on subtle personal criteria: evaluating whether a parenting displayed "good judgment";

utilizing intuition and "gut feelings" about cases; and superimposing their own ideas about proper parenting and proper homes. These criteria highlight the degree to which neglect is often ill-defined and difficult to separate from poverty. More specifically, caseworkers often seemed to attribute issues in a home to a parent's irresponsibility, when poverty was a likely cause or was at least exacerbating the situation. To illustrate these patterns, I examine three cases in detail: one described to me by Meredith, an African American caseworker in her mid-twenties who was relatively new to the job (she had been a caseworker for about seventeen months), another described by Marilyn, a Latina in her thirties who had been a caseworker for six and a half years, and a third that I learned about through observing a 1028 hearing.

Case 1: "Gut Feelings" and Class. The report in Meredith's case alleged that a teen girl was not in school; however, when Meredith looked at "the priors" (i.e., the prior reports) on the family, she saw that the mother had been noncompliant in the past so she was prepared to find something serious even though it was "only" an educational neglect case. When she was able to talk to the mother and assess the home, she found that the apartment was very dirty, a ceiling was falling in, there was little food in the house, and there were not enough beds for the children. The children reported that things were fine, the younger children were in school and doing well, and there seemed to be no serious safety issues. Therefore, Meredith and the more experienced coworker she took with her to conduct the investigation decided there was no reason to remove the children.

Meredith questioned the children's well-being in the home and asked her coworker if the conditions—the scarcity of food and lack of beds—might warrant a removal. Her coworker explained that the home situation was adequate but suggested Meredith could come back "to see how they live." Meredith was not satisfied with leaving the children in the home, despite her coworker's opinion, so she made other visits until the situation came to a head:

MEREDITH: Then I went, and it wasn't sitting with me. So I went back the next day. So the next day, I go back, and I see that just a head of lettuce and peanut butter and a half a box of pasta. No food.

TINA: When you say it wasn't sitting with you, what do you mean?

MEREDITH: Because, for some reason, it just felt like the kids were scared to tell me what was going on. I feel like there was a lot. . . . Instead of educational neglect, I feel like it should have been called in for a lot of other things. Like, when I first met the mom, I knew for a fact that she was abusing drugs because you see the brownness and the darkness on her lips and the way her teeth were so, the way she was so gray. She had marks on her arms, and I was just like . . .

TINA: Like she was cutting herself or something?

MEREDITH: No, like needle marks. So I was like, "This mom is using." I just felt that. I'm just like, "Something's going on." Even during the whole interview, she was playing with her nose. She was just like [sniffs], you know, fidgeting so much. I was just like, "You know what, let me just make sure." So *thank God* for the next day that I went, and I saw that they had nothing. And the mom, even, she was like, "Oh, I just went to try to get PA [public assistance] and food stamps," and she was like, "None of the money was there. I think I was sanctioned." So on and so forth. So I told my supervisor what I saw and everything like that, and she was like, "You know what, let's remove these kids." I said, "Thank you, God."

Meredith followed up on her hunch that the mother was using drugs and visited the home several times to see if things were really okay. The lack of food in the home was enough to justify removing the children. One reasonable explanation, that she simply couldn't afford food, was rejected, and Meredith assumed that insufficient food was solely a result of the mother's drug use. After the children were removed, the mother tested positive for marijuana and cocaine. The teen was placed in foster care (and was, at the time of the interview, in danger of having her own newborn removed from her care), while the younger children were sent to their fathers.

Meredith reported that after they were removed the boys admitted that they did not always have food, had only a few articles of clothing, and had seen their mother use cocaine. They did not divulge this information earlier, Meredith said, because they wanted to stay with her; in fact they were very distraught and crying when they were removed. She reported that they were doing well with their fathers and that she was happy she made the removal as the boys had more to eat and better living conditions with their fathers who both had steady jobs. It is interesting that Meredith did not report considering whether services might have helped this family; instead, she simply blamed the mother for the conditions. The conditions could have been due to the mother's drug use and her negligence, but these conditions could also signal problems associated with poverty—lack of access to drug treatment, poorly maintained housing, and welfare sanctions. Meredith might have assisted the mother with finding treatment and working out her housing and welfare problems. It was also not clear if the children's fathers had been paying child support while the children were in their mother's care; enforcing such payment might also have helped the situation.

During our interview, Meredith told me that, in general, she has been shocked by what she has seen as a caseworker: "I was raised in Long Island, so for me to be living in the city and seeing the way people live, it's just like, some of these things are so crazy to me." Although she did not make the connection specifically in her statements, it seems that this upbringing has conditioned how she thinks about her cases and her gut feelings about children's safety in their homes. When talking about going to the home in this case for the first time, she described being scared because the building was dilapidated and there were trashcans near the door (which likely meant rats, she added) and having to get up the courage to go to the door. She also described being shocked by the conditions of the home while her companion, the more experienced coworker, did not seem concerned and saw no reason to think about a removal. Her shock at these conditions led her to feel they were inappropriate for children and that the children needed to be removed to a better living situation. The discretion she was afforded allowed her to make visits until a removal could be justified.

Meredith's decision to remove the children in this case involved several factors. The prior reports on the family led Meredith to be worried about what she would find, and the mother's lack of compliance in the past signaled that she was not attempting to address the situation.[14] Second, Meredith relied heavily on her intuition that something was not right and on her assumption that the mother's behavior indicated a drug problem. Without solid evidence of the mother's drug use, Meredith returned to the home more than once until she was able to find conditions that allowed her to make the removal she felt was warranted. Third, Meredith's personal feeling that this was no way for children to live played a role in her decision to investigate until she could justify removal. Meredith found conditions of poverty such as these shocking because they contrasted so dramatically with her own middle-class childhood. It seemed easy for her to feel that these conditions are dangerous for children and to blame the mother for them. Rather than seeing poverty as the source of the problems in the home, Meredith blamed only the mother's drug use. The case was considered neglect on the part of the mother, and services were not seen as an appropriate response because Meredith felt the mother was responsible for these conditions and unwilling to work to remedy them.

Case 2: Compliance and a Mother's Judgment. Marilyn's case not only illustrates the role of caseworker assessments concerning parents' judgment, responsibility, and the home environments they provide for their children, but the case also illuminates how these ideas about judgment and responsibility, which are subtly tied to class and race, are used in deciding interventions in a case. This case involved a Latina mother who lived in a shelter with her three children (ages nine, six, and a newborn). She was smoking marijuana, not always getting her children to school, and leaving them with "inappropriate caretakers," that is, neighbors and friends in the shelter who had criminal and ACS histories as well as a boyfriend with a criminal history. Marilyn described monitoring the family for several months because she never felt that the children were at enough risk to be removed from their mother. A preventive services agency provided services to the family for more than four months. During the time that Marilyn monitored the case, the mother continued to use marijuana and, upon admitting her history of depression, was then sent for a psychiatric evaluation and medication. Marilyn warned the mother not to leave her children with inappropriate people; she was caught doing that, so Marilyn took the case to court to get court-ordered services and supervision.

At court, the mother was given conditions under which she could retain custody: she must get mental health and drug treatment; she could not leave the children with inappropriate caretakers; and she must keep her nineteen-year-old boyfriend out of her home, given his criminal history and the allegation that he was sexually abusing her older daughter. The condition that the boyfriend be excluded from the home stayed in place even after the sex abuse allegation was proven false. It is important to note the degree to which Marilyn's directives reached into all aspects of the mother's life, even those that didn't seem to present risk to her children (see also Appell 1997). While the court case was ongoing, on a visit Marilyn found the boyfriend in the home, the children said he was always there, and the mother continued to use marijuana. Marilyn made a surprise visit early one morning and found other friends sleeping at the apartment. Finally, after several months, the mother was late for a court appearance. At this point the judge asked ACS what they planned to do, and they decided to remove her children.

Marilyn emphasized that the mother's behavior—tardiness to court and allowing the boyfriend and others in the home—proved the decisive factor in the children's removal. The reasons to explain why she might have been late, such as lack of transportation, were neither investigated nor taken into account. Her refusal to follow directives was taken as evidence that she was not focused on her children and not properly maternal. It is interesting that the mother's continued drug use and her perceived lack of compliance with her mental health services (she had missed appointments) were not the decisive factors. On one level, the condition that the mother keep these people away from her children is reasonable; from the caseworker's point of view these people have criminal and ACS histories and therefore are potential dangers: "I explained to her . . . 'It's like you can barely take care of your own family *on your own*, and you're adding more problems by having all these strangers coming into your house around your children.' Not to mention she had, there was one prior case where the oldest child was almost killed at the age of two by her supposed fiancé. You understand? So now, you're showing me that you haven't learned from your prior experience, and you're still allowing people that you just met to be around your kids" [emphasis added].

The caseworker's comment that the mother could barely care for her family "on her own" not only paints her as an irresponsible mother who does not learn from past experiences but also discounts the fact that few parents care for their children on their own. Middle-class families regularly purchase child care or pay for after-school programs, often from "strangers," and many parents regularly have family and friends provide child care (Colen 1995; Hansen 2005; Lareau 2003). It is possible that this mother relied on her friends and partners to help with her children in the same way, especially given the lack of affordable, quality child care available for even working families (Douglas and Michaels 2004; Foderaro 2008; Hansen 2005; Michel 1998, 1999). Marilyn also emphasized that everyone with whom this mother was in contact had either an ACS or a criminal history or both, and she asked me, rhetorically "What are the odds of that?" The odds are actually very good, given the high rates of ACS and criminal justice involvement in the community served by Marilyn's unit, Central Harlem.

Marilyn also stated that she felt the children were at some risk, but not in *danger*, throughout these months of monitoring. The children never said they were harmed by the boyfriend or the other people the mother brought around them, and the allegations of sex abuse were quickly shown to be false. The times the caseworker caught other people in her home the mother was also present so she could supervise the children to ensure no one was harming them. Nevertheless, the mother was seen as continuing to place her children in danger and as unwilling to learn from her past mistakes and comply with what the agency saw as best for her children. Marilyn's description signals both that a household with "people in and out" was seen as automatically dangerous and that this mother was seen as more interested in her boyfriend and her social life than in protecting her children. Again, this assessment paints her as irresponsible and selfish. This view is also tied closely to stereotypes of irresponsible women of color and to implicit comparison with middle-class, white norms of relatively isolated nuclear families (Stack 1983).

Case 3: "Judgment," Class, and Credibility. In this case, the mother's judgment was questioned and used to assess risk to her child, a three-year-old who was removed due to the mother's alleged drug use, mental health problems, and "chaotic" life. The mother, in her early twenties, was white, received welfare, had previously been a victim of domestic violence, and was homeless after she left that relationship. The case initially came to the attention of ACS when neighbors, in an expensive building in lower Manhattan, called police with complaints of yelling and fighting coming from the apartment. The mother and her son were living there with the mother's boyfriend, a former Wall Street trader turned restaurant investor. According to the caseworker's testimony, the initial investigation showed that the domestic violence allegations were probably false, so the caseworker decided to mark the case unfounded, but she planned to visit the home a few more times before doing so. On one of these visits, the boyfriend told the caseworker that the mother had moved out, and he then revealed that the mother used drugs and that they had met through a mutual friend in a drug-treatment program. He also told the caseworker that the child had found the mother with a needle in her arm, passed out, and showed the caseworker drug paraphernalia that he said the mother had left in the apartment. He said he had offered to care for the child while she went to treatment, but she had refused and left. The caseworker also reported that the mother's therapist and the child's pediatrician had both expressed concern that the mother lived a "chaotic life" and did not provide stability for the child. The pediatrician, however, also felt that the child was healthy and well cared-for, an assessment shared by the caseworker.

When the case was first filed in court, the mother was asked to take drug tests, but both of the tests she submitted were inconclusive.[15] The mother had a record of negative tests from an out-patient program, but their testing policies allowed for the possibility that she had provided clean samples from someone else, so the caseworker did not believe these tests were accurate. The decision was made to remove the child on the basis of this information. When the mother became very upset with the decision, the ACS caseworker and the law guardian both concluded that she was mentally unstable.

The mother's attorney asked for a 1028 hearing and attempted to show that the evidence for her drug use was questionable: she had tested negative, and it was likely, he argued, that the boyfriend had made up the allegations of her drug use out of spite after she had left his house and broken off their relationship.[16] The attorney was mostly successful, in my mind. The caseworker admitted that only the boyfriend's word evidenced her drug use. The mother testified that the boyfriend drank excessively, tried to control her, and felt entitled to monitor her behavior because he wanted to "save the poor white girl on welfare." She denied current drug use (although she admitted past use) and argued that his allegations were vindictive, but she was not able to explain the inconclusive drug tests. As far as the mental health allegations, she admitted that she had been diagnosed as bipolar but was compliant with treatment until very recently when she had a Medicaid problem and was unable to fill her prescription.

During the hearing, the law guardian questioned the mother extensively, focusing on how she had met this man, when she had moved in with him, and why she stayed if he was alcoholic and controlling. The mother admitted she had not known him long and had not known much about him when she and her son moved in with him. She explained that she had to leave an abusive relationship with her son's father (he was incarcerated) and needed a place to live, which explained her move into the boyfriend's apartment, which was in a better neighborhood. She needed a place to live and left when things got too bad. The law guardian later told me that she focused on this part of the story because, although she was concerned about the drug use, she was equally concerned about the mother's judgment in deciding to live with this man after knowing him for only a couple weeks. She further told me that she had spoken with the boyfriend and felt he was telling the truth about her drug use. In her view, he was not "a bad guy" and had tried to help her out.

After all the testimony, each attorney presented his arguments about how to proceed in the case. The mother's attorney stated that the child should be returned because the child had been well cared-for and there was no solid evidence of her drug use.[17] The ACS attorney argued that the child should remain in foster care due to the mother's drug use. He argued that all the evidence for her use (the boyfriend's statements, the inconclusive tests, and the drug paraphernalia in the apartment) was conclusive and dismissed the idea that the boyfriend had made allegations out of spite. The law guardian argued that the child should remain in foster care due to the mother's drug history, not taking medication for her mental health issue, and showing poor judgment by moving in with a man she barely knew, who, according to her, drank and was controlling. All of this meant that the child would be at risk if returned to the mother's care.

The judge, in making her decision, stated that ACS had proven imminent risk and that the case was not, in her mind, simply about the mother's drug use or whether the boyfriend made up these allegations. She believed that the mother had a serious mental illness and a history of serious drug abuse, that she was not on her medication, and that she had not maintained a stable residence of her own for the child. She put a lot of weight on the information from the psychiatrist and the pediatrician who both felt that life was chaotic for the child and on the fact that she moved in with her boyfriend after only knowing him a couple of weeks. Thus, she ruled that the child should remain in foster care.

In this hearing, several factors played a role in the outcome. First, assessments about the relative credibility of the mother and her former boyfriend were used to conclude that the mother was lying about her drug use; his credibility was likely bolstered by his respectability (he had a stable life, an expensive apartment, and money) in contrast to the mother. His position was a stark contrast to an unemployed single mother with a drug history and psychiatric diagnosis who did not have a stable residence. Thus, her denials that she was a drug user were dismissed while his were not questioned, despite his own drug history. More important, officials questioned her judgment in moving herself and her young son into the apartment of a man she barely knew and deemed her "chaotic" life too risky for her child. Her testimony about her boyfriend's behavior, which her attorney attempted to use to undermine the credibility of his accusations, was, in the end, taken by the law guardian and the judge as further evidence of her poor judgment. The fact that she moved into his home to avoid homelessness was not even considered.

Overall, her "chaotic life" was seen as presenting a risk to the child. It was interesting that the child's pediatrician and the caseworker both decided that the child seemed well cared-for and did not point to anything specific about her chaotic life that had been detrimental to the child, but constant moving and living with unknown persons were seen as presenting risk and were therefore weighed more heavily than the things the mother had apparently been doing right. I argue that these assessments come from a certain ideal of raising children that is, in large part, class-based. Having a stable home given the mother's situation—unemployed, supporting yourself on welfare, leaving an abusive relationship—in an expensive city such as New York is nearly impossible for a poor woman. Her problems, however, were labeled as neglect and blamed on her individually; that is, nobody saw her chaotic life as an outcome of her poverty and her history of being subjected to violence and rather chose to interpret her behavior as acting irresponsibly, exhibiting poor judgment, and resorting to drug use.

Officials' Views of "Proper Parents" and Parenting

In their discussions of decision making, both caseworkers' and attorneys' discussions about parents provide evidence about their expectations and definitions of adequate parents and parenting. Officials generally discussed parents in ways that blamed problems on a lack of individual responsibility and drew on negative stereotypes of poor women of color. They often discussed parents in the racially coded culture of poverty discourse commonly used to talk about poor people, especially welfare recipients, more generally (Gilens 2000; Mullings 2005; Quadagno 1996; Roberts 1997, 1999; Williams 1995). Significantly, these discourses are overtly color-blind and make no direct reference to race (Mullings 2005), but, at the same time, it is clear that they refer to women of color. Negative views about poverty in the contemporary United States have become increasingly tied up with race so that any discussion about "welfare queens" or even simply "welfare mothers" assumes that these individuals are women of color who live in inner cities and can blame only their own irresponsibility for their poverty (Gilens 2000; Quadagno 1996; Roberts

1997, chap. 5; Williams 1995). Decision makers have picked up on this form of color-blind racism, and it likely conditions their views of their clients of color and how they make decisions in their cases; that is, the decision makers are much more likely to see the mothers they encounter as irresponsible and potentially dangerous to their children, rather than as loving but constantly struggling.

For example, Rafael, an 18B attorney, explained that he came from a family of Puerto Rican immigrants without much money, like many of his clients. He discussed his clients using a mixture of, on the one hand, culture of poverty discourse, and, on the other, complaints that the system blames people for problems that are not their fault. He complained about clients who wasted money on cable and cell phones and who told him they did not care if their child was taken because they would just have another one. He added that he wondered if they were so willing to have more children because they could get more welfare money. He also said that they would sign their children into special education classes only so that they could get Social Security money. Finally, he complained that too many immigrants were getting services when it was possible, under immigration law, to exclude them from the country altogether. In other words, he tended to see his clients as irresponsible, lazy, unworthy of help, and responsible for their own poverty; moreover, he thought they were taking money from the government that they did not need.

Marilyn, who described herself as being from the "same community" as her clients, had similar views. She told me that most of her cases involve families who live in public housing or shelters. When I asked her why she thought that was the case, she responded:

> Well, it has to do with, I think, arrested development. A majority of people haven't grown up and still have a teenage mentality, and they have arguments with neighbors, and they're calling in on each other and stuff like that. I think that within the educational system, they cannot relate to the service needs of the community. You know, the staffing. For example, most of the families that we service are a one-parent household and mostly women. You understand? Where the father may be incarcerated, out of the picture, don't *know* who the father is. It's very limited the support that they have. Unemployed, okay, no high school education. So it's a lot of really negative stuff that's already there. You understand? And if they didn't value an education for themselves, they certainly don't value it for their children. You know?

Later in our conversation she used this concept of "arrested development" again: "They [i.e., parents] haven't grown up. They haven't had the opportunity to become adults." She added that parents do not see their problems because they have never known anything else, so they do not seek out services. In these comments, she hints at the constraints parents face; however, her comments also pick up on discourses that blame individual irresponsibility for poverty. She, too, views her clients as irresponsible, even childlike, so they cannot, in her mind, be trusted to care for their children. She also feels this is why they are living in poverty in the first place. In short, their problems are related to personal failings (irresponsibility and lack of interest in education) rather than to structural inequalities. By seeing her clients as childlike she also justifies both incredible intrusions into the lives of some clients and directives relating to practically every aspect of their lives. The idea that these mothers (and fathers) have not "grown up" signals, in Marilyn's mind, that they are not responsible, cannot be trusted to do what they have to do, and make questionable decisions. Thus, intense surveillance and a focus on compliance, even regarding sexual partners and having guests in one's home (recall Marilyn's case above), are warranted. If mothers resist making the changes required, then removal of their children is a likely outcome.

Caseworkers judged mothers, in particular, on the basis of how focused they were on their children and viewed them through the lens of stereotypes of oversexualized black women (i.e., the "jezebel" stereotype; see Collins 1990). For example, I witnessed two home-alone cases in family court. In one, the mother maintained she had left her children home overnight with a babysitter so that she could avoid a more than two-hour commute to her new job by staying with her boyfriend. Caseworkers were suspicious of her claim to have hired childcare and believed she made up the story about the job and simply left them alone to spend time with her boyfriend. She was able to later regain custody, however, after proving she had been at work. Another mother, who was with her boyfriend when they both were arrested after a traffic stop, which brought the case to the attention of ACS, claimed to have left her nine-year-old child home alone for a few minutes while she went shopping. She did not regain custody after the judge decided that her story was not credible. The judge stated on the record that she believed the mother was not going to get food but was going to stay the night with her boyfriend.

These cases demonstrate the extent to which mothers had to prove that they were focused on their children and had to counter assumptions about their irresponsibility. The mother who appeared to be placing her desire for a night out with her boyfriend over her children's safety was not able to show she would not place them in danger again so they remained in foster care, but the mother who proved she was working to support her children was able to get them back. It is interesting to note the degree of suspicion these women, both poor women of color, were under; the judges assumed from the beginning that the women had cavalierly left their children in danger in order to fulfill their own sexual needs. This seems to be related to common images of black "welfare mothers" who represent "a woman of low morals and uncontrolled sexuality, factors identified as the cause of her impoverished state" and of black women more generally as oversexualized (Collins 1990, 78; see also Roberts 1997). Here, again, is the idea that poor women of color cannot be trusted to behave responsibly and to care for their children properly; decision makers at all levels assume they are irresponsible and careless mothers.[18]

Fathers were also held to particular standards, and, from the beginning, caseworkers often assume them to be "deadbeats" who won't be involved in their children's lives. It was not uncommon for them to be denied custody, although no petition alleging that they were neglectful or abusive parents was even filed. Fathers, attorneys, and parent advocates all reported that caseworkers often do not look for the fathers of the children they are removing to see if they are potential caretakers. I witnessed several cases in family court in which fathers who were not named as respondents and were not living with the mothers at the time when the children were removed came forward to get custody of their children. Although they had no allegations against them and there was no evidence that they might not be fit caretakers, judges did not grant them custody, and caseworkers told them to either find lawyers and file custody petitions or wait while the caseworkers "explored them as a resource." Caseworkers promised to get back to them about taking custody of their children after the investigations, but these delays were frustrating to fathers. Decision makers assume that the fathers will not be proper caretakers, and therefore, before gaining custody, the fathers must prove that they are responsible. One 18B attorney told me this happened all the time and that this cut children off from an entire set of potential family caretakers—not only fathers but also paternal relatives, who are rarely considered as potential kinship foster parents.

Custody was denied due to a criminal history (even if this didn't involve children) or due to drug use. Fathers are often assumed to be unfit and forced to prove they should get custody. Because children are usually living with their mothers, caseworkers do not take fathers into account even if they are involved with their children's lives. This theme came out in my conversation with Ramel, whose newborn son was removed from his girlfriend and him due to their drug use:

> RAMEL: I guess because I'm the father, I'm a male, and because—I've been seeing that, and at first when I went to family support services, it was like that, too. . . . I was kind of getting a little cold shoulder. Because a lot of males really, unless they show that they're serious about doing what they have to do, a lot of males don't get the respect that the female get, because it's the mother, and I understand that. . . . However, it's not fair.
>
> TINA: So you would say that maybe their attitude is "we'll wait and see about this one, and see if he disappears," or . . . ?
>
> RAMEL: Exactly, [laughs] exactly, exactly. And it's past fathers that put that jacket on this. However, you can't judge a book by its cover. I love all my kids.

Ramel felt caseworkers were approaching him with a "wait and see" attitude. If he demonstrated he was serious and not like other fathers who were uninvolved, then and only then would they work with him. Because decision makers assume that men of color are not involved and fit caretakers, it is difficult for them to gain custody of children (another clear example of stratified reproduction).

This situation is likely related to pervasive racialized stereotypes about "deadbeat" African American fathers who are seen as completely uninvolved with their children and as selfishly spending their money on themselves and their time with new girlfriends rather than with their children. Absent African American fathers are often blamed in the press and in some scholarly research, along with black mothers, for social problems facing black children such as high school drop-out rates, drug use, poverty, and gang activity (Hamer 2001). In this context, denying them custody can seem unproblematic (see also Reich 2005; Roberts 2002).

Parents' attorneys also felt that parents are held to a "perfect parenting standard" that is heavily based on middle-class norms. For example, Brandon, an 18B attorney, stated:

> So like a perfect parenting standard would be like, I don't know, definitely no drugs, no alcohol, completely spotless house, home all the time with the

> kids. You know? Kids are going to school, doing well in school. You're there to pick them up right on time. You're there to drop them off right on time. They're never left alone at school. They're never left running around outside past 8:00 when it's dark. . . . No corporal punishment. Everybody should be put in time-outs. Everybody should like, you know, it's sort of like this new psychology way of raising children, which I, frankly speaking, have a hard time with. . . . But that's what it seems to me. If you make any error in judgment with your children and the person who's hearing your case or prosecuting your case has a subjective view that that's not okay in their book, they're gonna come after you.

Here he describes a standard of perfection that is time- and resource-intensive with little room for errors in judgment. Meeting this standard requires ample time to spend with children, flexible work schedules with the ability to take time off, the means to purchase help with housekeeping or a partner with whom to share chores, the ability to cope with all personal problems, and insurance to pay for treatment if needed. It is a difficult standard to attain for the majority of parents involved in child welfare who are poor and raising children alone with little access to childcare, inflexible jobs with long hours, lack of health insurance, and so on. The philosophy behind these expected child-rearing techniques, that is, that children should be negotiated with and given "time-outs" rather than physically punished, is also not shared by everyone.

Judges and attorneys often disregard how parents' material circumstances affect their ability to care for their children or to comply with court and ACS directives. Instead, the judges and attorneys saw these parents as irresponsible and neglectful as two examples illustrate (see detailed discussion in chapter 7).

In one case the child was paroled to the mother (the allegations were not clear), and the caseworker reported that the child was fine in the home. When told that the mother was not able to be in court in the middle of the day because she was fearful of losing her job, the judge replied, "Did you tell her she could lose her child if she doesn't come to court?" The judge ended the hearing by directing the caseworker to tell the mother she would issue a warrant for her arrest if she was not in court next time. The judge completely disregarded the importance of the mother's job and the likelihood that she really was unable to take time off without the risk of losing her job and the income she needed to support her children (a catch-22 because lost income would also put her at risk of losing her children; see chapter 8).

In another case witnessed in family treatment court, a father was deemed neglectful because he had not protected his children from their mother when she went back to using cocaine. Both parents were Latino and eligible for assigned counsel; they had four children. The father provided ample testimony that he saw no signs she was using again and reasonably assumed she was drug free: she had completed a drug treatment program, and she was not losing weight as she did when she was using previously. He also explained that he worked two jobs and long hours almost seven days a week (generally from 6:30 A.M. to midnight) to support the family and allow her to stay home with the children. Therefore, he was not home to see what was happening. He was questioned by the judge, law guardian, and ACS attorney about why he did not either (1) move out with the children, (2) kick her out of the home and keep her away from the children, or (3) question her more about whether she was using. He clearly explained why all these solutions were impossible: he supports her, they could not afford to live apart, and she was the only caretaker. The judge made a neglect finding against him, stating that working was no excuse for not knowing about her drug use. She lectured him about how he needed to "protect" his children from his wife, and the children remained in foster care. The judge ended by telling the father that he should consider quitting one of his jobs so he could talk to his wife. She added that they should go to counseling to "open up to each other more." It was hard to imagine how this family could afford any of these solutions and hard to see how counseling would solve these problems that stemmed from their lack of resources.

It is important to acknowledge that court officials (but less so caseworkers) also recognized, at times, that parents are facing structural barriers (though they do not use that terminology). Many attorneys and judges acknowledged the fact that most of the parents in court are poor people of color, struggled to explain why that was the case, and asked for my opinion because they were truly trying to understand it. Their own theories about the disadvantages parents faced focused on them coming from "different worlds" than the attorneys and judges, on their poverty and lack of education, and sometimes even on the court system itself. For example, Brandon told me that: "You know, the attorneys and the judges, we come from a different world than where these people come from for the most part . . . and so their rules are different. What they do is different, and they're getting judged by a system that doesn't really understand them. You know what I mean? That's one problem." Bob similarly complained that the court either ignores how parents are different—as when judges used legal jargon to explain important facts like the ASFA time-line—or disregards the parents' perspective—as in the case of parents from the West Indies who did not see anything wrong with smoking marijuana but were told they were neglectful.

Rafael asked me, rhetorically, why all the parents in family court are black and Latino and answered his own question with "oppression." He further complained that judges thought they were better than the parents because they had more money and chastised caseworkers who brought parents to court when their children were late for school without bothering to investigate the reason. As examples, he cited one case in which the school bus was actually dropping the child off late and another in which the mother had to take both a bus and a train to get to a school that was far away. In both cases the mother was blamed, although she was not the cause of these transportation problems. He also pointed out that there were not enough people working in family court or ACS who spoke Spanish and could appreciate cultural differences.

Poverty and education were also acknowledged as barriers to meeting family court standards. Brandon explained, "But at the same time, those people don't have the money, they don't have the education. They don't have anything so [that] they can do what I call the perfect parenting thing. . . . They can't do it. And I don't even know how the wealthiest most well-off family can always be a perfect parent." Some attorneys thus *were* aware of the differences between themselves and parents and were trying to grapple with why they saw only poor people of color come through the courts' doors. At times they were able to point to the larger inequalities that impacted their lives. This is testament to the fact that working in family court is a difficult job, and many do it because they *do* want to help children and/or see defending parents as important. Their own jobs are difficult, however, and there is generally not sufficient time or resources to help all clients (see chapter 4).

Conclusion

Decision making around allegations of child neglect is complicated and involves the use of criteria that are neither clear-cut nor easy to apply. The legal definition of neglect is flexible and broad, encompassing a wide range of family issues. Most cases in the child welfare system involve personal issues faced by parents that place children at risk: drug use, mental health issues, and domestic violence. These problems are sometimes concretely linked to a lack of care for the child or evident signs of the parent's impairment; however, very often having these problems can, in and of themselves, be construed as constituting a "failure to exercise a minimal degree of care." Decision makers often assume that parents cannot continue to provide care for their children in the face of these problems and that removal is the best solution if parents do not quickly access help in a way recognized as legitimate by caseworkers. These problems can indeed present risk to children, but, by-and-large, child welfare does not deal with these issues when faced by white, middle-class families. In contrast, cases in which it was clearer that children's needs were not being met were actually less likely to result in the children's placement in foster care.

Caseworkers and family court officials are allowed a fairly large degree of discretion in their decision making. This discretion recognizes that every case and every family is different, and it ideally allows for flexible decision making in order to meet these diverse needs. This discretion, however, also allows for similar cases to be judged very differently and for officials to take into account subtle issues like a parent's judgment in how they run their lives or their ability to be responsible. These assessments are often influenced by discourses about and stereotypes of poor women and men of color, or made through implicit class comparisons, or both. Caseworkers and family court officials drew on racialized ideologies about the irresponsibility of poor parents and used these views to justify surveillance or removal of children. Although direct references to race were not made, these "color-blind" discourses are nonetheless racialized. Caseworkers talked about parents in ways that drew on larger stereotypes of both black women as irresponsible, careless mothers who are to blame for their own poverty due to their own poor choices and overly sexualized nature and black fathers as uninterested "deadbeat" dads. The presumption that poor parents of color are irresponsible and to blame for poverty makes it more likely that they are seen as risks to their children rather than as struggling parents who have something to offer them.

Although the law requires caseworkers and other decision makers to distinguish between neglect and poverty, this is easier said than done. Many of the families who come into contact with the child welfare system have lives constrained by very limited resources, and many of the problems that exist in these families can just as easily result from poverty as from willful negligence. Persistent issues—lack of health insurance or problems with Medicaid, lack of affordable childcare, inflexible job schedules, limited availability of drug and mental health treatment, inability to provide care for their children if in-patient treatment was needed, vulnerability to homelessness, and difficulties leaving abusive partners—were often central to the risks that children faced. Although caseworkers and decision makers were aware of these issues, they often saw them as the results of parental irresponsibility, poor judgement, or drug use, rather than as the roots of family problems. Caseworkers did not often acknowledge parents' very real struggles in the face of extremely scarce resources; instead, they labeled parents neglectful and dealt with risk to children through placing children in foster care and attempting to alter the parents' behaviors and attitudes through counseling. In these ways, the child welfare system creates and recreates stratified reproduction.

Overall, the definition of neglect used in child welfare has a tendency to take parental problems out of context by ignoring their roots in structural inequalities and instead blames individuals. In addition, the larger context of how parents care for their children is lost as they are judged almost solely on the basis of particular problems or particular moments in time. Rather than being seen as parents who need help, they are seen as neglectful adults, "risks" from whom children need to be protected. This label, which is enforced by legal means and difficult to overcome, makes it easy to devalue or ignore the care these parents have provided to their children while facing problems that are often not acknowledged.

7

Power in Child Welfare

Compliance and Rights

Once parents enter the child welfare system, they lose the ability to control many aspects of their lives, and caseworkers are given leeway to require a broad range of behaviors and services. Parents must defer to caseworkers, conform to all expectations and requirements, and agree with caseworker evaluations of their problems. Any other response can lead to a loss of custody, a delay in reunification, or a loss of parental rights. Not all parents are equally able to comply and show this deference, but their barriers are either seen as illegitimate or simply ignored. In fact, parental anger and resistance is seen as a confirmation that the parent is dangerous, unwilling to change, or both. Ideally the family court should act as a check to this state power and ensure that intervention happens only when necessary; rather than providing this oversight, family court too often rubber-stamps caseworkers' judgments with little scrutiny and provides parents with few opportunities to challenge allegations or caseworkers' assessments. The other job of the family court is to ensure that reasonable efforts are made to prevent foster care or reunify families. As a society, we have decided that agents of the state have the right to intervene, but they also have the responsibility to help children be safe in the custody of parents when possible and to reunite children when removals are necessary. The court rarely enforces the state's dual responsibilities, however, and parents have little ability to use the court to meet their needs.

Power Dynamics in the Investigation Process: Struggles over Compliance

In addition to the role of race, class, and subtle judgments about parents in decision making (chapter 6), compliance is a key factor that points to important issues of power. In the investigation stage of a case, caseworkers use compliance as both a shorthand to assess the level of risk a child faces in his home and a way to measure when risk decreases. Compliance is taken to mean that parents have acknowledged their problems and are taking steps to remedy them. At the same time, compliance is also a matter of the differential power held by caseworkers and parents in these interactions. It can be the decisive factor in the decision to remove or not, such that cases in which the situation seems to place the child at the same level of risk can be handled quite differently based on the level of parental compliance (Reich 2005). Parents know (and if they do not, then they are told) that the caseworker has the power to remove their children and that complying might allow the children to stay in their custody. Caseworkers also make it clear that they can take parents to family court if they do not comply. Thus, parents are pressured (intentionally or unintentionally) to cooperate fully, to comply with caseworker directives, to admit to their problems (even if they might not agree that problems exist or share the caseworker's idea of what they are), and to generally defer to the caseworker. If parents refuse, the state, through the family court, can enforce their cooperation. Thus, the caseworker is in a position of great power over the families on their caseloads.

Caseworkers look favorably on clients who are compliant in the sense of being cooperative with them, properly deferential and calm, and willing to do anything to keep custody of their children. They are suspicious if parents do not let them into their homes, do not answer all their questions, or do not comply with requests (such as a request to submit to drug testing), although all these things are within parents' legal rights. When parents refuse to cooperate in these ways, it is highly likely that they will, at best, be taken to family court, or, at worst, have their children removed. Thus, parents have little ability, practically speaking, to control the information they give to caseworkers, to adjust the requirements with which they will comply, or to shape the terms of the interaction (see Eubanks 2006 and Gilliom 2001 on the same dynamic in the welfare system).

Caseworkers also expect parents, especially mothers, to have an attitude perceived to be both properly centered on their child and eager to do whatever it takes to keep custody. Expressions of love for their children and the willingness to do anything are seen as positive, and other reactions register as negative. Amy, a white woman in her forties who worked as a caseworker for five and a half years, explained: if a parent says "'I do have a drug problem and I'm willing to go into services, please don't take my baby, I'll do anything, I'll do anything,' then you're much more likely to work with them."

Robert, one parent with whom I spoke, offers a prime example of the lengths to which some parents will go to prove themselves to caseworkers and to avoid further interventions in their family. He is a single father raising his two children after kicking their mother out of the home (ACS was involved) due to her drug use and an incident in which she threatened him and both children with a knife and slashed the children's bike tires. He has dealt with false reports made periodically by the children's mother. He told me that "when they [caseworkers] say jump, I just say 'how high?'" When a caseworker asked him to take a second drug test after the first was negative, he went voluntarily into a *month-long* out-patient drug-treatment program to be tested and prove to her he was not using. Here, he shows his deference in an exaggerated way and opens himself up to a high level of very personal and intensive surveillance so as to "get her [the caseworker] off my back."

In contrast, caseworkers view parents who do not cooperate or who react negatively with suspicion and take their behavior as a sign the child is at greater risk in the home. Caseworkers usually assume that they are hiding their problems, are unwilling to change, or both. If parents react in a manner that signals to the caseworker that they do not believe there is a problem, then the caseworker, once again, assumes that the parents are unwilling to change. Generally caseworkers see a parent who reacts in an angry or defensive manner as having an "anger problem" that requires management and counseling—that is, a parent who is likely to lash out at or behave violently toward the child. This is based on the assumption that if parents are not controlling themselves and being even-tempered in their interactions with the caseworker, then they probably do not control their anger around their child and are thus likely to hurt the child when the caseworker leaves. One caseworker, Marilyn, even stated that she feels a parent might retaliate against the child because they had to deal with an ACS case. She explained that, if a parent is arrested because he or she left a mark or bruise on the child, then Marilyn tries to place the child in foster care, even if there is a possibility to have the child cared for outside the system by an informal arrangement. She explained her rationale: "After a while, they may say, 'I'll take care of them temporarily,' but then who's going to take care of the kid when the mother comes out of jail? She's going to be angry with no services and may harm the child even more. It's done because, 'Now, you put me in jail.'"[1] Therefore, caseworkers take anger very seriously and assume that parents will take anger out on their children.

One mother, Irene, a Latina in her forties and the mother of five children, told me that she was sure that her angry reaction to caseworkers led to the removal of her children:

> This hospital had called ACS and said that the knee bruise, the bruising on her knees and stuff, was abuse and that if I knew what was going on, and I said, "As far as I'm concerned, she's a child, she plays, she gets hurt or whatever." And then they was like, "No, that's more than playing." I said, "Well, you know, y'all take it as whatever." So I guess I didn't speak right to the emergency worker that came out, because I got hysterical. I said, "Why y'all removing my kid? You know, I want to see my daughter." I was there. I wanted to let my daughter know she not coming home. So I told her . . . "I don't care what you believe you know. I know I'm not a bad mother. I'm do what I gotta do." So they removed all my kids.

Her denial that anything was wrong and her anger at the assumption that she caused her child's injury, she felt, led to her child's removal.

Caseworkers' concern with anger is an understandable response, especially in cases in which the child has been injured when being punished. Children are vulnerable to violence and anger, especially when they are young, and it is reasonable to wonder whether an angry outburst at the caseworker signals a larger problem. Anger on the part of a parent, however, is almost always seen as a problem, even in cases in which the parent's anger is justifiable, might not be directly related to the harm a child has suffered, or probably does not signal anything about how the parent will treat the child. Pamela, an African American who had worked at ACS for eleven years, told me a story about a woman who had a "hard life, went through a lot," including the death of a child at the hands of a former boyfriend. A hospital called in a report because she was speaking very harshly to her son who was going through treatment for cancer: "Her voice is very abrasive, and I told her, I says, 'I understand that you may not be beating him or hurting him to the point where, you know, doing it. I really think that the children, the way you speak is, can get you in a lotta trouble.' She went to court, had that same boisterous attitude. The judge got fed up and remanded the children." Here, again, it seems that the woman's "abrasive" attitude became the decisive factor in how the case was handled.

In addition to being compliant in the sense of being cooperative and even-tempered, there is pressure to share the caseworker's analysis of family/personal problems and to deal with them in a way that follows the caseworker's directives and timetable. Parents lose the ability to control their lives, to define what they want for their family, and to push for the help that they feel they need. Instead, because they are presumed to be unfit, they must submit to the opinions of experts (see below for more on this point). In Olivia's case, for example, the caseworker decided that having two children live with her in a single room was not adequate and that she needed to move into a homeless shelter. An African American woman in her early forties with seven children, ages eight to sixteen, she argued that she was weeks away from getting a Section 8 voucher that would enable her to find her own apartment and that they could manage for a few weeks. The caseworker did not accept the mother's view of the problem and the best solution, so the caseworker removed her children.

Compliance in the Reunification Process

Parents' attitudes and the proper performance of compliance are key in the reunification process as well. Demonstrating compliance is all-encompassing: a parent must attend everything one is sent to and be consistently on time, accept caseworkers referrals and maintain a polite relationship with them, show "commitment" to children and a willingness to do whatever it takes to regain custody, agree with the caseworker's assessment of family problems, show that one has "taken responsibility," and adopt attitudes that signal change.

Mary's Case

To illustrate the dynamics of this, I want to describe Mary's case in detail. Her case is typical in terms of the barriers that parents face and the delays they experience. Her case, however, is not typical in that there was more discussion than generally seems to occur about the service plan itself and why certain services were necessary. Although not entirely typical, I choose this example precisely because these discussions provide valuable data about the thinking behind how and why service plans are devised and when reunification is appropriate.

Mary is a college-educated, white, single mother, in her early forties, whose daughter, Julia, age nine at the time, was placed in foster care. This case is complicated in many ways, but there were three basic allegations: (1) Mary was not adequately feeding Julia, leading to her small stature (this was labeled failure to provide adequate medical care in the court petition); (2) Mary was mentally ill and a drug user, charges she steadfastly denied (she maintained she made statements about *past* drug *experimentation* and depression); and (3) Mary's apartment was unsafe, given its extensive clutter and rats. The case came to the attention of ACS after Mary voluntarily placed Julia in foster care for a few weeks when she was facing an eviction. Her landlord was attempting to remove all the rent-stabilized tenants and renovate the building in order to rent at full-market price. When Mary brought Julia back home, the agency gave her an after-care plan. She viewed it as voluntary so, although she did comply with some aspects of the plan, she did not follow it completely, nor did she answer the caseworker's questions about what she had been doing. For this reason, the caseworker reported Mary to ACS. Julia was placed in foster care on an emergency basis, following allegations of noncompliance and Mary's refusal to allow the caseworkers into her apartment.

After Julia had been in care for five months, no progress had been made on the service plan until, at a court appearance, the ACS attorney *directed* the foster care agency caseworker to create a service plan, which was to include random drug testing, a mental health evaluation, and individual counseling. At that time, Mary was told about the plan, but the caseworker refused to discuss it further or make referrals until another conference could be held. A month later no referrals had been made, and Mary, following the advice of parent advocates, asked to have a conference. Mary attempted to schedule the conference so that she could bring an advocate.

She was told this was not allowed, but she persisted. The caseworker then refused to schedule the conference so that the advocate could come and told Mary that the conference would occur nonetheless. Mary asked me to attend as moral support and to take notes for her, and I did. At the meeting, which began forty-five minutes late, Mary attempted to take control by introducing me and stating what she wanted to discuss, but the caseworker's supervisor interrupted her and told the caseworker to run the meeting. This was a clear signal that the caseworker, and not Mary, should have power over the conversation about Mary's family and her needs. After the usual preface about rules and a rundown of what had happened in the case thus far, including the new service plan, Mary asked why she was not told about services earlier. The caseworker replied that this delay occurred because she had spent her time filling out paperwork (which *is* long and cumbersome) to possibly move Julia to Ohio to live with Mary's sister, a college professor. She added that Mary was not her only client, the implication being that she did not have time to do everything Mary expected of her. The caseworker then explained that the services would need to be done in a specific sequence: first, a mental health evaluation (these appointments often take weeks to get), then individual therapy (there are very often waiting lists) and, finally, a parenting class (they only start every seven to thirteen weeks). When Mary protested that this sequence would take a very long time and asked to start a parenting class while waiting for the evaluation and therapy, she was told this was not possible.

By yet another conference, four months later, Mary had been assigned a social worker, Rebecca, to help with her case, but she still had not received referrals for all of her services. A mental health evaluation was completed, but it had been conducted by someone Mary was referred to through the homeless shelter system. Mary and her daughter had also begun family therapy a couple of weeks prior (with a counselor at the foster care agency), but a place for individual therapy still had not been found, and, therefore, the caseworker had not begun looking for a parenting class. I attended this conference as well, and, thanks to persistent questioning by Rebecca, I was able to gain insight into how caseworkers think about service plans and reunification more generally.

Rebecca asked the caseworker a question that I never saw asked, at least not directly, at any other time during my fieldwork: How will you know when progress has been made and you are ready to recommend that the child be returned? The caseworker looked puzzled and did not answer for a few seconds, but then she said that Mary's therapist would determine her readiness. Rebecca countered by asking: But what change do you want to see? The answer this time was compliance: we want to see she is going to therapy. This back and forth about what specific change was desired and how the caseworkers would determine when reunification would occur continued in this vein for nearly an hour. Rebecca attempted to get specific responses, while the caseworker gave her vague answers or those that boiled down to either "compliance" (i.e., that the mother was going to the appointments) or "everyone has to do *x*." The caseworker's supervisor became frustrated with the caseworker's answers and pushed her to be specific and to link the services and criteria to the reasons the child was in foster care in the first place. After that comment, the therapist at the agency did jump in to state that Mary's mental health history meant that she might be in need of therapy.

The most specific information Mary received about what specific changes the caseworker expected of her remained vague: (1) she must take responsibility for why her child was in care and deal with those issues, and (2) she must interact more "positively" with Julia by being more relaxed and enjoying the visits rather than focusing too much time and attention on Julia's grades and her meals and coaching her to speak properly. This requirement was especially disturbing to Mary. Crying, she told the caseworkers that the visits were her only time to be a parent and ensure her child's needs were being met. The caseworkers did not give a rationale for these measures of change, but it was clear that they believed that Mary did have a mental illness, something along the lines of obsessive/compulsive disorder, which meant that she "expected too much" of Julia and was clinging to a rigid idea of a proper diet despite the fact Julia did not like it and was not eating. Apparently, this is why they presented, eventually, these specific behavioral changes; the caseworkers held that Mary's changed attitude would signal her agreement with their assessment and her acceptance of normal behavior. Rebecca commented to me, after the meeting, that the caseworkers were essentially considering neglect not feeding a child what she liked.

Mary's psychological evaluation through the shelter system found no serious mental health issues, but this convinced neither the caseworkers nor the judge so Mary was ordered to get an evaluation through family court a few months later. That evaluation diagnosed her with Munchausen's Syndrome by Proxy: she was purposefully making her child ill so that she could get attention from doctors; this was the diagnosis, despite the fact that *inadequate* medical care had been an initial allegation. The evaluator also added, Mary told me, "that because I'm so deeply angry at the [agency that made the report]—and I mask it with intellectualism, I have deeper issues I'm covering up—since I'm admitting no wrongdoing." In other words, she was also seen as hiding her mental health problems.

Mary had a quite different analysis about her actual problems and the help she needed to resolve them. She was adamant that her main problem was actually a housing issue—that is, her dilapidated apartment and eventual wrongful eviction—and she was anxious to get help to either pay her rent arrears or get another apartment. She continued to maintain that she was feeding and caring for her daughter adequately and that she was neither mentally ill nor a drug user. Regarding the mental health evaluation conclusion that she was "covering up" and not admitting to the problem as defined by child welfare officials, she commented: "Yes, I'm angry. Why admit to something I didn't do?" Mary's views meant that, in the eyes of those evaluating her, she was not dealing with her real problems and working to fix them. Thus, she was not ready to have her child returned.

Along with her child welfare case, Mary also had to deal with her housing issue and her public assistance case, both of which required her time and often conflicted with court appearances and visitation. She was forced to miss a housing court appearance that was scheduled on the same day as a family court appearance and had to miss visits with her daughter while dealing with what was basically the gutting of her apartment by her landlord in an effort to force her out so that he could charge higher rent. She was eventually evicted and lost her court challenge of his actions. After being chastised by the judge, that "if you have the choice between visiting your child and waiting for the plumber, you had better visit your child" (as if she were in the middle of a voluntary bathroom renovation), she made sure not to miss future visits. In addition, she was kicked out of her Back-to-Work program when she refused to take a job until she was told what the schedule would be to see if it would fit with her visiting and appointments schedule. She eventually had to close her public assistance case for a time and did not always have enough money for food (she lost weight during the case). Her case thus worsened her poverty (for more on this, see chapter 8).

After Julia had been in foster care for two years, Mary was able to see her daughter, unsupervised, for several hours each Saturday, and through *her own efforts* she was able to find an apartment, was in counseling, and had completed a parenting class (she had to get a referral from Rebecca). Given that she had done these things, the agency did not file a termination of parental rights case (despite being allowed to under ASFA). Because she refused to allow the caseworkers to inspect her new home until she got money to make repairs—in a catch-22 where she could not get this money until the caseworkers stated when Julia would be returned and they refused to do so without the inspection—there was no plan to return Julia, and the caseworkers were planning to send her to Ohio instead (something that Mary did not support). Mary's sister was eventually given full permanent custody of Julia, and Mary was appealing her case when I last talked to her, a little more than four years after her daughter was placed in foster care.

This case illustrates several common dynamics in the reunification process and the common roadblocks parents face in regaining custody. It illustrates the cookie-cutter services plans that are often created and how requirements expand and explanations for why a parent presents risk to their child shift over time (see also chapter 5). Caseworkers initially created a service plan that looked very much like any other parent's plan and, when pushed to justify these services, often fell back on explanations that "everyone must do this." As the case went on, their analysis of Mary's problems shifted and expanded, as one would expect under a therapeutic approach (chapter 2). Although the caseworker's and evaluators' view of Mary and her problems had elements of the original allegations (the mental health issue and the child's inadequate nutrition), the new version was different in important ways. The allegations of drug use were dropped (although she had to continue to submit to random drug tests), but her mental health and Julia's care became clearly linked in a much more serious way than in the initial allegations.

Second, Mary's case shows the importance of what I call performing compliance. Although Mary did not refuse to comply with any specific service, her anger and refusal to accept the caseworkers' view of her and their analysis of her problems lead to Julia's continued placement. In a therapeutic approach (chapter 2), this is understandable: Mary did not make the wholesale changes in her life that the caseworkers thought were necessary to make her a better mother. By continuing to insist on defining her own needs and problems, Mary did not adequately show deference and compliance. Finally, this case illustrates many reasons services are delayed. Delays in creating a service plan and making the necessary referrals were caused not only by time constraints faced by the caseworker but also by the time she devoted to other priorities, namely finding a possible permanent place for Julia, which took time away from the process of reuniting the family. From Mary's perspective, she had trouble complying with her visiting schedule while also juggling housing and public assistance matters.

Performing Compliance

Performing compliance has several components. First, caseworkers place a huge emphasis on attending the services required. In the reports to the judges that update them on the progress of the cases and discuss the progress toward reunification, the caseworkers note whether parents have been attending and been on time to all classes, appointments, conferences, visits, and meetings. Even when missed visits and appointments were attributable to medical issues, to the foster mothers' failure to bring the children to visits, or to legitimate problems with transportation or scheduling (parents' attorneys told me they saw these issues frequently, and the parents I came to know faced them regularly), the caseworkers generally included the absences, and they reflected negatively on the parent. When Mary's caseworker said, regarding her therapy requirement, that "we just want to see you are going," she was certainly not alone.

On the one hand, using attendance as a measure of compliance is a matter of practicality, given the difficult and unclear factors necessary to gauge when a parent has made the changes necessary to regain custody of children. Apparently there is so much faith in education, therapy, and "programs" that the system assumes mere attendance means that change will occur. On the other hand, attendance is used to measure whether parents have their lives together enough to show up regularly and if they are committed to their children and willing to put the effort into attending. Parents who show responsibility and commitment in this way are thought to be better able to care for their children and to display control of their personal life and willingness to change as necessary. The logic of this view is understandable, but this line of thinking also struck me as evidence that caseworkers doubted parents' love for their children and so required proof of it. In addition, structural factors often make it difficult for parents to show up consistently and on time; many parents simply did not have the resources to comply. Using attendance to judge readiness to regain custody ignores these factors and reframes them as lack of compliance, lack of interest in children, or unwillingness to change rather than as issues of poverty (see chapter 8).

Second, parents must show their commitment to their children. Many parents, like Destiny, a young Latina mother of three, reported that getting into as many "programs" as they could was one way to prove commitment:

> She [a parent advocate] said to try to get involved in as many programs as you can, and when you go to court, just say what you're doing so they could see that you busy, you trying to get your kids back. And we supposed to have somebody, like, you know, professionals that works in the program or something vouch for us, saying that we doing all these programs. Because she said it doesn't matter when the caseworker's speaking to say, you know, whatever. It matters when somebody else comes in and says, "Look, they been trying to do what they gotta do to get they kids back."

Caseworkers do generally take being involved in services as a sign parents are committed to their children and willing to do anything to get them back, as long as they agree that the services and service providers are appropriate. Involvement also evidences that the parents have "gotten themselves together" and are now able to be active citizen/parents who are willing to do whatever it takes to improve themselves. If the professionals involved with these services have positive things to say about a parent, then this praise usually carries a lot of weight, provided that the caseworker views the professionals as appropriate. Mary told me on numerous occasions that she felt she was being asked to prove that she loved her child by doing what the caseworkers asked and by prioritizing services and visitation over her efforts to secure housing and a source of income. These priorities are reasonable from a middle-class perspective but not from the perspective of a poor parent struggling to make ends meet. Parent advocates, caseworkers, and some ACS attorneys, law guardians, and judges also told me that parents who "didn't wait around for their caseworker" for referrals but took initiative to seek help independently were viewed favorably for taking responsibility and showing a desire to get their children back without relying on outside help (see also Smith and Donovan 2003). Moreover, decision makers valued such action as another sign that the parent had changed, assumed responsibility, and demonstrated a willingness and ability to parent on their own.

Third, parents must take a deferent attitude with caseworkers. Parents' attorneys, like Bob, were straightforward about the necessity of a proper attitude: "If the caseworker doesn't get along with your client or doesn't like your client, your client is dead . . . whether she does everything or not, she's dead in the water, chances are she's gonna, you're gonna, lose." In his experience, caseworkers can refuse to give services or "spin" reports to make the parent look bad. But if the judge's decision depends upon determining the credibility of either the parent's or the caseworker's explanation of the events, then the judge usually assumes the caseworker to be more credible: "If it comes down to crediting the client, or crediting the caseworker, the caseworker's gonna get the credit all the time. . . . They [the judges] know that the caseworker is lying or is just incompetent because that's their job [i.e., judges are supposed to evaluate whether or not witnesses are trustworthy, and they experience poor casework frequently]. And the judges will take their word for it. . . . If it comes down to one or the other, then they're gonna trust caseworkers." In these ways, caseworkers have the power to define case progress, but parents have little, if any, ability to challenge the caseworkers' evaluations of the situation. This reality is especially problematic when it comes time for the courts to decide whether reasonable efforts have been made in a case. Judges frequently complained about caseworkers not making reasonable efforts toward reunification, but the judges rarely used their power to hold caseworkers accountable (see also chapter 4).

When I asked Sandra, an 18B attorney, if she found her clients were helped by the services they were offered, she stated:

> I can't think of anybody who's gotten any decent services, actually. Well, I shouldn't say that. A very, *very* small number. . . . Nobody seems to think, really, people are going to get better. It's simply the passage of time, and if they've sufficiently toed the line and stopped being belligerent and become more, have become more *supplicant,* more like *supplicants* and stop having that edge of fighting ACS. If they've successfully done that, then ACS thinks everything's fine. *If they preserve any sense of their own independence* and belief in fighting this through . . . they're absolutely cooked. (emphasis added)

After talking with parents and closely following their cases, it seemed to me that Sandra is correct in this assessment. Since parents are seen as having failed to be responsible and are in need of wholesale personal transformation, they are required to submit to the advice and views of experts who can tell them what they should be doing differently. If parents are unable to defer to the better judgment of experts, or if they continue to fight suggestions and argue they do not have the problems they are said to have, then they will have trouble regaining custody.

In Emma and James's case, for example, their relationship with their caseworker became so bad that they would practically shout at one another (I witnessed one of these incidents), and eventually the caseworker avoided them as much as she could and just handed them referral letters rather than discussing services with them. A white couple in their forties, they had their daughter removed at birth due to mental health allegations and inadequate housing. They found service providers on their own and made their feelings known: the caseworker was unqualified, and they could do a better job of deciding what they needed and where they could get it. They also talked about choosing service providers as their right and shared the common perspective that those chosen for them would act as surveillance rather than help. Although they completed the list of services required, the caseworker either decided their services were not appropriate or simply ignored what they had done; the caseworker told the judge that the couple had been doing nothing. Her attempts to paint them as noncompliant seemed to stem from a feeling that they weren't deferring to her. An attempt to have their services recognized by the family court failed, and the judge explained that, although the caseworker needed to talk to them about what they were doing, the parents ultimately would have to follow her directions.[2] After their daughter had been in foster care for more than two years, these disagreements were never resolved, and for this reason, among others,[3] it seemed that the agency would move to terminate their parental rights. This case showed a common pattern: caseworkers expect parents to simply follow their directives. Parents who questioned what they were being asked to do or tried to control the situation too much faced delays in reunification. The system saw such parents as unwilling to admit their "real" problems and change.

Finally, parents must show that they have taken responsibility. In general, I found that parents who came to agree with caseworkers' definitions and analysis of their problems and showed proof that they would do anything to fix them were successful in getting their children back. Parents who refused to admit wrongdoing, blamed others for what they were going through, or could not prove they were adequately remorseful and willing to change were likely to have their children in foster care for longer or even to have their parental rights terminated. Many judges required parents to specifically admit wrongdoing in court and show remorse or some other sign that they had taken responsibility. A social worker at the Legal Aid Society[4] told me that she specifically wanted to see that a parent was not one "who spends a good deal of their time sort of fighting the system, fighting with the case workers, finding fault what other people are expecting them to do" before she felt the child was no longer at risk in the home. She felt that an attitude of "fighting the system" meant the parents were not taking responsibility and were trying to deflect attention from themselves and their problems so that they did not have to address them. Instead, she told me, she wanted to see that parents were using the experience of having a child in foster care to "really gain more in terms of their parenting approach." Any sense that parents might have insight into what they needed, or should be partners in planning their lives, was completely absent.

Attorneys also talked about how parents needed to stop expecting to get help without making enough of an effort to improve themselves. Brandon, for example, told me that:

> I try to tell these people that now you're at a crossroad. Here you are. I'll help you . . . but you have to make a decision. The drugs have to stop. You're hitting your kid, you have to stop. Your house is messy, clean it up. Why are you on welfare? You're twenty-five years old. . . . Go to McDonalds and get a job. . . . I tell them, I'll write you letters. . . . Forget about, you know, McDonalds only pays me, you know, $6–7 per hour. You know what I tell 'em? You're gonna get benefits. You're gonna get all this other stuff. . . . Start making decisions for yourself and we'll help you. . . . You sit them down and, you know, I don't coddle them. I yell at them. I seat them in a corner, I scream at them. I ask them why they're being stupid. What are they doing? Do they want to lose their kid forever?

This kind of talk about parents is related to the culture of poverty discourse and draws on the ideology that the poor need to take responsibility and be forced, even harshly and paternalistically, to work to end their poverty. It ignores structural constraints faced by parents and overestimates the likelihood that low-wage service jobs will significantly improve parents' lives.

Social workers engaged as parent advocates recognized this tendency and attempted to help parents use their child welfare experience to "really change." For example, Emily, a white woman in her thirties and a social worker at the Bronx Defenders, who clearly felt the system was biased and unfair, told me that she has to make sure she does not just commiserate with parents about the system but also helps them get something out of it:

> But we're here now and we have to figure out a way . . . to get something from this. And it's like a very sick discussion because it's like most people don't feel like they need to get anything from, you know, ACS or child welfare. They're very comfortable with their role as parent, or mom, or dad. And, you know, really having discussions around . . . definitely more with isolated families, that parenting is not instinctual. . . . And if we're saying that . . . we're gonna take your children, then we have to explain why and put in . . . supportive services that will actually change what their idea of parenting is and . . . that's the hardest part of the job.

Here she talks about the therapeutic nature of her job. Instead of fostering an attitude of fighting the system, she encourages clients to accept efforts to change their parenting and actually make those changes.[5] Part of her job is convincing them they are in need of the help offered.

To further illustrate the importance of performing compliance, I want to contrast two cases with very different outcomes. Caseworkers often used parents' attitudes and compliance as part of the rationale for either refusing to increase visitation or decrease supervision, which must occur, in most cases, before a child is returned. For example, I witnessed one case in which a mother's unsupervised visits were suspended *only* because she acted "inappropriately" toward caseworkers during visits. The caseworker admitted that the mother did not behave toward her children in a way she found problematic, but she felt the mother was acting unstable and should not have been allowed unsupervised visits.[6] In contrast, Stephanie, an African American mother, lost custody when she gave birth to a second child who tested positive for drugs, but she was able to get them back more quickly than most of the cases in my study. She described what she thought made the difference. She was very "proactive" and basically did her attorney's work for her (made all copies, got all necessary records). She had good "rapport" with the courts because she never "acted out" and "was dressed appropriately" and "spoke appropriately." And, finally, she never missed a visit. Her lawyer also commented that she was "very passionate about this," which was also helpful. Stephanie emphasized "not acting up" and stated that in the "toughest of times . . . when I was still in my early recovery, you know, I never acted out, I never acted out and, sometimes it was just blatant lies." She summed up what led to her family's reunification by stating that "I had established myself as being trustworthy again." She is clear that having the correct attitude was key.

It is important to note, however, that Stephanie was far more able to prove her commitment and trustworthiness than most of the parents who come in contact with child welfare. She is college-educated, with a master's degree in social work, and was able to keep a job throughout the entire process (which is rare, see chapter 8). She thus had various important resources. Her education and job allowed her to "dress appropriately" and "speak appropriately." Her job was flexible enough that she could attend court, meetings, and treatment, and it gave her resources to keep in constant contact with her lawyer and make the copies needed. Her social work training, in particular, allowed her to understand what was required and probably made it easier for others in the system to respect her. She was thus far more able to be active in her case and do things "on her own." These material resources and cultural capital played a role in her ability to make herself "trustworthy." They also allowed her to interact with the decision makers in her case in such a way that they would be willing, as she described it, to tell people that she was "decent." Further, she was seen as "passionate" because she was compliant, engaged, and "proactive," but not "angry" because she was able to control her emotions and could talk to decision makers as a colleague, given her similar background and education. Because of her resources, she had an easier time proving she was an active and responsible citizen/parent who could take charge of her life and make changes without outside help. Most parents, however, are not able to comply in this way.

Barriers to Compliance

Poor parents of color, who form an overwhelming majority of child welfare clients, face very real and very common barriers. Too often the system does not acknowledge these barriers. Despite their circumstances, parents are expected to be able to deal with their problems relatively quickly and to take action, often with little assistance. Before a general discussion of these issues, I examine in detail a case example, taken from a 1028 hearing

I witnessed because it illustrates common barriers to compliance as well as the standards of proper parenting that require resources not available to most parents.

Case Example

This case involved a primarily Creole-speaking Haitian immigrant, working as a school bus driver, who had been taking care of his nine-year-old daughter for about a year (the child previously lived with her mother in Haiti). He was accused of medical neglect and inadequate guardianship for leaving his child for an hour or two before and after school with "inappropriate caretakers," namely two teenaged family friends who lived upstairs. Since the child began living with him there had been two incidents in which she had a seizure. The first time this occurred, he was at work, and the family upstairs called for an ambulance. Apparently the hospital or the EMTs called ACS when they realized that there was no adult present. According to the caseworker, she found no problems with the home. The child seemed well taken care of, was in school, reported her father used no corporal punishment, and appeared healthy apart from the seizures, which, it seemed, happened rarely. In light of this, the caseworker offered services: she told the father to put the child in day care after school, attempted to provide a visiting nurse to ensure the child took her seizure medication, and monitored the father's treatment of the girl. The caseworker, however, felt that the father was not cooperating; he had not followed up when given child care vouchers, had not picked up her medication for a few days, and had not taken his daughter to a specialist as recommended. The second time she had a seizure, the father was apparently present, but the caseworker still felt he was not doing enough to ensure she was getting medical care and adequate supervision. Therefore, she scheduled an elevated risk conference to decide how to proceed, but the father did not attend.[7] He testified in court that he was told the conference had been canceled. After this, they removed the child.

According to the father's testimony, he had problems using the child care voucher he was given and then had been unable to get another one because the caseworker was on vacation. When he finally received another voucher, the second seizure occurred, and his daughter was removed. He explained that he had tried to give his daughter the medicine, but she sometimes refused to take it. Finally, he described how he worked long hours in order to support her, which left him little time to deal with her appointments and sometimes made it difficult to get her prescription. He further stated that he would be willing to find child care for her and to let a nurse into his home to ensure the child took her medicine.

The ACS attorney questioned him about his compliance in an effort to prove the caseworker's assessment that he was neither taking her condition seriously nor taking steps to keep her safe. In his answers, the father outlined very consistent and plausible reasons for not doing these things—his schedule, lack of communication between himself and the caseworker, and language barriers. Especially striking was the ACS attorney's question asking him if he had changed his work schedule to care for the child after he learned of her condition; the lawyer implied that changing his schedule would somehow have been as easy for him—an immigrant working at a relatively low-wage job, in which hours are set, for an hourly wage—as altering a schedule might be for a middle-class professional with a more flexible job, personal days, and sick leave.

After all the testimony, each lawyer was given a chance to state a position. The father's attorney argued that his client was willing to comply with all services and that the child had clearly been well cared-for. He further pointed out that leaving the child for a couple of hours with teenagers was a babysitting arrangement and not inadequate supervision. I noted that this is also the kind of arrangement readily available to someone in this father's position, while more formal child care or an after-school program might have been prohibitively expensive for him to arrange. It also seemed that he trusted the teens, and they acted appropriately when the daughter's first seizure occurred. The law guardian also supported returning the child home, in part, she said, because this was what the girl wanted and also because it seemed that the father was new to the United States and to dealing with a child with a serious medical condition. Given that his primary language was Creole and that the doctor and the caseworkers provided instruction in English, he simply needed more help. In the ACS attorney's summary of the case, he clearly laid out why the child would be at risk in the home. He made the argument that the caseworker was a credible witness, who had tried to work with the father and provide services that would have reduced the risk to the child, but his noncompliance not only placed his child at risk but also led them to believe that things would not change. The attorney moreover highlighted the fact that the father had not attended a case conference, which implied that he was not taking the situation seriously enough. He was portrayed as a careless and irresponsible father rather than as a single parent with little time and money.

Largely because the law guardian supported the child's desire to return home (see also Guggenheim 2005), the judge returned the child with intensive services and stated that the case "cried out" for preventive services: help in understanding the doctor's orders (either through an interpreter or by written instructions) and a visiting nurse or other person to help with the medication. She further ordered the father to obtain formal child care to ensure adequate supervision given the child's medical condition. She added that if the teens upstairs *must* babysit they *must* be told about her condition and what to do. The judge, the law guardian, and the ACS officials agreed about why the child was at risk: the father did not ensure she took her seizure medication, and he left her with caretakers they viewed as inappropriate. That these caretakers were entirely reasonable and offered an affordable arrangement with which he felt comfortable did not matter. The caseworker's testimony that she believed the child was, generally, well cared-for did not outweigh the factors that were thought to place her at risk.[8]

These officials differed, however, in terms of how to deal with this risk. I was able to talk to the law guardian on this case, Michelle, a white woman in her thirties, several months after it occurred. When I asked her about a case that she felt was "borderline," in which she had a hard time deciding what position to take, she mentioned this case. She told me that the child had told her very clearly that she wanted to go home, but, as a law guardian (whose job is to represent the child's interests), she was ambivalent about taking that position because she was worried about the child's medical condition: "I was very concerned, obviously, about the seizures. . . . But I spoke to my supervisor and [he] said if the father testifies and says that whole, you know, 'we'll make sure to give the medication, we'll do this, and we get in-home services,' then I should support the child. . . . I felt uncomfortable, but after talking to the supervisor, I felt better. That's what I wanted to do, but I was just worried about the medical part of it." Michelle's comments in court also signaled that she felt the father was not intentionally being neglectful, nor did she find him a poor caretaker; rather, he needed help. The fact that her client wanted very much to go home meant she was inclined to support sending her home, and she was able to feel she was not putting the child in danger because services would be in place. ACS officials, however, felt that the father's supposed refusal to comply meant that services would not alleviate the risk to the child. The caseworker believed that the father was not timely in following up with the services that ACS required, while the reasons why these things might have occurred—his long and inflexible working hours and his difficulty understanding English—did not change her view that the child was in danger in the home. Instead, the caseworker saw the father as irresponsible, individually blameworthy, willfully noncompliant, and, therefore, a risk to his daughter.

Michelle told me that, for the months when the preventive agency was in place, "things were going beautifully. We thought the case would be dismissed, like things were going great." When the time limit for having preventive services was reached, however, the ACS caseworker who had originally investigated the case and removed the child was sent to monitor the family. Things quickly "fell apart," and ACS asked the judge to remand the child. Although Michelle was not certain what had happened to bring about this outcome, she felt that the father's lack of trust in the caseworker meant he was not always returning her calls or cooperating with her and that this had been the problem. In the 1028 hearing the father testified that he did not trust the caseworker because she lied to him, so this seems a reasonable conclusion. This case not only evidences the role of parents' attitudes and compliance but also offers another example of the tension between investigating/policing and helping/supporting and how this often inhibits effective service provision. This focus on compliance, without full acknowledgment of the real barriers faced by parents, was a common theme.

Lack of Appropriate and Accessible Services

Getting services that fit with a parent's schedule and are convenient and appropriate to their situation can be very difficult, but only some caseworkers (those who focused on service provision more than investigation, see chapter 5) were fully aware of this. A conversation I had with Carl, an African American in his late twenties who had been a caseworker for five and a half years, captures the difficulties clearly:

TINA: Do you feel like you have services to refer people to that are what they need and that are helpful?

CARL: No, no.

TINA: No? Can you explain more?

CARL: . . . [For example,] she's in this certain area, but they don't offer the service she needs. It's offered by, let's say if she lived in Coney Island, it's offered here in Williamsburg. Problem.

TINA: Yeah, big problem. Opposite ends of Brooklyn.

CARL: . . . The family may go for two, three weeks, and then the next thing you know, they're calling on the phone. . . . They don't think it's working. We [the caseworkers] don't even think it's working. . . . [Take] substance abuse, it's a good program, but it's not what Mom needs. . . . Mental health services, that happens to probably be the worst. We have mental health services that do not actually address a client's mental health problem, and they have to refer the client out. And with referring the client out, they refer a client to a place they can't get to that's not easily accessible. . . . If she lives in Brooklyn, we're sending her to the Bronx for a mental health services test. How can she do that? And then when she can't make it back home in time to pick up her children, call the case in once again because she's being neglectful.

Carl recognizes these barriers, but a lack of available services constrains his efforts. Many caseworkers, however, do not even recognize these constraints. For many parents, if there is a delay in getting services due to these issues or an insurance problem, as in Joan's case (see chapter 5), caseworkers often feel the parent is refusing to comply or simply delaying. They usually feel that the delay places the child at risk so they might either remove or refuse to return the child; they rarely take these barriers into account. In this way, again, parents' problems are individualized, and caseworkers assume parents should be able to deal with their problems and "take responsibility" for their own lives despite constraints. A few caseworkers, like Carl, are more aware of the constraints parents face and are more flexible in their expectations. He told me he resists telling parents they have to do services and taking them to court when they have not done them unless absolutely necessary. Despite Carl's approach, I found that, in general, caseworkers expected parents to deal with problems individually while ignoring the constraints they faced; if parents did not comply, then removal was often the result.

Lack of Referrals and Bureaucratic Delays

As discussed in chapter 4, many caseworkers did not make referrals, and parents had to resort to constant follow-up. Many caseworkers and judges framed this situation as a display of "responsibility," "commitment," and an ability to be "proactive" on the part of the parent rather than as a failure on the part of the caseworker. Caseworkers viewed parents who did not follow up as uncaring and uninterested and felt parents were thus not willing to change, not taking responsibility, and not ready to regain custody (see also Smith and Donovan 2003). Caseworkers did not take into account difficulties in following up, such as lack of a telephone, something that was common among the parents I met. Instead, whether parents "engaged in" services or not was seen as their individual responsibility and a measure of how much they wanted and deserved custody. Even when parents were approved for help, bureaucratic rules and overwhelming caseloads can cause delays. It was common in family court and in support groups to hear parents complain that they were waiting for vouchers for services, or for checks to be sent to landlords for deposits and rent, or for money to be able to buy clothes and supplies for children. These delays sometimes unnecessarily delayed reunification (see chapter 8 for more on this topic).

In addition to barriers to compliance that stem from the side of service provision, parents face numerous constraints in complying. First, keeping up with all aspects of a case is extremely time-consuming. For most parents it was quite literally a full-time job. Parents must attend various meetings and appointments, and these usually mean hours, or entire days in some cases, of waiting and commuting. Trips to family court often mean almost an entire day of waiting. Various conferences and meetings at the foster care agency occur frequently, and visits with children occur weekly or twice-weekly. Appointments for services are often only within normal working hours and can be daily, as in the case of drug programs. Parenting skills classes occur once or twice a week for twelve to fifteen weeks. Parents often had long commutes, sometimes taking hours and requiring multiple trains and buses, because services were not all in one place and their child was likely to be placed with an agency far from their home.[9]

In addition to juggling the requirements of a child welfare case, many parents were subject to the requirements of various other agencies: welfare, public housing, Medicaid, and possibly the criminal justice system and/or housing court. This sometimes made it nearly impossible to attend all meetings, appointments, and visits and to be consistently on time, especially when parents had little or no money for transportation. When I asked Carl if finding services that fits a parent's schedule was a problem, he replied: "Definitely. I think that's the most [common] problem that we come in contact with, with families is that the scheduling. Mom works or they're working long hours, they're working two jobs, they're working double-shifts or they're working extra hours to make extra money. Some services don't work on weekends. And they'll say, 'On the weekend, I'll do it.' 'It doesn't work on the weekend, now what?' So we're back in that vicious cycle of repetition. I think that's a lot of it." These reasons for missing appointments, being late for visits, or not getting to services, however, were generally not acknowledged as valid and rarely noted in court reports as explanation for a parent's supposed noncompliance, just as they were often not recognized during the initial investigation and risk assessment.

For example, I witnessed a termination of parental rights hearing in which one of the grounds for the termination was that the father did not consistently engage in therapy. He explained that neither he nor the caseworkers could find a clinic with appointments outside of his working hours. Because he had already lost a previous job due to absences connected to his case, he decided not to risk losing another, so he went to appointments when he could and skipped when he had to. This was not accepted as an excuse for his "noncompliance" by the judge, and his rights were terminated. Ironically, the other grounds for termination were that he did not have his own housing but lived with a girlfriend, their apartment was a walk-up, and his child was in a wheelchair. This situation likely had to do with his limited income. This kind of no-win situation was common: if you miss therapy, you have not changed; if you lose a job or cannot find housing because of therapy, you have not made an adequate "plan" for supporting the child. Even judges who are more sympathetic to these kinds of problems and will direct agencies to help parents with these issues, still generally lecture parents about the need to find a way around them, even in the absence of any help, in order to get their children back.

Given these issues, Bob, a white 18B attorney, told me that he has completely changed his mind about services for his clients: "You know, they would pile services on the clients. And I used to think that I'm helping the clients because you get into this, and this, and that, and ultimately what you see . . . [is] that the more services that you're piling on these people and the more hoops that you're asking them to jump, the greater the probability is they're not gonna get their kids back, and now I will fight what I think are unnecessary services." He explained that he has found that more services also meant more opportunities to generate either delays or negative reports about parents, given the prevalence of skeptical professionals' opinions and the more mundane matters of missing or being late for appointments and visits.

Mistrust, Anger, and Resistance

In addition to these material reasons for delays, there are emotional reasons as well. Many parents had reactions that stemmed from lack of trust in caseworkers and/or a belief, based on how their case had been handled or past experiences with unresponsive and punitive state systems, that "the system" or individuals within it had no interest in actually providing help. Many parents feel that caseworkers were judgmental, looked down on them, and could not be trusted because anything you told them could be used to keep your child in foster care. Some parents view foster care caseworkers as agents of surveillance and punishment (although parents do not use those words) rather than help. This view is understandable given that caseworkers literally do supervise them with their children and record details about their behavior during visits, which are then used to assess the possibility of reunification. Many parents have also come to mistrust caseworkers during the investigation stage (see chapter 5), and I found that not all parents distinguish between ACS caseworkers and foster care agency caseworkers. This is another example of the problems created by a system in which helping and policing are so closely intertwined.

Often, parents talk about caseworkers "not liking" them or "having it out for" them. I surveyed parents in parenting skills classes and asked them to rate their views of their caseworkers. These parents were very early in their cases; most of them had had children in foster care less than eight months. In addition, given that parenting skills classes are often difficult to find, these parents had cases that were going well in terms of adequate referrals for services. Nevertheless, almost 30 percent reported negative views about their relationships with their caseworkers. Among the parents who had had children in care for longer than eight months, the percentage reporting negative views of their caseworkers jumped to 50 percent. Among parents who seek help from CWOP and other organizations, the numbers were even larger because this is often a reason for seeking help. Even parents who held less negative views of caseworkers reported that having to deal with new caseworkers as their case progressed set them back in terms of being able to trust a caseworker enough to form a decent working relationship.

Mistrust and anger often lead parents to delay engaging in services or to resist referrals from caseworkers. For example, a few parents I met asked me to suggest places they could get counseling because they did not trust their caseworkers and thought that any therapists they recommended would only report negative things back to the caseworkers. Other negative reactions stemmed from anger at both state interference into their lives and the judgmental way they were viewed and labeled. Such anger often led to delays in compliance. Leslie, an African American mother, for example, told me it took a long time for her to begin talking to a counselor: "Three years. I had to battle with myself, get myself together, you know, see a therapist, which I was angry. You know, I didn't wanna see my kids taken away, and I'm like I wanna see them. But I had a very good therapist. She stayed with me, she worked through it with me; she's very nice, very nice."

Joan commented that, more generally, African Americans have a hard time believing that state structures like the child welfare system might be helpful, so they spend their time fighting these systems (see chapter 5 on negative perceptions of ACS). "I'm not sure why that is," she commented, but she admitted that she used to feel this way until, after finally coming to grips with her addiction, she saw that some people can provide help without looking down on you: "But she's becoming, now, because I'm going to the [drug treatment] group, I'm seeing her [the foster care agency caseworker] less as the enemy. Because I didn't want anything to do with none of them. But I put myself in this position. And it's hard to swallow. And I see a lot of them girls [other mothers in her parenting class] angry [and constantly complaining] 'the worker, the worker.'" She further explained that her drug addiction had deep roots and was difficult to deal with:

JOAN: You just can't stop like that. You just can't. Even, I don't care how many courtrooms, you just can't stop like that.

TINA: Yeah. Well, especially, it sounds like you had a pretty long history.

JOAN: I've had a long history of it. Yeah. I've got five years here I don't do it. And then when you do it, and it's never because I just feel like it. It's what's happening in my life at the time. My grandmother didn't raise us to go to therapy. We was, whatever goes on in your house stays in your house. And to come to grips with the idea of therapy took a *long time*. Then to come to the idea, to the grips of this thing as a disease took a long time. Because I was just, I was just *bad*. You know, I'm a bad mother, I'm a bad person.

Joan initially had a very different orientation to therapy and treatment than her caseworkers. She was not only uncomfortable with the idea of talking to someone about intimate matters but also angry at her position. She was able to overcome her resistance eventually, but if parents are not able to comply with the caseworkers' plans, then reunification is very difficult.

Different Priorities

Finally, what seemed to be a lack of compliance to caseworkers sometimes stemmed from parents disagreeing about what they most need. During one permanency hearing, for example, the caseworker complained to the judge that a mother refused to go to drug treatment until she could resolve her money and housing problems. The mother was lectured and told that this was her last chance to enroll before the goal would be changed to adoption. It was common for caseworkers and judges to downplay parents' concerns with material problems like housing and money and argue that they needed to "get their priorities straight" and instead get the services caseworkers required for reunification. This was clear in Mary's case. Several mothers, including Leslie, told me that caseworkers specifically told them they needed to "work on themselves first" and worry about financial matters later. This view fits with a therapeutic perspective in which personal problems and behaviors are viewed as most important and what is in need of change, but, as I discuss in chapter 8, parents who had not arranged for housing and income are often not able to regain custody. This therapeutic view also ignores evidence that issues related to poverty are at the root of many problems deemed neglect by the child welfare system (see chapter 1). All of these very legitimate and common barriers were too often ignored or framed as only individual failure rather than the result of social inequalities—a situation that perpetuates relations of stratified reproduction.

Courts as a Venue for Weighing Competing Rights?

Daily practices in family court—both empowering and disempowering parents—are important to examine. The purpose of family court is, ostensibly, to find a balance between parents' rights to their children and children's need for safety. Further, the courts, ideally, should scrutinize child welfare practice to make sure officials are following the law by (1) supervising families and placing children in foster care only when necessary, and (2) making reasonable efforts to prevent removals and reunite families. In other words, family court should act as a check on the power of the state to interfere unnecessarily in family life and to ensure that it carries out its responsibility to provide help when interventions are made. As described in chapter 4, however, most time in family court is spent with routine bureaucratic matters, and, when substantive issues in the cases are considered, far more time is spent dealing with visitation, services, and the child's foster care placement than is spent determining if the family intervention (removal or court-ordered supervision) is justified and if the allegations in the case are true. In other words, the judges spend most court time reviewing and administering the activities of supervising a family or monitoring a child's placement and the parents' service plan. In contrast, the courts spend very little time scrutinizing the decision to become involved with a family in the first place and the nature of that involvement. One 18B attorney, Sandra, a white woman in her forties, described what goes on in family court:

> . . . [It's] an administrative procedure to try to change the behavior [of parents] that some caseworkers find problematic. At its extreme there are people, and I can see this, that can't at any given moment, or maybe forever, raise children, and they present too much of a problem to the raising of children. But I would say that they make up a very small percentage of the people that are in family court, and many people in family court are simply there, it seems to me, because they make caseworkers nervous, and it's not law in the sense that, the legal arguments are so often unavailing, and if the judge just gets some sense that some child is gonna be hurt or some judge is gonna be blamed, they'll err *invariably* on the side of removal.

It is not law, as she knows it, in the sense that legal arguments and discussions of parents' rights make little difference in the context of the very real fear that a child might be hurt and the state might be blamed. Instead, the proceeding becomes about altering parental behavior and dealing with matters related to the child's foster care placement. Emily, a social worker at the Bronx Defenders, echoed Sandra's statement:

> You could go sit, anybody could go sit in Family Court, and you can feel, see, and experience, you know, in my view, civil rights violations all over the place.

> So it just feels so dirty, and every time I'm in there, I'm like this, "I can't believe this is happening!" . . . I mean, our new attorneys are gonna be trained as litigators. They are going to be asking for 1028s; they're gonna be filing motions; they're going to be pushing the legal practice, which it's kind of asleep over there. I feel like they're, the legal practice is very, you know, sloppy, from just being allowed to. You know, it's not individual fault, it's just kind of been an allowed system.

These comments reflect what I observed in family court: parents have very little opportunity to challenge either state interventions in their lives or the allegations in their cases.

Legal Rules in Family Court

Because family court is a civil rather than a criminal court and because of the nature of its cases, the prevailing legal framework deliberately makes it relatively easy for child welfare authorities to prove a parent has abused or neglected his or her child. First, the standard of proof in family court is a "preponderance of the evidence"; that is, it is more likely than not that the allegations occurred. In addition, various rules of evidence are loosened, given that, in these cases, the evidence available about what happened is often limited. "The acts charged almost always occurred behind closed doors, and the victims may be too young to testify in their own behalf. Even an older child who could tell what happened to himself or to a sibling may be unwilling to do so, out of fear or dependence or love for the perpetrator. . . . In its procedures and evidentiary rules, Article 10 attempts to provide due process to the accused, but at the same time to accommodate the special problems of proof present in a child protective case" (Schechter 2006, 371). In other words, the law takes into account the difficulty of proving these cases and loosens the rules to accommodate this difficulty.

For example, if the state offers proof that the child's injuries were unlikely to have occurred but for the parent's acts or failure to act, then this is seen as proving that abuse or neglect has occurred unless the parent can prove that the harm happened another way. This can be difficult or nearly impossible for parents to do, in many cases. For example, in one case I encountered, a mark on a child was thought to be a burn, caused by the father, but he and the mother both said that the child was injured in a fall. The child remained in foster care along with his two younger siblings (when I met them it had been nine months). Because the parents had no solid proof the child had fallen, the father was kept from having *any* visits with the "target child" (i.e., the injured child).[10] Thus, in practice, this rule means that parents are often automatically assumed to be the cause of harm to their children, and it can be very difficult to prove otherwise.

The most common rule at issue in family court applies to cases of parental substance abuse: if it is proven that the parent used drugs or alcohol to the extent "that would ordinarily produce a state of intoxication or substantial impairment of judgment" then, again, the burden shifts to the parent "to prove that the child is not likely to be harmed" (Schechter 2006, 372). If the parent cannot prove nonimpairment, then the child is deemed neglected. I never witnessed an attorney attempt to argue that a parent's drug use was not affecting their child. I did observe, on only a couple of occasions, an attorney attempt to argue that there was no proof that the parent was using drugs at all; such arguments were unsuccessful. In general, if there is any evidence of parents' illegal drug use, their attorneys strongly urge them to either admit their use in court or waive their right to have a trial. It is almost certain that the judge will make a neglect finding anyway, and settling without a trial allows the case to move forward faster. Any illegal drug use, from cocaine to marijuana, is thus considered almost automatically harmful.

Bob described how he sees the rules of evidence and what counts as proof in family court: "I think the point is that the deck is stacked against the parent to begin with. The rules of evidence [what is allowed as evidence], for example . . . is stacked against them. For example if you took a case in Criminal Court on the same charges with the one in Family Court, first of all, it's a higher burden of proof [in Criminal Court], and the reason they made a lower burden in proof [in Family Court] was to, you know, to actually catch these guys, but it becomes so low, okay, that it's ridiculous." In terms of the balance between parents' rights and children's safety, the scales are tipped to make it easier to prove that children are at risk from their parents and often very difficult for parents to prove they are fit parents who do not present risks to their children (for legal analyses, see Chill 2003; Guggenheim 2007; Wilkinson-Hagen 2004). Apart from these matters of formal procedure, daily practices in family court also create situations in which parents' rights are too often inadequately protected.

Petition Writing

When a case is brought to family court, ACS attorneys screen the case, and, if it is to be filed, they write the petition. They aim to craft a document that will get the relief they want (supervision of the family or placement in foster care) and allow them to prove the case later. For example, specific dates of drug tests might be put in to emphasize that a parent is still using despite being in treatment. At other times, dates are left out to skirt the issue of a parent who is not in treatment but has also not been using recently. Brandon, who was an ACS attorney before becoming an 18B, discussed writing petitions in general: "You draw up the petitions at ACS, 'cause I used to do it, you beef 'em up. They're like resumés. You know what I mean? If somebody does something you exaggerate it. You put it in the best way that's gonna get you the relief that you're asking for." Sandra felt that many petitions would not stand up in court for this reason and suggested to me that "everybody should just take a deep breath and put them [ACS] to their proof [which is rare, see below] because their cases fall apart *all* the time. *All the time*." She felt that questions should be raised about allegations rather than assuming they are completely true and supported by evidence.

In my observations of the intake process, I witnessed this kind of "beefing up" on a few occasions. For example, I witnessed a case in which a mother was accused of neglecting her daughter by not ensuring she went to school, not getting her medical treatment for hip pain, and kicking her out of the home with nowhere to go. It was not entirely clear to the caseworkers, however, that the mother had actually been the child's caretaker when she was not in school or not getting medical attention (i.e., it was not clear these problems were the mother's failures). There were also at least three stories about the day the child was either, depending on the story, thrown out of the house or left. The ACS attorney eventually decided that the story about the child being thrown out was likely "bullshit," but it was left in the petition nevertheless because it was the most serious allegation and the one most likely to result in foster care placement. Since initial hearings to approve the sought-after intervention and fact-finding hearings to determine the truth of the allegations are very rarely thorough (see below), exaggerations like these are often not uncovered and stand as a record of the facts in the case, a pattern that makes a neglect finding more likely and influences the services that a parent will be required to complete.

The Initial Hearing

In the initial hearing, the judge is asked, essentially, to find that the case warrants government intervention into the family and that the agency has acted properly. In general, I found that these serious decisions were made relatively quickly, in a proceeding that lasts only a few minutes. As discussed in chapter 4, it is extremely rare for a judge to raise any questions about what ACS requests to do in a case. Most of these questions consider where children would be placed; most ignore the question of whether intervention in the family was warranted and necessary. Only twice did I witness a judge who found a removal to foster care was unwarranted. On only a couple of occasions did I see the judge hold a full-blown hearing with careful questioning of not only ACS and the steps already taken but also the proposed solutions to resolve the case. To the contrary, most of the time judges defer to ACS in terms of assessing risk and authorize the ACS-proposed solution on the basis of the petition alone, with almost no questioning or scrutiny. In addition, law guardians rarely ask for full-blown hearings, although they are charged with ensuring that the children's needs and interests are protected, and, presumably, this includes avoiding unnecessary removals (see Guggenheim 2006 for discussion of why law guardians tend to practice in this way).

Lack of clear evidence and exaggerated claims generally are not discovered by questioning the caseworker about what she learned and how she investigated. It was very rare, in my experience, for the judge or the law guardian either to seriously question and oppose what ACS asked for or to question the ACS caseworker about the exact efforts made to prevent removal. The practice of having a *pro forma* hearing at this stage is so ingrained that attorneys from the Bronx Defenders told me that when they attempted to force questioning and scrutiny at these hearings they were "hazed" by fellow attorneys, which included heckling when they asked detailed questions and pressed for full-blown hearings.

This situation is, in part, due to overloaded court calendars that leave little time for full hearings (see chapter 4). At the same time, this is also related to the "*New York Post* law" phenomenon and to the fact that the judge is appointed by the mayor and reluctant to go against another city agency (Lansner 2007). These factors create a situation in which judges have very little incentive to challenge ACS when they seek to intervene in families and significant incentive to avoid challenging ACS practice.

In addition, the fact that most parents' attorneys are relatively poorly paid and overworked means that they do not always have the time or interest to fight these interventions vigorously.

1028 Hearings

Once a child is placed in foster care, parents have the right to ask for a 1028 hearing in which ACS must prove the child would be at imminent risk in parental care. If ACS cannot prove risk, the child is returned immediately. As far as I know, no one keeps statistics about how often 1028 hearings occur and their outcomes, but my observations in court and my interviews with attorneys strongly suggest that they are rare. I only saw seven 1028 hearings and six requests for such hearings during my court observations. In an additional three cases, hearings had been held in the past. Attorneys told me that they rarely requested these hearings because they felt they could not win them; not only were they unable to prepare and were therefore disadvantaged compared to the ACS attorney who has all the facts of the case, but also the attorneys felt that, if a removal had been made, the situation was probably so bad that no judge would send the child back home. As Brandon, an 18B attorney of Indian descent, put it: "I think the majority of reasons why you don't [ask for a 1028] is because on a remand it's, because a case is so bad. . . . Take a dirty house. If your house is in that condition on the day that I ask for the hearing, you can't win the case." In other words, certain issues are simply seen as presenting risk to the child, and it is relatively easy for the agency to convince a judge a child is at "imminent risk" (the standard for removal) if left in the home. Again, judges are under pressure to avoid any situation in which they might be blamed for leaving a child with his or her parent if a tragedy were to occur, and so the judges are likely to agree that the risk justifies a removal. Therefore, 1028 hearings are usually only held when an attorney feels the removal is very questionable.[11]

Despite barriers that kept many attorneys from asking for 1028 hearings, attorneys from the new institutional providers and one 18B attorney, Sandra, had a distinctly different take on these hearings. The institutional providers told me they were planning to "really litigate" these cases, including allowing clients to exercise their right to a 1028 hearing. These lawyers are able to do this, in part, because they had smaller caseloads and support staff (such as social workers and paralegals), that 18Bs cannot afford. In addition, they are overtly committed to social justice and feel that parents need strong advocates. Sandra found 1028s similarly important and told me she limited the number of cases she handled so that she actually has time to do them. She felt that asking for 1028s shows her clients that she is willing to make noise and fight for them and shows judges that parents want their children and will fight to get them back. Sandra thought this might cause the judge to look more favorably upon her clients. For this reason, Sandra thought 1028s were important. The attorneys who did push for their clients' rights in these more vigorous ways were very much in the minority in family court. One ACS attorney felt that these attorneys were asking for such hearings far too often, which was only slowing people down and wasting time. The vast majority of parents thus did not get this kind of vigorous representation.

Settlements and Fact-findings

In terms of legally concluding a case, the judge must make a finding, through either a fact-finding hearing (similar to a trial in criminal court) or a settlement, about whether the parent has neglected the child.[12] Settlements avoid time-consuming trials, in terms of both time before the judge and time spent by the lawyers preparing their cases. They also avoid the hassle of finding large chunks of time in which to conduct a trial, which is extremely difficult. In my experience, settlements, which practically always result in a neglect finding against the parents without a trial, were by far more common than trials, which is similar to practices in criminal court as well (Feige 2006). One judge told me specifically that she finds she has too many cases to allow her to manage things fairly and expeditiously. She thus pushes for the parties to resolve as much as they can among themselves (i.e., avoid a trial) as long as the children are safe and their needs are being met.

A parents' attorney stated directly that the system does not work if parents do not make admissions; this was simply the family court equivalent of plea bargaining in criminal court. He further complained that fact-finding hearings are likely to be adjourned if an attorney or caseworker is not present or if records needed for the trial are unavailable (even if this omission was due to attorney error), which leads to cases dragging on. If his client (i.e., a parent) is late or misses a court date, then it is likely that the ACS attorney or the judge will a hearing by inquest. This means that the judge looks at the evidence presented by ACS, but the parent's attorney is not allowed to present a case; the parent will almost certainly be found to have neglected the child, without the parent even having the opportunity to defend himself or herself. I witnessed this occurrence several times in family court and met two parents to whom this had happened. Emma and James, for example, showed up for the hearing a couple of hours late (they said they were confused about the time). The inquest found that they had neglected their daughter. The judge agreed to "vacate" (i.e., erase or nullify) her earlier finding and scheduled another hearing for several months later, but not all judges will agree to do this. It was apparent that parental absence is taken as evidence that the parents do not care about their children and have insufficient interest in doing what is necessary to regain custody.

In general, parents' attorneys told me that they often avoid going to a trial because it seems that the allegations are basically true, and the trials are just a waste of time. As Brandon put it, "You can try the case if you think that it's tryable, but you know, most of the time the allegations are kinda true. There's not really a way to get them off. So I would say settlement." In my experience, a parent who actually wins a trial is exceedingly rare, and one attorney who has worked in family court for years has claimed, citing statistics from the court, that judges rule for ACS in 99 percent of fact-finding hearings (Lansner 2007). One ACS attorney, Marcus, a white man in his early thirties, told me a story that illustrates the ease with which ACS attorneys can win their cases. When he took over a case from another attorney, both he and his supervisor felt, at the very least, it would be difficult to prove. In addition, some of the allegations did not fit under the definition of neglect so he was considering withdrawing the case. Specifically, there were three allegations: (1) the mother had threatened someone physically, but there was no good evidence of this, she denied it, and it was not clear the child was even present; (2) she had left the child with someone in a homeless shelter for twelve hours; and (3) she had refused to take a parenting class. Marcus told me that the first two allegations were "borderline" about whether they could be defined as neglect because they did not present risk to the child and were not a failure to exercise a minimum degree of care, while the third allegation definitely could not be considered neglect. In presenting his case at the fact-finding, he did not ask any questions about item three, but the judge did and then entered a finding of neglect on the basis of *all* the allegations. This is one extreme example to show the gross inclination of most judges to find that parents are neglectful, despite the allegations' seriousness, their likelihood to cause harm to the child, or even their inclusion in the legal definition of neglect.

There remains a final factor in why trials are not common: when a child is in foster care, the judge has already determined that the child was at risk, and, as long as the allegations fit the legal definition of neglect (which, if they did not, the case *probably* would not have been filed in the first place), it would be practically unthinkable to later rule that the parent did not neglect the child, especially since, given the normal pace of family court, the child has likely been in foster care for many months, a year, or even more. On a very commonsense level, a trial, reopening the question of whether neglect occurred, would raise the possibility of having to admit there was not really a problem and there had been no legal basis for denying custody. The fallout from that admission would be tremendous: lawsuits, press coverage, loss of jobs, and so on. Even if the family was "only" under ACS supervision while the case was ongoing, it would still be hard to then find the parent had done nothing to neglect the child.

For these various institutional and legal reasons, the vast majority of parents who have cases in family court come out with a finding of neglect against them. This legal finding has important consequences: such neglect is held against them if they became involved with the child welfare system in the future, and it bars them from jobs at places such as daycare centers, medical settings, and schools (see chapter 8 for more on this issue). It is also an extremely hurtful process for many parents who felt they did care for their children, despite their problems and the allegations against them. Being labeled neglectful was profoundly contrary to how they understood themselves as parents. Finally, this family court process has a tendency to lend legitimacy to negative stereotypes of unfit parents of color (see chapter 8). Again, formally, parents do have legal mechanisms they can use to defend themselves, but, in practice, they will almost certainly be labeled neglectful if their case is brought to court.

Language and Views of Parents in Family Court

In addition to these overt aspects of family court practice, more informal aspects of behavior—the language that is used, jokes that are told, and how court personnel discuss parents—help to create a general climate in which parents rights are not adequately protected. These practices work in two ways. First, they help turn what is actually a profound set of decisions about intervening in families into a routine bureaucratic matter that happens with little questioning. Second, they signal that parents are seen mainly as a set of problems that place their children at risk rather than as struggling parents in need of help (in terms of either personal problems or legal advocacy). This general atmosphere effectively makes supervision of these parents, the removal of their children, or both appear to be the best approaches to dealing with risk to children.

Family court deals with issues in a technical and bureaucratic language that masks both the decisions' human consequences and their enormous impact. This language makes it seem that the issues being discussed are not families and the difficult decisions surrounding if, when, and how the state will become involved in their lives. For example, when children are formally placed in foster care, the term used is "remand" rather than "removed" from their home and their parents or even "placed" in foster care. If child is removed from their home and placed with a relative who will not be a formal foster parent, that child is "paroled" to this caretaker. The state also uses the term parole when a child remains in a parent's home and the parent is subject to supervision by ACS and has to comply with certain conditions (such as engaging in particular services or not using corporal punishment). The term parole is generally used to refer to criminals who are released under supervision before their sentences have been completed; the term is used in family court because a similar process is at work—the child is released to the care of someone (a relative or a foster parent) who will be supervised. Caseworkers from ACS visit the home to check on the child and are able to move the child to another home if they see fit. In the case of a child being paroled to a parent, the term most closely resembles the usual use of the word; that is, the parent is accused of either harming the child or presenting some risk to the child and will therefore be supervised and given a set of requirements to fulfill. In fact, Dorothy Roberts (2002) has commented that family court requirements read very much like parole orders, but a parole here occurs before it has been decided that the allegations are true. This sequence differs from the criminal context, where the truth of the allegations must be judged first and supervision of the person is authorized only if the allegations are found true. Again, this signals the presumption, often made from the beginning of the case and rarely questioned, that parents are risks to their children and require supervision.

It is also common in family court to hear family members, loved ones, and caretakers referred to as "resources" for the child. I am not entirely sure where this term comes from, but it takes the parent/child relationship out of the realm of emotion or even biological ties and reframes it in terms of what parents have to offer to children that will benefit them in more instrumental ways. The terminology also refers to material resources and emphasizes what children need from their parents in order to grow up to be more productive citizens. By establishing these criteria, many poor families in court seem to have little to offer their children.

These terms are not only jargon, but they also serve as a way for lawyers and judges and, to a much lesser extent, caseworkers to distance themselves from the enormity of the decisions being made and the emotional consequences their actions have on families. Instead of asking to remove a child from their parent and send them to live with a stranger or a relative, for example, the ACS attorney asks the judge to "remand the child to a foster care resource" and for "the respondent to be allowed visitation two times per week," clinical descriptions that mask the reality of the proceedings,. Lawyers from the Bronx Defenders were very clear that they felt the language used in court allowed ACS and court staff to push to the back of their minds the enormity of their actions. They felt that officials like to "dance around" the consequences by using legal terms rather than naming the actual situation.

Although different methods of distancing oneself from the removal process are sometimes used by everyone who works in this system, family court personnel are more likely to use language to create distance, in large part because they are more able to do so. Judges and attorneys are almost never present at a removal and do not get to know parents as parents and human beings; instead, they mainly learn about parents from court records and testimony. In these contexts, parents are generally reduced to negative characteristics or labels, such as drug user or domestic violence victim, while their lives and the contexts in which they live are absent. Also, many of the attorneys I met in family court were young, often directly out of law school, and many of them do not have children. Several attorneys even specifically brought up this issue in interviews and commented that, because they did not have children, they had to imagine what a removal would be like for a family often through acknowledging how they might have felt as a child. Moreover, some attorneys who represent parents stated that they felt that not having children made it easier for law guardians and ACS attorneys to be judgmental about how parents care for their children and, by extension, easier to feel a removal is justified. In an informal discussion I heard one 18B attorney, when told that ACS was participating in an upcoming "Bring Your Children to Work Day," quip: "But they don't have children. They're not allowed to, right?" Although he was joking, the idea that childless ACS attorneys were preferable clearly referenced the fact that having children when employed in these positions would only make the job harder.

Caseworkers, however, are more likely to see parents with their children, to see their homes, and to spend at least a little time getting to know them and seeing how they parent. Caseworkers must physically remove children, and therefore they must find other ways to "desensitize" themselves, as Marilyn put it. The practice of distancing through language is not surprising, given that these decisions are difficult but necessary, and it is understandable that they discuss decisions in ways that make them routine and transform families into cases. However, turning family court matters into bureaucratic routine often means that officials make these decisions quickly, with little scrutiny or attention to the actual impacts on families.

I often also witnessed disrespectful or callous comments made about parents and families by attorneys between cases or in hallways and elevators. One 18B, for example, talked about how parents are "all messed up" or how they were all "stupid" because they "admit to using drugs." This assumption—that all parents are messed up or unfit to raise children—seemed common among court personnel. I heard attorneys and court officers openly make fun of parents and their problems between cases, laughing about their explanations for their behaviors. For example, in one case involving domestic violence, the mother denied that things were as bad as the police reports said and stated that she wanted to stay with her partner. After the case, her attorney laughed about her denials and made jokes about how ridiculous he found them. This presumption that parents deny problems, which implies they are unwilling to change, makes it easy to argue that the best solution is to deny them custody of their children because offering help seems futile. These kinds of jokes and comments also included extended family members that parents wanted to be kinship foster parents for their children. On one occasion, I heard a law guardian make jokes about how messed up the parents were and laughingly comment, "You think I'm going to consent to send the child with their relatives? I don't think so!" The overwhelming perception that parents are not fit to retain custody extends to family members as well.[13]

There are several ways to read this kind of joking and disrespectful talk in family court. First, the courthouse is a tough place to work. After only a few months of observations I myself grew to dread walking into the building because of the emotional toll and difficult circumstances. It is therefore understandable that joking behavior occurs as one defense mechanism to cope with the job. Second, none of the families that come before the court is without problems of one sort of another so these derogatory comments come from seeing both family after family who present similar issues and parents who either deny existing problems or cannot cope with them. I, however, found these kinds of comments and jokes troubling. At least on some level, the negative comments are related to the fact that the vast majority of parents who come through this system are black and Latino and most live at or below the poverty line, while the attorneys and judges are more uniformly white and from middle-class backgrounds. Because of these differences, attorneys and judges have likely never experienced the conditions under which most of these parents live. In addition, they are exposed to only a portion of these parents' lives—namely allegations from particular moments in time or labels like "drug addict" or "domestic violence victim." All these factors make it easier to see parents as only the sum of the problems they are facing or merely a set of risks to their children, rather than as parents who love their children but are struggling. This limited view makes these signs of disrespect more common and leads to a subtle perception of parents, from the moment they walk into the courthouse, as risks to their children and unfit parents who are undeserving of help.

Conclusion

An imbalance of power between parents and child welfare officials and decision makers is a prominent feature of the child welfare system. The parents who are caught up in this system must take steps to prove that they are responsible parents who have their lives together enough to care for children. Proving this requires deferring to the judgments and requirements of child welfare decision makers while remaining calm, cooperative, and properly focused on their children. Parents are often held to standards that are attainable by middle-class families, but difficult to reach for poor and even sometimes working-class parents. Parents were expected to be able to quickly access help for drug abuse/addiction or mental health problems, to ensure their children were always adequately supervised, to provide their children food and safe housing, to always provide prompt medical attention, and to create a "stable" and violence-free life for them.

Caseworkers and other decision makers weigh parents' compliance heavily and use it as shorthand to evaluate whether parents are serious about making changes that would benefit and protect their children. If parents comply and share the caseworker's, judge's, or law guardian's analysis of their problems, then they are perceived as "taking responsibility" and working to change the situation, thus alleviating the risk to their children. Necessary services, however, are often unavailable, and caseworkers often have neither the knowledge nor the time to make adequate referrals. Furthermore, the ability of parents to comply is profoundly structured by race, class, and gender inequalities, but this is rarely taken into account. Too often the system ignores the barriers to compliance many parents face, barriers stemming primarily from poverty, inflexible jobs, lack of transportation, or lack of health insurance. In addition, parents who are uncomfortable or unfamiliar with therapy or distrustful of state systems due to past experiences, as were many women of color I met, also had difficulty performing compliance. In many ways, if they want to retain custody of their children, parents must give up the ability to make basic decisions about their lives and relinquish their own analyses of their problems and how to solve them.

Although the family courts are ostensibly about ensuring that the decision to become involved in family life so intimately is made carefully and that parents' rights to their children and to the help they need to be adequate parents are protected, daily practices in family court do not meet this goal. Family court provided little in the way of meaningful oversight and judicial scrutiny of ACS caseworkers and their decisions. Although the purpose of bringing cases to court is to provide parents with an opportunity to defend themselves and challenge state interference into their lives, crowded calendars and prevailing attitudes and practices mean that this generally happens only in a *pro forma* way, and few parents are able to protect their rights. Day-to-day practices in family court, in part because this court deals almost exclusively with poor people of color, make it quite easy to intervene in families, either by placing them under court supervision or by denying them custody of their children. Too often officials *assume* from the beginning that parents are unfit, while institutional practices make it difficult to challenge these state interventions into family life and provide little incentive to try.

Many parents felt that they had no advocates in family court. I found that I was able to observe family court freely when I came on my own, but when I accompanied a parent I was questioned about my presence and usually barred from the courtroom. I came to attribute this difference to officials being suspicious of anyone who might be present as an outside advocate for a parent. Recognizing this, parent advocates often told parents that they needed to be their own lawyer—bring in their own evidence, request hearings directly, and learn about the law and their rights—and parents were generally told they would have to insist upon their right to bring someone with them to court. These accepted practices and prevailing attitudes actually play important roles in re-creating stratified reproduction and inner-city poverty.

8

Re-creating Stratified Reproduction and System Change

> "We . . . are treating the symptoms of poverty. If we don't start . . . looking at having better outcomes for parents, we'll never have better outcomes for children, and it's very simple and basic, but people seem to think it's like this very foreign concept." (Emily, Bronx Defenders social worker)

Given the overwhelming issues associated with the child welfare system and the gross inequality that accompanies its functioning, I feel compelled to use my research to suggest some practical contributions to both the analysis of the larger role of the system in contemporary American society and to the development of a more equitable future for children. I clearly recognize a role for child protection: children are vulnerable to violence and to willful, severe neglect by parents. A mechanism to investigate reports of maltreatment and to find alternative caretakers for children in situations in which they are in danger is necessary. I also acknowledge, and celebrate, the people who work in this system who are well intentioned and try to serve families as best they can under constrained circumstances.

At the same time, the system that exists in the early twenty-first century is deeply problematic. Tying help for parents struggling with poverty, drug abuse, domestic violence, and mental health issues so strongly to law enforcement and investigation undermines the ability of this system to provide help. Despite good intentions, the system too often becomes punitive. The discretion afforded to caseworkers, coupled with a lack of concrete guidance on how to separate neglect from poverty, leads to blaming parents and removing children when services for the entire family might provide effective remedies for these situations. This system operates within a profoundly unequal society in which racialized stereotypes of "unfit" black mothers, "deadbeat" men of color, and "broken" inner-city families are ubiquitous. These stereotypes subtly, and unconsciously, affect decision making. Perhaps more importantly, this system has always been tasked with dealing with the (real or perceived) family problems of the poorest members of our society in a culture in which poverty is seen as an individual failing. This almost necessarily means it will place blame on individuals and deal with them punitively.

The child welfare system is asked to deal with the profoundly detrimental effects of social inequalities with few resources and practically no ability to confront the roots of family problems: lack of income and meaningful jobs, lack of decent housing, the stress of living in poverty and parenting in difficult circumstances, and few services to deal with issues such as drug abuse and domestic violence. As one 18B attorney told me:

> There are a lot of people who have a lot of problems, and, you know, the mother who's twenty-one years old, who has been in foster care all these years herself and is AWOL from foster care, gets pregnant and has a child, but has no job, has no education beyond an eighth grade. *Maybe* an eighth grade, not even an eighth grade that I would think of as an eighth grade. Has huge mental health issues, has nowhere to live. What can I do for that person? No, really, what can I do for that person? . . . I'll certainly do everything I can, but I can't get her housing. I can't stabilize her life. I can't get her a job. Even though I very often get judges to allow me to get a social worker to try and help, but there's a limit to how much *they* can do.

In short, even the most well-meaning and competent professionals cannot change the larger social system within which poor people of color live and raise children.

The child welfare system, in its structure, its daily practices, and its interactions with other state systems in the context of few resources simply cannot do much to make the lives of families better. Beyond an analysis of how the system fails, however, I argue that the system, as currently arranged and constrained, plays a role in actually *re-creating the very inequalities* it must deal with on a daily basis: poverty, racial stereotypes and inequalities, and relations of stratified reproduction. Officials are trying to do good things for families and vulnerable children. Too often, however, intervention makes things worse.

Perpetuating Poverty through Child Welfare Practice

My most surprising finding was that involvement with the child welfare system tended to perpetuate and sometimes worsen poverty. For many of my informants, child welfare was one factor in deepening poverty or in making a relatively stable economic situation precarious. As much research has demonstrated, the current structure of low-wage work and disappearing public benefits has made the economic position of poor people in general more insecure in recent years (Goode and Maskovsky 2001; Hays 2003; Mullings and Wali 2001). For my respondents, the child welfare system was another element in this uncertain landscape while the focus on personal transformation, without equal attention to material conditions, sometimes made their situations worse. While studying these issues, one must keep in mind that this particular form of state practice disproportionately impacts people of color and thus, along with systems of policing and incarceration, plays a role in re-creating a particular form of racialized, inner-city poverty.

Of the twenty-eight parents in my study, almost half (thirteen) lost substantial portions of income and/or housing during the course of their involvement with child welfare. Four became homeless, and one was almost evicted; she had luckily lived in the same building since childhood, and the landlord was willing to wait for rent. Two parents were homeless prior to their children's placement in foster care and were about to get an apartment, but this was delayed by their child welfare case. Seven parents either lost jobs or were unable to work due to their child welfare involvement. Most of those who lost jobs were able to avoid homelessness by moving in with relatives or receiving financial help from family members. My findings likely underestimate the numbers of people who were substantially less well-off after child welfare involvement because of the difficulties of collecting data from those who lost either homes or phones.[1] In contrast, only nine parents were able to maintain a relatively stable economic position, and several less typical factors enabled them to do this: (1) they had middle-class jobs and education; (2) they had stable working-class jobs and two incomes; and/or (3) they were not heavily involved in the child welfare system. Even parents with educations who had worked at steady jobs, however, were vulnerable to worsening economic conditions. Simone described her position within this vulnerable group: "I guess by all practical purposes I'm a poor person, now. As a person that's worked and going to college and to have been put in the system and now having to go on welfare because I had to do things. So finances is just a whole new—I keep feeling like I'm living someone else's life."

The situations of the parents who experienced deepening poverty are complicated, and their child welfare involvement was one of several factors that contributed to their worsening economic conditions. Some were already in precarious economic situations, which led to their involvement with child welfare (as in Mary's case, see chapter 7), but, for others, things became worse after the government benefits on which they relied were reduced or cut off when their children were removed from their care (sometimes improperly due to a lack of communication between agencies), a situation that left them vulnerable to homelessness. For example, Salina, a former foster child with little education who had worked on and off during her life, was unable to make ends meet when her children were removed:

TINA: So can you go through, when the kids were home with you, what you got, food stamps, Section 8, public assistance, all that stuff, and then what changed after?

SALINA: All right. When they was home they was paying the rent. They was paying at first $166 a month, the welfare. Section 8 was paying $1,011 and 90 something [cents]. . . . I was getting $786 in food stamps and the cash I was getting $141. And now that they not in here, I get $155 in food stamps and $37 in cash. The rent went up, so welfare pays $239 or $241, and Section 8 still pays . . .

TINA: So your rent is still getting paid.

SALINA: It's still getting paid. It wasn't getting paid for a whole eight months . . .

TINA: . . . No rent. From either program, neither welfare nor Section 8?

SALINA: No. Section 8 still paid.

TINA: Okay. No rent from welfare. Okay. . . . At this point, you have rent arrears like $4,000?

SALINA: Right.

After her children were removed from her care, her rent subsidies and food stamps were dramatically cut, which lead to her falling behind on her rent. She was not evicted only because her landlord was willing to wait for payment. It is also important to note that she was able to give me great detail off the top of her head—she was clearly keeping track of every penny as she struggled to make ends meet.

For other parents, like Destiny and Spencer, their child welfare case derailed their efforts to secure stable housing. They were living in a family shelter and were about to get a housing voucher when their children were removed; then they had to move to a single room in a couples' shelter with no access to a kitchen and start the process of securing housing all over again. They faced continual issues with transportation to and from their jobs program, parenting and anger management classes, court, and visits. Their food stamps were cut because they were in a non-cooking facility, but they had continual problems with their cash assistance being cut as well. They both reported not having enough to eat, which was especially troubling since Destiny was pregnant with twins. They also felt humiliated by paternalistic shelter rules which Destiny found especially hard with her pregnancy. They were not allowed in the building between 10 A.M. and 2 P.M., were not allowed visitors, and were awakened each morning at 7 A.M. Spencer was actively looking for work (he had stacks of job ads, flyers for job fairs, and a set of books to help him study to take the transit worker's test next to their bed), but he felt that the little bit of extra help they needed so they could get on their feet was not forthcoming after they lost custody of their children:

SPENCER: They're [the jobs program] trying to get me a job, but then it's also a problem for me to get a job because I have a criminal record [from crimes committed as a juvenile], like I say. I don't got a GED or high school.

DESTINY: All the appointments.

SPENCER: I got a lot of parenting class, I gotta go to parenting class 5:00 to 7:00, and now I'm going to start the anger management class, just to get that out of the way, on Tuesdays from 5:00 to 7:00. And then . . .

DESTINY: The courts.

SPENCER: We don't have no money for no carfare. We don't have no food money . . . I don't have clothes for employment, job interviews, or anything. And, like, it's like a whole mess-up they doing over here, and they not helping us actually for nothing.

Other parents lost their jobs as a direct result of their child welfare case (as in Joan's case; she was a nurse's assistant), or they lost jobs when they had to take time off to deal with their case and their services. Yet others felt they had to quit their jobs to prove they were sufficiently focused on their children and dealing with their problems. Judges and caseworkers frequently lectured parents about needing to focus on their cases and would dismiss concerns about work as illegitimate reasons for missing appointments and visits. For example, Nicole described quitting her job after a caseworker refused to change the time of her visits to fit her work schedule and give her time to travel to the agency: "But they [said] 'Oh, she got a job. Oh, her job is more important than her kid.'" Several mothers reported they were told they should not be working and needed to "work on themselves first." They either had to apply for public assistance or rely on family members when they took this advice. Ironically, under current welfare policy, public assistance cases require all recipients to focus their energies on finding a job (any job) or require mandatory work assignments. Caseworkers at that agency are often inflexible in allowing parents to combine job searching and/or mandatory work assignments with other obligations. Thus, many parents were caught in an impossible conflict between different agencies with different policies.

Job loss was also common because reunification is literally a full-time job. Reunification activities were generally incompatible with the jobs parents had or were likely to get in low-wage service industries in which schedules were inflexible and unpredictable and missing work very often meant losing the job. For example, Ramel, who was homeless prior to his child's removal from him and his partner, had planned to get a job but was not even going to look, he said, because his criminal record meant that any job he would be hired for would not allow him the flexibility he needed to attend services and see his son. Most parents told me it was either impossible or extremely difficult for them to hold a job because keeping up with their case was extremely time consuming: many appointments, entire days waiting at court, hours waiting for caseworkers (every conference and meeting I attended started at least forty-five minutes, and sometimes more than ninety minutes, late), and hours on the phone or traveling to offices to follow-up on services and referrals. Constant follow-up was further complicated, for many, by not having a phone. A simple follow-up on a referral that might take minutes with a phone call might take hours with lengthy travel to an agency only to find a caseworker out of the office or unavailable. Most appointments took place during working hours, and service plans usually involved various agencies that were not necessarily near each other in addition to regular visits with children.

Most parents had to juggle their appointments while relying on public transportation, which can involve time-consuming or circuitous routes. For example, services several miles apart by car might take an hour by train and bus. Whereas a person with money might be able to schedule several appointments in a day and move between them relatively quickly and easily, parents had to go to great lengths to cut down on transportation costs, making everything take longer. A public transportation trip at the time of my fieldwork was $2, an unlimited ride Metrocard was $76 a month, and cab fare for a short ride was $8 to $10. Most agencies do not give unlimited Metrocards, which were simply not affordable for my informants. Instead, if agencies provide transportation at all, they provide a card with one to two rides for travel to a particular appointment. Attorneys and service providers often made comments that they found "excuses" about lack of transportation ridiculous, but these costs added up quickly when people had little money. Many of my informants couldn't afford basics like toilet paper, much less $6 to $8 a day for multiple trips to appointments. Many of them thus spent lots of time walking, and being late for appointments was almost inevitable; yet being late was taken as a sign that they didn't have their lives together or just didn't care. The impossibility of making it to various appointments via public transportation and walking was rarely taken into account.

In addition, since services can be hard to find and waiting lists are generally long, there is little ability to negotiate convenient times and locations that allow parents to juggle all their responsibilities. Although, in theory, agencies are supposed to accommodate parents when scheduling visits, meetings, and services, in my experience they were scheduled for the convenience of the caseworkers or foster parents, often at times that were impossible for parents. In very rare cases, judges ordered changes in visitation to accommodate the problems of juggling visiting with other services and jobs while relying on public transportation. For example, one day in court a mother's attorney complained that she was only allowed one-hour visits but traveled about an hour each way to get there (two buses and a train). The ACS attorney agreed to increase her visitation to two hours. Although this kind of change is *possible*, parents generally have practically no ability to change the days and times of visits. Most caseworkers work to accommodate foster mother's schedules and expect parents to come when they are told.[2] Not attending is seen as proof parents don't care and won't change. As mentioned in chapter 7, it is also fairly likely that the child will be placed in a part of the city far from where the parent lives, a problem that also increases the chances of being late or missing appointments.

Mary, for example, closed her own welfare case because caseworkers refused to negotiate work requirements around her visits with her daughter. When I saw her about a year after her child welfare case started, she had lost a noticeable amount of weight and was barely eating. Similarly, Joan faced many barriers in getting drug treatment to retain custody of her daughter. After she lost her job, she and her partner were "barely making it" on his off-the-books exterminator's income, even though their rent was low while they were living in his grandmother's brownstone in the middle of Brooklyn. Joan found an out-patient program that would accept her but it required an hour and a half on trains to the Bronx:

> When I went to the program that day it said my insurance had lapsed, so I had to go apply for welfare, which means there's a forty-five-day waiting period. I came up to the Bronx without welfare, without Medicaid for a good two months barely making it. The counselor told me if I can get the $2 to get to group, he'd get me home. And that was our agreement. "[Joan], just as long as you come, if you can show up here, I'll get you back home." Before my Medicaid even kicked in. So they [caseworkers] seen that I was willing, but when 1199 [union] insurance ran out, I was left without nothing. And they knew all this. They didn't call anybody to expedite anything. It's like they wanted to take her. When they went back into my records, like they wanted her gone. I want to sit and blame. But if I hadn't did what I done she wouldn't have been gone anyway. But I needed the help. I needed the help.

In this example, Joan's child welfare case created a situation in which she had few resources to deal with her drug addiction and then her inability to get treatment was used to justify removing her child.

Eva, a Latina in her forties, offered another example:

> And I'm just looking for work right now. But then the thing is, I've gotta look for work that's a little flexible because of all this going on. Because when I was working at the cleaner's, I told the guy, "Listen, I have to leave early on Monday and Wednesday, so I could get to Staten Island [from Brooklyn for visits with her daughter]." And at the beginning he was like, "Okay, I'll let you do it this week, but whatever it is, you need to take care of it because I need you here." . . . He wasn't happy with it, but how do I, ACS couldn't change [the visits], you know what I mean? I gotta find something that's gonna be flexible. Like, for example, the home health. You can tell them, okay, I can work these days but I can't work these days.

Being a home health aide was not actually an option for Eva, given her child welfare case. She enrolled in training, but parent advocates told her not to bother due to her history. She ended by telling me: "So my whole life over this case all around is just screwed. Like I go for the job and, you know, even this, what I'm doing right now with [home health aide] training. I was just doing it and hoping for the best. It might be that I finish it and then they tell me, 'Oh, you can't.' I don't know what else to do, though."

When parents are unable to prove they have adequate housing and income for their children, foster care agencies often refuse to reunify the family even if there are no other barriers. Although most officials were very reluctant to *remove* a child *solely* for lack of income or housing, these issues were commonly the reason for delaying reunification or even terminating parental rights (see also Reich 2005, 130). Carrie, a law guardian who had been an ACS attorney and caseworker previously, discussed the problem:

> Housing in New York City is a mess. It's just horrible. Even for working people it's just so difficult to find affordable housing. Housing's a major barrier to reunification. [If an apartment needs repairs in order to be safe,] it's sometimes a battle . . . but a lot of it does get done once it's raised, especially when ACS helps raise it. Some of it is just that people don't follow through. They're so just beat down by all the different systems that they think that just 'cause they've said it once that that's complaint enough, and it wasn't

> done so why bother again. But there are procedures. You have to fill out the right paperwork, and you have to follow up and ask them. . . . I think some of it's just failure to take some of it seriously, or just failure to be able to handle all of it, and deal with so many bureaucrats in a day. But yeah, it definitely comes up, and not having space for kids comes up, particularly upon reunification.

Although Carrie suggests that parents can overcome these very common housing barriers, parents had a difficult time doing so in many cases. Salina's experience shows that ACS helping to raise an issue with a landlord is not necessarily effective. Her apartment was actually dangerous (there had been electrical fires, there were water leaks, and a ceiling was caving in). She wanted the apartment fixed but was having a difficult time getting her landlord to fix everything:

> SALINA: So I'm trying to get them to fix everything. I mean, you know, the landlord is stingy so he don't even want to fix nothing. So just yesterday I was in they ass, like, now they like, "Okay." [Henry (her boyfriend)] was in they ass, so now they send me a letter talking about, oh, he's not on your lease, so he can't be there. 'Cause if Section 8 found out, that's a problem but now all a sudden after four years. So now that he [the landlord] got to kick in the money and got all these fines from the city.
>
> TINA: Then he wants to mess with you [i.e., find a reason to kick her and/or Henry out despite being fine with him living there for four years].
>
> SALINA: Right.

Her attempts to get the landlord to make needed repairs brought threats of eviction and delayed the return of her children. Other ways to secure safe housing, such as living with a family member, are also generally ineffective. Children are not often released to parents in this situation; either the family members' child welfare or criminal history is problematic, or the agency views the arrangement as "unstable."

Agencies are supposed to help parents with obtaining housing and applying for government benefits, but not all caseworkers are knowledgeable about the procedures or willing to provide enough of this help. In some cases, workers were not aware of the money available to help parents with housing and jobs. Even when parents were aware, parent advocates and parents alike reported that agencies erroneously told them they were ineligible. Children can, in fact, be released to their parents if they are in the shelter system,[3] but many caseworkers were either unaware of this practice, told parents it wasn't allowed, or withheld that information because they felt that it was not a stable plan for the children. Parent advocates at the Child Welfare Organizing Project (CWOP) tell parents about this possibility (see later detailed discussion of CWOP). I saw two cases of children who were returned to their parents in the shelter system in a matter of days when parent advocates from CWOP intervened after the parents had waited months and had been told that the only barrier to returning their children was their lack of housing.

Even when parents were approved for housing help, bureaucratic rules caused delays. For example, a father, who was not caring for his son when he was removed from his mother's home and had no accusations of abuse or neglect against him, waited months to gain custody because he did not have his own apartment. When I saw the case, the child had been in foster care for more than a year, even though seven months earlier the father had been approved for an ACS housing grant to pay a deposit on an apartment and buy furniture. His lawyer complained that he had already lost two apartments because he did not receive the grant check quickly enough so the landlord had rented to someone else. The lawyer asked for a court order that the father get the check that day, as he had an apartment and a lease and needed the money to pay the deposit. The ACS attorney argued strongly *against* the order and complained that ACS could not release a check until they knew he had an apartment. According to the rules parents cannot get this money directly (parents are not trusted with it), but they are approved for specific amounts for rent, deposit, and/or furniture and issued checks written to landlords or stores. Instead, the attorney promised it would be done "expeditiously." The judge, as frustrated as the father, ordered ACS to get the check within a week. He even threatened ACS officials with contempt, which is extraordinarily rare for this judge who is very soft-spoken and even-tempered.

It is particularly short-sighted and, I would argue, punitive to ask parents to focus solely on changing their behaviors (such as anger or drug abuse) and on doing everything possible to prove they care about their children while their financial and work lives deteriorate. The system participates in making it harder for parents to support themselves, in the name of reforming them, and then sometimes refuses to allow reunification solely on the basis of inadequate housing and income—allegations that, if they came at the beginning of a case, would be deemed simply poverty and not a reason to remove children.[4] In Salina's case, caseworkers were prepared to return her children after she proved she was no longer using drugs. They even told her oldest son that he was going to be coming home on a particular day:

> [The caseworker], she kept tell my son, "On the 13th, y'all coming home." And I told her, "Don't tell them that because you never know what the judge gonna say." He's expecting now to come home on the 13th. Thirteenth come, he called me right after court, like, "We're coming home. You're coming to get us?" . . . I'm like, "No. Now they're talkin' about my apartment's got to get fixed up. So now we got to wait until they fix the apartment up for y'all to come home." So after that he just lashed out. That's why he's acting out like that [stealing and refusing to go to school]. That's what I feel. . . . He [her son] got to know I can't come to him and be like angry because I was in his situation. My mother never came to get me out of foster care. I signed myself out at twenty-one. So my family was never there for me. So me right now, I'm an angry person, but I don't take it out on nobody. That's with me, I don't talk to nobody so that stays in me.

Not only did caseworkers delay reunification for housing issues, they inadvertently perpetuated the problems in this family by creating intergenerational patterns of emotional trauma.

Overall, parents were often placed in terrible catch-22s: forced to choose between work and needed services, or between work and visiting their children, or between losing a stable place to live and losing their children. These situations could even lead to a complete loss of parental rights, as in the case of the father whose rights were terminated due to his lack of compliance with therapy and his lack of housing (see chapter 7). An important finding of this study is that the child welfare system itself can become one factor in deepening parents' poverty. If parents are not able to show evidence that they have adequate housing and the means to care for their children, then reunification will not occur. The child welfare system thus plays a role in re-creating poverty, which is then used as a further reason to deny custody to parents—a clear example of the re-creation of stratified reproduction. This situation usually affects families of color, those most likely to come in contact with child welfare.

"This System Just Sets Them Up for the Next One"

It is important to note that poverty and inequality are perpetuated among the children who are placed in foster care as well. Although I did not have access to as much data about the children in these cases (except through parents and the reports of law guardians in family court), my observations and interviews point to some important patterns that have been more fully explored by other researchers (see, e.g., Jonson-Reid and Barth 2003; Pecora et al. 2003; Reilly 2003). In court, I was struck by the large numbers of children who were labeled special needs, were involved with the juvenile justice system, or were not doing well in school. Special needs ranged from behavioral problems in the foster home or at school, to children who were in special education classes, to students who had been placed in therapeutic foster homes, to children taking a combination of psychotropic drugs. It was not always clear, from the information I was able to access, how many of these children had these problems before they were placed and how many had developed these problems after, or maybe as a result of, foster care placement. Parents, however, told me that these problems developed *after* their children were placed.

Several parents told me that their children were only put on medication, given a mental illness diagnosis, or put in special education *after* they were removed from their homes. They felt that situational behavioral problems, stemming from removal, were dealt with inappropriately. Parents often resisted the labels given to their children and felt that such labels were used to place children in educational settings where they were simply warehoused. For example, Irene described the effects of foster care on her children (she is referring to them by their ages at the time of the interview, not when they were in foster care):

> When they took my kids from me, my twenty-one-year-old was an honor roll student, and all the kids, they were all regular ed kids, all of them. When they came back out of the system eighteen months later, they were all special needs. Each and every one of them. . . . My fourteen-year-old who's in private school now he was ADHD, on medication. The fifteen-year-old was hyperactive with bipolar disorder. The twenty-one-year-old was drinking alcohol and had dropped out of school. And then, the baby had a speech impairment problem, and it was addressed through early intervention. Like, I took him to early invention when he got back. . . . The fourteen-year-old . . . right now, he's in a

> gifted program. So I really worked, you know, hard to get him off medication and do whatever I had to do to make it right, but they still have issues. Like, they still have a lot of feelings on what happened with them in foster care, so.

Irene clearly blames the foster care system for creating problems and describes her efforts to undo the damage she felt the system created.

Many parents also told me that delinquency and school attendance problems were results of foster care. Parents complained that foster parents neither ensured school attendance nor expected children to do well in school. Parents felt this was setting their children up for failure. For example, Salina described her situation:

> You [the foster mother] can't let him do what he want to do because now he's doing bad in school and what are y'all telling him? Y'all ain't telling him it's wrong. Y'all ain't telling him it's right. Y'all just letting him be. So now he's like, "Whatever. They ain't getting mad at me 'cause I'm bad in school." Over here [at my house], you couldn't do that, no. . . . Now they trying to rush them to get them home because he's doing bad in school. He's not graduating. He's not passing this year. He just graduated from sixth grade. He's not doing good. He's got to repeat the grade this year. So I'm like, come on, you see all the work that—I worked hard to get him where he's at now. And now look at him. Now he's to where he don't care. He don't care. . . . He's stealing. . . . So you're telling my son it's all right to steal, it's all right to do bad in school.

In addition to the lack of guidance and supervision in foster homes, many parents reported that they had been told they could not be involved in their children's schools, even if this was not the case. Parent advocates confirmed this was a common problem. This also seems to contribute to foster children having poorer school outcomes than other children (see also McDonald et al. 1997; Zetlin, Weinberg, and Kimm 2004).

In other cases, child welfare involvement made existing issues that children faced worse. For example, Claudia's inability to deal with her teen son's anger led to her calling ACS for help. She was initially offered services, but his issues were not adequately addressed. After an incident in which he showed violence toward her and she retaliated, she was arrested, and her son was placed in foster care for a year and a half. During this time, mental health treatment was not provided, and he deteriorated, becoming angrier and cutting school (something he never did in her house). She complained numerous times that the foster mother was not taking him to appointments and not ensuring he was in school, but she was told by caseworkers that they "couldn't tell her [the foster mother] how to run her household." By the end of his foster care placement, an angry and sometimes violent child who still was an "A" student was failing, frequently absent from school, and had a juvenile delinquency case. Rather than getting help for her son's behavioral issues, Claudia felt that ACS made the situation worse. Being placed in foster care and not being pushed to do well in school started him on a path that was likely to end with him having inadequate education and a criminal record that would make future employment difficult.

Parents also reported that being investigated or losing custody damaged their relationships with their children because their children no longer fully trusted them. Both Irene and Leslie described how their children stopped coming to them with their problems, which made it harder to be an effective parent. They also felt it was hard to discipline since their children had lost respect for them. Leslie explained the issue:

> Once you . . . lose your kids through the system, they're judging you. Every small mistake you make, they're [your children] holding you accordingly. It's not the same where they had that healthy fear of you. Like, I remember those days. You know, I was never harmful to my kids, but they respected me. But once they went through the system, that left and I never got it back. Never. And that really bothers me. . . . I'm lacking now because they don't look up to me. They're looking up to my sister and her husband [they were the foster parents], so when they come home, they really don't really have any respect. . . . I've been fighting ever since. I've got a little bit. It seems like they acknowledge me now, but still every day is a struggle . . . it seems like we're closer now, but I had to battle just to get where I am with them. Let them know that I care, let them know that I'm not gonna let them get taken away again.

Although these issues need more research, I believe that trauma from foster care removal that is either not adequately treated or used to place children in school tracks that are not fully educating them, foster parents who do not adequately enforce school attendance and achievement and other rules, and loss of parental authority might account for the poor outcomes among foster children documented by other researchers (Armstrong 1998; Courtney et al. 2011; Kapp 2000; Munson and Freundlich 2003; Pecora et al. 2003; Ross, Conger, and Armstrong 2002; Shin 2002).

When these children are placed in classes that are more about controlling their behavior than providing an education or when they are routinely suspended for unruly behaviors, their education suffers, a trajectory that leaves them vulnerable to joblessness and homelessness as adults.

Some child welfare officials agreed with parents' views of how the system damaged children. A law guardian who represented teens expressed dismay that she routinely received plans for teens ageing out of foster care that included "discharge to homelessness" even though this is illegal:

> But the main problem that pretty much all of my clients have, is trying to find housing and find a job. They don't even know where to start because you'll find that the agency's independent living programs don't really teach them anything. . . . A lot of times, what we say, is this system just sets them up for the next one because you'll have eighteen-to-twenty-one-year-olds in foster care. They're supposed to be able to live independently, but what does independent living actually mean? A successful transition to independent living means they got their Section 8 or NYCHA apartment. . . . That being a measure of success is really sad, but that's the reality.

Emily, a social worker at the Bronx Defenders, summed up the ways that child welfare actually perpetuates family problems and inequality among the families it serves: "It seems like it's not about saving poor children. It's about actually telling people who are in these families that they're unfit, you know, parents, that they actually aren't worthy. . . . We're coming in saying that you're not doing it right and we, you know, are gonna remove them, but we're not gonna do it any better, either." The child welfare system, then, does not necessarily provide adequate care to children when parents are unable. Instead, the social problems of poverty, lack of education, crime, and mental health issues facing these families are perpetuated or, in some cases, made worse by child welfare intervention.

Community-Level Effects

In chapter 5, I discussed the patterns of surveillance that not only lead to a high concentration of child welfare involvement in poor and minority neighborhoods but also draw service providers and community members into this system of surveillance. In this context, many poor families of color were afraid of "catching a case," and this fear did, at times, strain relationships and cause parents to be reluctant to seek out needed services or divulge their problems, for fear of losing their children (Roberts, Hill, and Pitchal 2006). In conversations with parents and parent advocates and in support groups, I found a profound fear of ACS and a pervasive sense that the agency did not investigate thoroughly and placed children in foster care without doing enough to help the family. The agency was widely perceived as unnecessarily tearing families apart. Most parents and many parent advocates and activists felt that placing children in foster care was the main purpose behind the agency; the aims of protecting children, making families stronger, or helping families get back together were lost. Many people felt that because ACS and the foster care agencies are paid for keeping children in foster care there is a financial incentive to place children in foster care and then drag out foster care placements when the children might have safely stayed in the home.

This belief is not far off: funding is indeed skewed toward foster care and adoption. ACS itself recognized this problem and in 2005 announced a plan entitled "Protecting Children and Strengthening Families: A Plan to Realign New York City's Child Welfare System." Among other goals, it aims to focus on services for families rather than foster care by changing funding priorities:

> As a system, child welfare gets what it pays for—foster care drives the funding and the services. As a result, close to two-thirds of families never receive in-home support services, aftercare is not funded at all, and 75 percent of the time neighborhood-based services are not in a family's plan. Reinvesting means taking advantage of the savings produced by the declining foster care population to recycle money back into the very support services—preventive, quality foster care and aftercare—that help reduce admissions and lengths of stay in the first place. (NYC Administration for Children's Services 2005)

Moreover, the process of supervising foster care placement takes up most of the time of caseworkers and the courts while parents wait months for either simple referrals or the most basic of services. Thus, parents' feeling that caseworkers are not working to help them or their families is an accurate description in many cases.

This basic lack of trust in ACS extends to anyone who might report a family—foster care agencies, doctors, school officials, neighbors, friends, and family members. The widespread fear of "catching a case"—that is, the feeling that results from how reports are used as weapons, how schools threaten parents with calling ACS if they do not pick up unruly children, and how doctors and other service providers call "just to be safe"—leads many to be wary of asking for help or even divulging family problems. For example, Leslie was very reluctant to trust anyone and refused help from several agencies even when she had trouble securing mental health treatment for her son who was failing in school and frequently cutting classes. A parent advocate at one foster care agency described to a parenting group how she avoided taking her sons, whom she described as rambunctious boys who had bruises and other injuries fairly often, to the doctor when they were injured because she feared continued reports. Others talked about the need to be cautious in divulging family problems to anyone or getting into disputes with neighbors since child welfare reports might follow.

In this way, the surveillance system that these families are subject to extends outward by involving its subjects in watching each other. At the same time, many parent advocates and parents with active child welfare cases talked about the need to involve authorities when children were legitimately in danger. They wanted officials to investigate, especially in the case of severe abuse. They also sometimes advocated making calls when families seemed to have no other resources. It seemed to me that communities were desperate for support at the same time that they criticized how it was too often accompanied by separation of children from parents (see also Roberts 2008). This phenomenon has been present throughout child welfare history (see chapter 2).

Parents and activists felt that the presence of ACS in their neighborhoods made it more difficult for everyone, whether they had been involved with ACS or not, to be a good parent. Irene explained: "I try . . . to steer them toward the right way, but sometimes it's difficult because . . . ACS has a hold on you. . . . I feel like you can't even discipline your kid. You can't even bring your child up and say, 'You know, you can't do that.' Because they give these kids rights that they shouldn't even have." In neighborhoods in which ACS involvement was highly concentrated, parents in general felt that their parenting was under scrutiny and that they couldn't command the same respect or enforce rules to the same degree. Some found that older children in the community felt empowered to defy parents or used ACS as a threat against parents, who worried that this attitude perpetuated problems of crime and lack of education when children were lost to "the street."

Extensive and regular ACS intervention in poor communities of color thus affects these communities as a whole. This finding parallels what researchers have found when studying effects of policing and incarceration (see, e.g., Clear 2009; Goffman 2014; Mauer and Chesney-Lind 2002). ACS intervention plays a role in straining community ties and in making children more insecure. Further, by discouraging people from divulging problems and seeking help, this state agency helps perpetuate problems that are already concentrated among the poor and people of color and undermines its own mission (see also Roberts 2008). How can people come together to push for social change if they are suspicious of each other? How can neighbors and kin pool resources to deal with poverty and lack of services (Stack 1983) if trust is broken? How do children stay healthy and parents get help for mental health and drug issues if they are distrustful of doctors, schools, and service providers? How can children grow up to be valuable and productive members of society when parents lose authority?

Re-creation of Stratified Reproduction

> "I do think that there's this somehow acceptance that poor people can't parent." (Emily, Bronx Defenders social worker)

Daily practices in child welfare are an outcome of stratified reproduction, but they also help to reproduce it. Caseworkers and family court officials draw on class-biased and racialized ideologies about the irresponsibility of poor women and use these to justify surveillance or the removal of children. Although direct references to race were not made in interviews or in court, these "color-blind" discourses are nonetheless racialized. Caseworkers talked about mothers in ways that drew on larger stereotypes of black women as overly sexualized and irresponsible, careless mothers who are to blame for their own poverty due to their poor choices (Collins 1990). This was clear in how Marilyn described her clients as having "arrested development" (chapter 6) or when Pamela told me that her clients "have to learn" that

> you can't have all these kids with all these different fathers and, you know, expect to be okay. It's not gonna be okay. . . . Sometimes the system itself, you

> know, fails everyone. Because if you're allowing them to stay on Section 8 for years and years, and they're cutting that down now where you have to, after five years, you have to be on your own. And I think that's pretty good because it's "I don't have to work. I can stay home. My rent is paid. I get food stamps. I have cable, food, a nice decent apartment. Why should I work? I get SSI for one or two of my kids. Why am I working?"

Her statements draw on stereotypes of poor women of color who have too many children and are lazy and unwilling to work (Mullings 1995; Quadagno 1996; Roberts 1997; 2002).

These stereotypes lead to harsher evaluations of clients, which makes it less likely they will be seen as mothers who have something to offer their children and more likely that they will be seen as risks from which children must be protected. These views, underlying recent policy changes that have limited the availability of services in the child welfare system overall (see chapter 2), tend to define poor parents of color as undeserving of help and play a role in caseworkers' decisions about how to allocate scarce resources. Daily practices that deny help to parents, ignore the root causes of family problems, and often worsen the conditions of parents' lives thus offer a self-fulfilling prophecy: they make it more likely that parents' problems will be perpetuated and that parents will have a hard time regaining custody.

It was often clear that the caretaking work of parents involved with child welfare was not valued and supported. The positive things women had done for their children are often not taken into account in decision making, and it often seemed as if any value they had as mothers was either denied or ignored. Instead, they were viewed as merely the sum of various personal problems that put their children "at risk." This picture makes the agency's decisions to supervise them or remove their children, rather than to provide services, seem the most appropriate. Decision makers frequently see mothers as irresponsible and assume they fit stereotypes of women who selfishly put their own needs before those of their children. Caseworkers often believe that mothers do not wish to change their lives or are unable to learn from their mistakes, and the caseworkers also assume that fathers fit stereotypes of either absent, "deadbeat dads" who reject involvement as caretakers or violent, criminal men who should be kept away from children (see chapters 6 and 7). These views create situations in which increased surveillance, mandated services, requirements about acceptable partners with whom parents could have relationships, and even the removal of children seem to be reasonable solutions to family problems rather than a focus on the real assistance parents needed with drug addiction, housing problems, and domestic violence. This "parent as problem model" (McConnell and Llewellyn 2005) is a prime example of how state practices build on relations of stratified reproduction. By continuing to define parents by what they lack, by not adequately providing the services that might enable them to better care for their children, and by creating situations in which parents actually had fewer resources to care for their children than they did before becoming involved in child welfare, the system reinforces and re-creates the idea that these are unfit mothers and fathers.

The family court system also plays a role in the creation and re-creation of stratified reproduction. Although the stated purpose of family court is to provide a forum in which the rights of parents are balanced with the safety of children, officials are under enormous pressure to avoid making a decision that ends in tragedy (see chapter 4) and are thus apt to make overly cautious decisions. Family court is often a rubber-stamp to ACS decision making about state intervention and quickly moves to the business of dealing with the supervision of families and children's placement in foster care. Daily practices in family court thus create situations in which the vast majority of parents *will* be found to have neglected their children. The legal finding of neglect removes problems from the realm of structural inequalities of race, class, and gender and into that of individual culpability, thereby further reinforcing stereotypes of unfit parents. The designation stays with parents until their youngest child is twenty-eight years old and makes it more difficult for them to retain custody in the future. In addition, a neglect finding places almost permanent suspicion on parents' ability to be adequate caretakers and might exacerbate poverty, especially for mothers, by limiting job opportunities.

Service providers also have a tendency to label parents in ways that build on stereotypes while simultaneously re-creating them and giving them legitimacy. Mental health services providers were often discussed by parents' attorneys and parent advocates as problematic in this way. Brandon explained this pattern:

> There's an MHS [Mental Health Services] Clinic in the family court. And basically if there's a question, you know, is your client all there? They'll send 'em up there. I always have a problem with the person getting sent up there because I have never seen a report come out of that office that says there's

> nothing wrong with them. Every time a report comes down there's something wrong with them. Every time that a parent goes to an agency psychologist, I don't see any positive reports. Counseling: never any positive reports for the family. . . . So it seems to be this big institution of complacency. . . . I'm not saying they do it intentionally, but I don't think there's any, any actual like caring left. I think that if there was a young person who went in there, they might be more motivated to handle the situation differently. Evaluate a person's needs. Understand where they're coming from. The whole thing. But I think once you get caught up in volume and once you get caught up over the course of time and you realize who your employer is, who is these foster care agencies who make money off the kids staying in care the longer period of time, I think that you become completely, what's the word, jaded maybe? And it happens to everybody. To me, to everybody who ever works in the system.

Service providers thus help reinforce views of parents that allow the state to deny them custody of their children.

Finally, the experience of going through child welfare damages some parents and permanently ruptures family ties. Nathan, a parent advocate, explained, "I had people that gave up. Got tired of going to court. Gave up, you know. . . . You go to court, you can't talk. People telling you to shut up. Your lawyer's not listening. Your lawyer lookin' crazy. People from the ACS lookin' at you like somethin' is wrong with you and, it's just how they knock your spirit down so low. Sometimes it's hard to bounce back." In this way, and for some parents, this experience simply perpetuates "broken" families and ultimately confirms the stereotype that poor people of color don't care about their children. That these experiences are so heavily concentrated in poor communities of color strengthens and legitimizes the prevailing view that these families are broken and require intervention by the state.

Causes for Optimism

There are some signs that child welfare in New York City has been changing in ways that might be beneficial to the poor families of color caught up in the system. During my fieldwork, attempts were being made to give parents more input into their cases and to provide them with better legal representation. New institutional providers have taken over some of the representation of parents in family court, and they were working to advocate more strongly for parents. These attorneys hope to change the culture of family court by more strongly challenging ACS. As one of their social workers stated, they planned to "really litigate these cases" and pressure ACS "to be a lot more thoughtful on these petitions. And truthful." In other words, the new attorneys were attempting to change prevailing practices that often authorize ACS plans for families with little scrutiny and leave parents without strong advocates for their rights. They are also able to provide parent advocates and social workers to help parents access needed services and understand the family court and reunification processes. The parents I met who were represented by these lawyers reported that they had a better experience in family court and with child welfare in general.

I spent time in family court with both lawyers at the Bronx Defenders and with one of their clients, so I was able to see how they approach parents firsthand. When they were assigned, they made a point to sit with the parent to go over the petition and explain what it said, to tell them what would next happen, and to ask the parent for her side of the story. This allowed the lawyers to begin preparing a case on the parent's behalf and to gather information that would immediately put her in a favorable light. The initial conference also provided information that sometimes enabled the lawyers to intervene and attempt to change or stop proposed ACS interventions. These institutional providers were more willing to request full-blown hearings and to push the courts to question ACS officials. Furthermore, they had parent advocates talk to the parent to provide emotional support and referrals for services.

They are able to do all this, in part, because they have lower caseloads, support staff to help with other aspects of their job, and colleagues who can cover for each other. More importantly, however, they practice in this way because they are committed to social justice and to ensuring that their clients receive high-quality representation while understanding the process. The new institutional providers offer a hopeful sign that the city and the courts themselves had recognized many problems endemic to family court and were attempting to remedy them. The parents I met who were represented by these attorneys had much better experiences in family court. Because these lawyers waited with parents (as much as they were able) until their cases were called, the parents felt they had an advocate. As the institutional providers take over more of this work, it is possible that at least some of the practices described earlier might change.

In addition, and perhaps most important, the activists and parent advocates at the Child Welfare Organizing Project have been doing vital work in assisting and supporting parents involved with ACS. Their weekly support groups, held at the time of my fieldwork in the Bronx, Manhattan, and Brooklyn, provide an important source of information, advice, and emotional support for parents. These groups were truly inspiring in how they were able to share information effectively and coach people through the process of dealing with their child welfare cases. Moreover, they provided a safe space where people could vent frustrations so they could remain calm in dealing with caseworkers and service providers. They begin every meeting by reciting the Serenity Prayer,[5] a copy of which is tacked to the wall alongside posters of black women leaders in history. The significance of these things became clear to me as I spent more time at CWOP and with parents navigating the system. The single most common piece of advice that CWOP gives parents is to keep emotions under control. If parents do not control emotions, then it is likely that caseworkers will be concerned about their ability to be a safe parent. The Serenity Prayer is a weekly reminder to parents to fight to change things in their cases while remaining calm and letting go of things they cannot change. This advice was especially important in dealing with often unresponsive bureaucracies and caseworkers. Parent advocates at foster care agencies also echoed this advice as did social workers assigned to parents.[6]

CWOP was also instrumental in working for larger structural changes in the child welfare system and in its daily practices. Most significant, the organization worked to create a role for parent advocates. CWOP created its own parent advocate training curriculum and secured funding to provide stipends for a cohort of parents who had been through the system to attend training each year. The parent advocates trained at CWOP have been able to secure employment at ACS or at foster care agencies; not only do they help parents navigate the system, but this service also provides an important employment avenue for those whose options are limited by neglect findings.

In my experience, problems with services were among the main reasons parents sought out parent advocates, along with generally unresponsive caseworkers and lawyers, the myriad barriers to regaining custody that crop up in cases, such as lack of housing, and the need for emotional support in dealing with "the system" or a child in foster care. Parent advocates can relate to parents and provide a valuable source of emotional and practical support. Most have been in contact with ACS (many have regained custody of their children), live in neighborhoods with high concentrations of families involved in ACS, and are similar in race/ethnicity and class to parents affected by the system. Many of the parents I met were helped by parent advocates who not only provide referrals for services and important advice about dealing with attorneys and caseworkers but also share knowledge about particular agencies and stories of their cases so that parents knew they were not alone. When possible, CWOP advocates attend conferences and intervene with caseworkers when parents' needs are not being met or their cases are not moving forward.

In addition, parent advocates often had a much better record of making referrals and finding openings than did caseworkers. They often have experience with service providers and are more likely to know what is available in their neighborhoods. For example, I witnessed a case in family court where ACS planned to remand a child because of the mother's drug addiction and her refusal to go into an in-patient program without her baby. The caseworkers maintained that there were no openings in any mother-child program, and she had to go into whatever program they could find. It took the parent advocate only two phone calls to find an opening at a mother-child program and to get an intake appointment for the following day.

The invaluable service parent advocates provide is a testament to the fact that most parents who are involved with the child welfare system are loving parents and citizens who can make valuable contributions to their communities and display a commitment to social justice. Seeing their work made my fieldwork, which was often emotionally difficult, more bearable and gives me hope for the future. These incremental changes in the courts and the increasing role of parent advocates are important and will help to ameliorate some of the persistent problems faced by families who come in contact with child welfare.

Despite these changes, these is still a need for a shift at ACS from a focus on foster care to family services and reunification so that unnecessary removals and unnecessarily long foster care stays might be avoided. These changes, however, will not solve the larger social problems that are at the root of why some families are likely to be affected by child welfare while others are not. Nor will these changes deal with the larger societal conditions that put both children and parents at risk. Larger social inequalities of race, class, and gender are fundamental to why some families are involved with child welfare and underlie many conditions that are harmful to children. Living in poverty and dealing with institutional racism present profound risks to children as do underperforming schools, inadequate housing and health care, dangerous neighborhoods, drug use, and domestic violence. Many of these problems disproportionately affect children of color who are also made less secure by being subject to removal from their families. Unless all families have access to adequate resources to raise children, some children will always be at risk for maltreatment and will not have the opportunity to thrive. As long as stereotypes of both irreparably broken black families and black women who are irresponsible and unfit mothers persist, it is likely that more black children will be involved with child welfare, especially given the ways that race and class intertwine to create conditions that make it difficult for poor women and men of color to raise children.

These persistent social inequalities are desperately in need of change if we truly want all children to have the opportunity to grow up to be healthy, educated, and productive citizens. All children need better access to high-quality education, health care, and safe play spaces and neighborhoods. Parents must also be helped to create stronger families. They are desperately in need of education, job opportunities, health insurance, access to mental health and drug treatment, safe housing, and support in raising children, including affordable childcare. Rather than expecting a system that has been tasked with investigating and responding to charges of maltreatment to act as a triage center for dealing with the most pressing family problems rooted in poverty and inequality, there is a need for large-scale change. The child welfare system should focus only on the task for which it was created—investigating and intervening in cases of abuse and severe and willful neglect—but this can only occur if universal programs that allow all citizens to have access to health care, education, and jobs are created and supportive services for those who struggle with mental health issues and drug abuse are adequately funded. Only when inequalities of race, class, and gender are lessened for all, will families and communities be stronger and will children truly have a chance to thrive.

Notes

Chapter 1 Introduction

1 All names used throughout this book are pseudonyms.
2 Section 8 is a federal program administered by the Department of Housing and Urban Development (HUD) and local Public Housing Agencies (PHAs) for very low-income families. They find their own apartment, and, if it is deemed acceptable and safe, the local PHA determines the amount of rent that will be paid on behalf of the family and the family will be responsible for the difference.
3 71.1 percent of those cases in which evidence of maltreatment was found had experienced neglect, 16.1 percent had experienced physical abuse, and 9.1 percent sexual abuse (U.S. Department of Health and Human Services 2010).
4 Native American children are also overrepresented in the child welfare system, but this population is outside the scope of this book.
5 Statistics can be accessed on the Administration for Children's Services Website, NYC 2013 Community Snapshots: http://www.nyc.gov/html/acs/html/statistics/statistics_cd_snapshot.shtml.
6 New York City is divided into fifty-nine Community Districts (CDs). CD boundaries are drawn by the Department of City Planning and are meant to fall along neighborhood lines.
7 Data from the Administration for Children's Services Website, NYC 2013 Community Snapshots: http://www.nyc.gov/html/acs/html/statistics/statistics_cd_snapshot.shtml.
8 They are broadly representative of the child welfare population in general and of the parents I saw in family court. The vast majority of the parents I interviewed were either black (fourteen) or Latino (twelve; either Puerto Rican or Dominican) and all were American-born. Only three parents (all mothers) were white. Twenty-two parents are mothers while seven are fathers. Eighteen of the parents I interviewed lived at or near the poverty line. Among the parents living in poverty, three work at low-wage service-sector jobs; ten rely on government assistance (most of these parents have worked in the past but were unable to due to their child welfare cases);

two are supported by family members; and three combine government help with off-the-books or informal work. At most, these parents have a high school education, and some, like Salina, dropped out of high school. Seventy-one percent of my total sample was living in poverty. In contrast, only six parents had college degrees and had worked in professional or social service jobs and five were working-class with more stable jobs such as clerical positions, nurse's assistants, unionized building workers, or the like.

9 Child welfare systems in other parts of the country, especially in areas with large numbers of Native American families, are also overwhelmed, but the dynamics are much different and beyond the scope of this book.

10 In Brooklyn I sat with the same judge, while in the other boroughs I chose a different courtroom each day and watched all the cases heard there. I was also allowed to observe the intake process (in which the lawyers for ACS speak with caseworkers and then draft the petitions to file in court) in two boroughs. This was invaluable in terms of learning about the investigation process and how decisions are made. Finally, I shadowed two lawyers to observe their practices at first hand.

11 I do not talk about specific cases I heard about in these groups unless the parent explicitly gave me permission.

12 It was common for parents to ask if someone could come to court with them, not to advocate on their behalf (although a few wanted this), but to have moral support and company. I made it clear to parents that I was not able to advocate for them, but I was happy to attend to give them someone to talk to or to take notes for them about the hearing. I did ask these parents if they wanted to be included in my study.

13 I formally interviewed thirteen lawyers (six parents' attorneys, four ACS attorneys, and three law guardians) and two judges. They were overwhelmingly white (eleven out of the thirteen attorneys and both judges) but included a parents' attorney who identified as Puerto Rican, an ACS attorney of Middle Eastern descent, and a law guardian of Indian descent. Both of the judges and seven out of the thirteen attorneys are women. This fits with the demographics of family court attorneys, judging by whom I saw around family court. Most judges were also white women (fifteen out of twenty-five), although there were also five white men, three men of color, and two women of color. I interviewed thirteen child protective staff members, including ten caseworkers and three supervisors/managers. The caseworkers had been in that position from a year and a half to ten years. Most of them (seven out of ten) had worked as caseworkers for five to seven years and were more experienced than the average caseworker currently at the agency, which has been plagued by high turnover. Ten of the caseworkers/managers are minority (seven African American women, two minority women, and one African American man), ten are female, and three are male. Most of the caseworkers are young (in their mid-twenties to mid-thirties).

14 The survey asked parents for basic information about themselves, their families, and their cases; how satisfied they were with their caseworkers and lawyers; and about any problems they had in getting needed services. In interviews, I asked parents to recount their cases and experiences with the child welfare system; describe their daily lives including how they support themselves and their children; discuss what their neighborhoods and their children's schools are like; explain any problems they have had meeting basic needs such as income, medical care, and housing; and talk about issues such as drug abuse and domestic violence.

Chapter 2 A History of Child Welfare in New York City

1 There is a parallel history to be told about the role of child welfare in the "civilizing" of Native American populations, but it is outside the scope of this book (see Briggs 2012).

2 Polsky acknowledges that the therapeutic approach has never been the only approach taken. Other ways of understanding what makes some groups marginal, as well as issues such as lack of funding, can lead many agencies to adhere to a therapeutic approach unevenly or not at all. The same is true of public child welfare agencies and child welfare policy.

3 Bruce Bellingham (1990) argues that these aims were not reflected in the actual work of the child-saving organizations. According to his analysis, Brace's methods built on poor families' existing fostering practices (in which children would be placed with others due to family hardships or in order to learn a trade), and parental unfitness was alleged in only a few cases. Mason refers to the placements brokered by the CAS as "involuntary apprenticeships" to both recognize the continuity with older practices and to highlight the coercion involved (Mason 1994, 78–80).

4 Brace's innovation in placing children in individual homes would not be implemented on a broader scale for several decades.

5 Mary Ellen was actually indentured by the city after the woman her parents hired to look after her stopped being paid and took the child to a poor law official. The family she was indentured to was actually her natural father and his wife (the child was illegitimate, and the charity did not know this fact). Her father then died, and her stepmother remarried. Then the abuse began. A charity worker learned of it and approached the Society for the Prevention of Cruelty to Animals (which had been founded in 1868 and had the power to enforce animal cruelty laws and remove animals from owners) for help. Their lawyer found a legal justification for removing Mary Ellen. Based on the child's testimony in criminal court, a jury found her stepmother guilty of assault, and Mary Ellen was placed in an orphan asylum and later with a farm family outside the city (Pleck 1987).

6 I focus on SPCCs in general due to a lack of information about the New York Society in the published literature.

7 New York State law regarding child "cruelty" at this time reflected the concerns of these child-saving organizations. In 1877 an act "for the protection of children" was passed. It included, in this order, the following conditions under which a child (defined as under the age of fourteen) could be found to be subject to placement in an orphan asylum:

- A child found begging or begging "under the pretext of selling;" a child found in public for the purpose of begging
- A child found wandering, homeless or without "proper guardianship or visible means of subsistence"
- A child destitute, "either being an orphan or having a vicious parent, who is undergoing penal servitude or imprisonment"
- A child who "frequents the company of reputed thieves or prostitutes or houses of assignation or prostitution, or dance-houses, concert saloons, theaters and varieties" (Laws of New York 1877, Chapter 428)

The law reflected concern with the behaviors of poor families and children, with a focus on behaviors thought to be immoral but that were likely part of families' economic survival strategies.

8 Physical cruelty made up only 6 percent to 13 percent of cases in Philadelphia between 1878 and 1935 (Pleck 1987).

9 A 1942 municipal ordinance denied public funds to agencies that refused to take children from all racial groups. It did not help the problem of lack of placements for African American children because religious agencies did not have to accept children outside their religious groups. In practice, only the Protestant agencies were faced with the loss of funding, and many simply relinquished public funding rather than accept black children. Those who were held to the rule gave various excuses and made it known that anything above a fairly small percentage of black children was unacceptable (Bernstein 2001, 56). Puerto Rican children are not mentioned in these discussions, and it is likely they were accepted by Catholic organizations.

10 In 1943, a public scandal occurred when police were called to a boys' shelter to restore order. Shelters were then investigated due to overcrowding and poor conditions. The investigation found that children did not have shoes and were punished by being isolated in two basement rooms with no furniture (one also had no windows). Another report stated that 140 children shared 73 beds on Labor Day 1955 (Rosner and Markowitz 1997).

11 Judges were reluctant to label any white child delinquent "because of the long-term consequences for future employment, army service, and self-image" (Rosner and Markowitz 1997, 1846). Either these consequences were not seen as important to avoid for black children or judges acted pragmatically to ensure they could be placed somewhere. Overcrowding at training schools eventually led to a policy under which judges could place children in city jails (Rosner and Markowitz 1997).

12 Filed in 1973, *Wilder v. Bernstein* argued that the entire foster care system was unconstitutional due to its public funding for religious agencies and because foster care denied black children equal protection under the law and violated their right not to be detained without due process (Bernstein 2001). The case of the lead plaintiff, Shirley Wilder, a teenager at the time, typified many of the problems faced by black children in need of placement. After the death of her mother and grandmother, she was sent to live with her father. After running away multiple times due to beatings and harsh treatment by her stepmother, her father finally brought her to family court to have her "put away." The court found she needed a residential center and psychological help, but she was rejected by every private agency and had to be placed in a state training school after spending several months in a detention center that was supposed to have been closed more than a year before. Conditions at the center were found by a federal court to be "so hazardous and unhealthy that they amounted to cruel and unusual punishment" (Bernstein 2001, 8). The eventual settlement, fourteen years later, required that children be placed on a first-come, first-served basis so that black children would have better placement opportunities. A study conducted two years later found that the settlement was not being followed, and, most disturbingly, although the system was now serving black children almost exclusively, differences in skin tone affected the likelihood a child would find placement (Bernstein 2001, 373). The attorney for the plaintiffs filed contempt motions claiming that the settlement was not being upheld, and this issue was fought until 1999, when the settlement was incorporated into the decision in another class-action suit, the *Marisol* case.

13 Doctors were reluctant to report such injuries as possibly caused intentionally by a parent, either not wanting to go to court or fearing libel suits (Pleck 1987, 167).

14 Reports increased nationwide from 9,500 calls in 1967 to almost 300,000 in 1975 to 669,000 in 1976, leading one expert to equate child abuse reports to 911 callers who were unable to distinguish "between life-threatening crimes and littering" (Ashby 1997, 137, quoting Douglas Besharov).

15 One nationwide study, conducted in 1963, found that more than "51% of children served by public agencies were either in foster care or receiving some kind of foster care" (Lawrence-Webb 1997, 23).

16 Mondale's first bill was vetoed by Richard Nixon who objected to its funding of public child care; however, a narrow focus on child abuse meant he was eventually successful. As Mondale once quipped: "Not even Richard Nixon is in favor of child abuse" (quoted in Pleck 1987, 176).

17 Nationally, the number of children in foster care rose from an estimated 272,000 children in 1962 to 319,800 in 1972 (Tobis 1989, 105). In New York City, the numbers of children in foster care hit a peak of 24,732 in 1975, up from 16,121 in 1960 (Tobis 1989, 103).

18 According to the psychological parent theory, children's different sense of time and need for continuity requires "a stable and uninterrupted relationship with one caregiver" (Erickson 2000, 82). This theory has been criticized for being based on limited observations and ignoring evidence that children can and do form multiple attachments. It is also based on the realities of white, middle-class, nuclear families and does not take into account patterns of shared childrearing common among African Americans (Stack 1974). Nevertheless, it has been widely accepted and used to create policies that aim to give children a permanent home and caregiver relatively quickly rather than allowing parents sufficient time to deal with the issues that led to foster care placement (Erickson 2000).

19 The law also made adoptions easier by reducing the amount of time for adoptions to be finalized and providing funding for adoption services.

20 Federal money spent for child welfare increased dramatically from 1981 to 1995 (from $0.5 billion to $4.1 billion), but the percentage that went to preventive services decreased over time (Roberts 2002, 142). By 1988, 77 percent of funding available for foster care, adoption, and child welfare (including prevention) went for foster care and adoption (Pelton 1989, 97), and by 1993, the federal government spent $0.12 for every $1.00 spent on foster care (Roberts 2002, 142).

21 As Pelton and Tobis point out, changes in the numbers of children exiting foster care also contributed to the increase. In the late 1970s and early 1980s there was an increase in the numbers of children leaving foster care and then a decrease in those rates and a new "revolving door" phenomenon in which children were in care for relatively short stays but were likely to be placed again (Pelton 1989; Tobis 1989). This change seems to be linked to waning support for family reunification as well as to a willingness to remove children, which is linked, in turn, to a larger conservative political climate and lack of support for helping poor families of color.

22 Often testing protocols were in place only in public hospitals and applied to women who had not had prenatal care or were on Medicaid (Roberts 1991). According to Zerai and Banks, these policies were "less a means of protecting children exposed to cocaine *in utero* than they are a way of repositioning and anchoring poor Black women within a system of 'unjust power relations'" (Zerai and Banks 2002, 6–7).

23 The numbers of beds decreased rapidly as private agencies stopped making them available in response to ongoing efforts by the city to regulate them (Tobis 1989, 188). Multiple stories in city papers attributed the crisis to larger numbers of children who needed placements and attributed that problem, in turn, to crack cocaine, although these children were removed from their parents for various reasons (see, for example, Kerr 1986).

24 A story in the *Atlantic Monthly*, for example, portrayed group homes and other institutions as pleasant and orderly. Although intimacy was absent, "in the paradoxical world of 'child protective services' an institution may be the first home some children have ever known, providing their first chance to sit down to meals with other people at regular times, blow out birthday candles, and be taken care of by adults who do not hit or even yell" (Weisman 1994). The conditions in poor homes were thus implicitly or explicitly compared to foster care, and foster care was made to seem the more appropriate place for children.

25 Although written after ASFA was passed, an article in New York's *City Journal* sums up the concern: "The nation's foster care system has given rise to an unnoticed and deeply troubling reality: not only has it accepted the inevitability of legions of abused and neglected children, but it has made them into an integral part of the inner-city economy. For every child put into foster care, the foster family—which may be complete strangers or only a slightly different configuration of the child's birth family—gets a subsidy two to three times larger than what ordinary welfare pays. Whole communities of grandmothers are living on the money they receive for their abused or neglected grandchildren. Welfare advocates treat foster care payments as just another routine way to pump government money into troubled neighborhoods. . . . The foster care system . . . allows families to accommodate, and even profit from, their dysfunctions" (MacDonald 1999, 42).

26 These quotations are from the text of the law itself—Public Law 105–89.

27 Reasonable efforts can be denied in the case of an abandoned infant, a child whose parent has committed murder or manslaughter of a sibling, or a child whose parent has committed a felony assault resulting in serious injury to a child.

28 If the child is cared for by a relative, if a compelling reason why termination would not be in the child's best interests is documented, or if the state has not provided the services in the parent's case plan.

29 These funds are in addition to subsidies already provided to families who adopt a child from foster care. These benefits are not means tested, and, interestingly, minority children are often automatically defined as special needs or hard to place (Ortiz and Briggs 2003, 51–52).

30 Others have argued that ASFA is good public policy because it emphasizes safety and finding permanent homes for children. Some have criticized it as not child-centered enough because it contains exemptions to time limits, does not adequately fund preventive services, and leaves intact the financial incentive to keep children in foster care longer (Bartholet 1999; Erickson 2000; R. M. Gordon 1999).

31 The lawsuit, known as *Marisol*, charged that the Child Welfare Administration (CWA) was failing at practically all aspects of its job—from protective and preventive services to monitoring foster care and permanency planning.

32 This general attitude was also reflected in the judges Guiliani appointed. Among the eleven he appointed who are still on the bench, three were former prosecutors in district attorney's offices, two worked for the city law department prosecuting juvenile

delinquents, two were ACS attorneys, and one was a former criminal court judge. The others had worked in the mayor's office, in appellate courts, and as a law guardian. It should also be noted that the commissioner of ACS at the time, Nicholas Scopetta, did, however, push neighborhood-based foster care as a model for a new system and spoke publicly about the need for more drug treatment services and preventive programs as budget cuts under Guiliani had taken a toll (Bernstein 2001).

Chapter 3 The Life of a Child Welfare Case

1 For example, the mandated reporter I spoke with (she is a therapist for children in a school in a very poor section of Brooklyn) told me about calling the SCR twice in order to trigger an investigation. The first person she talked to did not accept the report so her supervisor advised her to call later. The new operator, with the same information, accepted the report. This anecdote illustrates the differences of opinion (Besharov and Laumann 1996; Hutchinson 1993; Tumlin and Geen 2000) and the difficult judgment calls involved.

2 I was told by several caseworkers that particularly difficult cases—fatalities and those that involve severe abuse or situations that might end up in the media—are sometimes given to particular caseworkers who are very experienced and can be counted on to do a thorough and competent investigation. I even heard that one of these caseworkers took a leave of absence after having a nervous breakdown from the pressure of being assigned to difficult and high-profile cases.

3 These factors were found to be correlated with subsequent abuse or neglect in a sample of cases from the city.

4 One caseworker told me that closing an indicated case without services does happen, but the agency is trying to get away from the practice. I asked why this might happen, and she gave me this example: "Let's say you suspect that the parent uses drugs, but the parents refuse to come in for a drug test . . . and the mom's behavior indicates that she might be using drugs . . . and she did use drugs a few years ago. But there's no evidence right now to say that she does. Legally, you can't file the case because your kid is going to school, he's happy, he's healthy. You might indicate that case, but there's nothing to file, and the mother refuses services. There's nothing you can do with that."

5 As one caseworker put it: "Because if there's immediate danger in the home, I'm not waiting for a court order to tell me to remove the kid. If the kid is unsafe, I take that kid out, regardless of whether I have a court order or not."

6 Informal arrangements avoid foster care, but they still ensure a child is removed from a situation perceived as dangerous. For example, a grandmother might file for temporary custody, or, if one parent hit the child and is willing to leave, an order of protection will be obtained to exclude the parent from the home. In this case the parent might be mandated to obtain services, but he or she will have to pay for the services out of pocket. In that case monitoring of the family to ensure the order of protection is followed is often, but not always, done.

7 This rule is generally, but not always, followed. One law guardian complained that it is not always done, and a couple of the parents I spoke with reported it took longer for their case to be brought to court than what is supposed to happen by law.

8 The shorthand 18B refers to the section of the law that authorizes assignment of counsel to the indigent.

9 They submitted proposals and were given contracts. The institutions chosen had been taking child protective cases for several years, but parents had to find out about them and ask to have their cases accepted. They were then fairly small and could not take on many cases. Under the new contracts, they are given all cases that come to court a day or two each week, and, with the new influx of funds, they are hiring more staff. At the time of my fieldwork the city planned for these private agencies to eventually take about half of the cases. These institutional providers, in my experience, provided more advocacy for parents and were more effective (see chapter 8).

10 A person cannot be certified as a foster parent if the person has an ACS or criminal history or if evidence of drug abuse or other similar problems is found. In addition, the apartment must be safe and have adequate space, including separate rooms for boys and girls.

11 Less commonly, permanent custody or a plan for independent living, if the child is old enough, can be the goal.

12 Under a new ACS initiative, some agencies are holding conferences every three months. This will likely become the procedure for all agencies.

13 Some parents are able to speak with their children over the phone, but I found that this is often prohibited. Foster parents do not always want this contact, and there is a subtle tendency on the part of caseworkers to keep foster parents and biological parents from speaking and cooperating. This separation occurs, despite the rhetoric about the two parties being "co-parents" in the lives of the children, a theory that circulates among some at ACS and foster care agencies.

14 Not all male biological parents are legal parents.

15 It is also possible to terminate a parent's rights on the basis of a mental illness or mental retardation that "presently and for the foreseeable future" makes them "unable . . . to provide proper and adequate care for a child" (New York State Social Services Law, Section 384-B).

Chapter 4 Fear and a System in Crisis

1 There have also been attacks on the system for intervening unnecessarily in families and interfering with parents' rights (Bailie 1998; Chill 2003; Guggenheim 2005, 2007; Wilkinson-Hagen 2004). These criticisms, however, are most often leveled by lawyers and are rarely in the mainstream media.

2 Compstat was a management strategy that mapped crime using Geographic Information Systems technology, tracked investigations and policing tactics, and instituted weekly meetings where NYPD leadership met with precinct commanders to discuss patterns in crime and policing and to come up with strategies to reduce crime and improve quality of life.

3 He told the ACS attorney that only after caseworkers had tried to find a program would he agree to find that the agency had made reasonable efforts and rule on whether to remand or parole the child.

4 Marilyn, the caseworker who has only seven cases, describes herself as a veteran (she has been at the agency six years) and talked explicitly about her skills at "moving" cases. In other words, she conducts investigations quickly and has the institutional knowledge that enables her to transfer cases to other workers. Aaliyah, the caseworker with thirty-two cases, works currently in an FSU (Family Support Unit) and is not investigating. Instead, her job is to monitor families with monthly or biweekly

home visits (usually for a designated period of time by court order) and check that they are getting and complying with the proper services. When she worked in a "Hospital Unit" she had an average of twelve cases. She is an experienced worker (she has been at the agency for five years) and commented that she was good at working her caseload down.

5 The lowest number came from a new attorney who reported she hasn't worked her way up, as it were, to the caseloads carried by her colleagues, while the high number came from an attorney who only represents teenagers who are close to ageing out of foster care (she has a full-time social worker to help with her cases).

6 18B attorneys, being independent, have more control of their working conditions. Law guardians and ACS attorneys, because they work for organizations, have specific intake days and cannot really turn down a case, unless they can convince a coworker to take it. This difference is one reason the city gave contracts to institutional providers. They work more like the Legal Aid Society or ACS in that they could set up intake teams and ensure that attorneys are assigned to all the cases on a particular day.

7 This rate was only increased in 2004 from $40/hour for in-court time and $25 for out-of-court time. I was told by attorneys who were practicing before the change that they stayed in court as much as they could, which made it difficult to have detailed meetings with their clients.

8 I received several estimates of turnover. One manager told me that caseworkers stay an average of eighteen months and that in her part of Manhattan they lost twenty caseworkers in one month. Another told me he heard the average time people are staying is a year and a month. He also said that six and a half years ago he went through training with a group of twenty-seven people and only five are still at the agency. Carl, who is also a union representative, told me that the agency grossly underestimates turnover. He said that the agency only retains about 20 percent of the people they hire.

9 Parents have separate cases, and what happens, legally, with regard to one does not carry over to the other. If the mother had won the 1028 and the father had not asked for it, then the child would have been returned to her, but not to him.

Chapter 5 Policing versus Helping in Child Welfare

1 In one case involving a poor family I witnessed in family court, a father living in the home without an independent source of income promised he would not leave the children alone with their mother. The children were still removed, and no one considered help with child care to prevent a removal.

2 This attorney takes very few clients and mainly handles termination of parental rights cases for foster care agencies. Her attitude is that parents should be given very few chances and that moving to permanency very quickly is most important. She refuses to be on the 18B panel because she wants to be able to "pick and choose" her clients, presumably only those she really wants to fight for. That she chose this family is telling, but, beyond that, she had the time to fight for them vigorously.

3 That she is adept at this is evidenced by her extremely low caseload (at seven cases she was the only one below ten; see chapter 4).

4 A "modified behavior" chart with rewards and consequences for specific behaviors.

5 She has been hospitalized in the past and was "acting out" (not going to school,

being very disrespectful, smoking, and having her boyfriend over when her parents were not home). They got into a fight about household chores and the boyfriend. Her daughter hit Irene, and Irene bit her in the ensuing physical struggle.

6 The other class was conducted by an activist for parent's rights who had very simple rules that he did not enforce. His class is in no way typical, and other parent advocates warned parents against taking his class because they doubted it would be accepted by caseworkers.

7 He added, as further evidence of the family court evaluators' bias, that their policies dictate that any recommendation of "return to parent" must be reviewed by supervisors, but one that recommends continued foster care does not. He speculated that this level of scrutiny is why he has yet to see a positive report.

Chapter 6 Defining Neglect and Risk Assessment in Practice

1 The New York State Family Court Act, Article 10 Section 12 defines a neglected child as a person under eighteen
"(i) whose physical, mental or emotional condition has been impaired or is in imminent danger of becoming impaired as a result of the failure of his parent or other person legally responsible for his care to exercise a minimum degree of care
"(A) in supplying the child with adequate food, clothing, shelter or education in accordance with the provisions of part one of article sixty-five of the education law, or medical, dental, optometrical or surgical care, though financially able to do so or offered financial or other reasonable means to do so; or
"(B) in providing the child with proper supervision or guardianship, by unreasonably inflicting or allowing to be inflicted harm, or a substantial risk thereof, including the infliction of excessive corporal punishment; or by misusing a drug or drugs; or by misusing alcoholic beverages to the extent that he loses self-control of his actions; or by any other acts of a similarly serious nature requiring the aid of the court; provided, however, that where the respondent is voluntarily and regularly participating in a rehabilitative program, evidence that the respondent has repeatedly misused a drug or drugs or alcoholic beverages to the extent that he loses self-control of his actions shall not establish that the child is a neglected child in the absence of evidence establishing that the child's physical, mental or emotional condition has been impaired or is in imminent danger of becoming impaired as set forth in paragraph (i)."

2 In family court, a finding of "imminent risk" is necessary to place a child in foster care. If it is thought the risk is less, but the behavior of the parent seems to fit the rest of this definition, then the court can mandate services.

3 "Excessive corporal punishment" fits under neglect and is different than what fits the legal definition of abuse. Abuse must include certain sexual acts or injury not caused accidentally, "which causes or creates a substantial risk of death, or serious or protracted disfigurement, or protracted impairment of physical or emotional health or protracted loss or impairment of the function of any bodily organ" (Family Court Act, Section 1012, e, i).

4 This part of the definition was used to include issues like refusing to press statutory rape charges against a child's boyfriend, refusing to bring a child back home from psychiatric hospitalization when the parent felt the child was still a danger, and shoplifting by a parent.

5 An ACS attorney from Queens, Katherine, told me they focused on the *risk* of serious harm in defining abuse: "But once you start hitting the child like near the face, by the eye, that can easily be pled as an abuse case because you've got a protracted risk of blindness. You know? Losing your eye." In contrast, in the other boroughs, it would depend on the severity: if the child was slapped and a red mark was left that would be neglect; if the parent hit the child repeatedly with an object across their face and they had serious swelling and a black eye that would be abuse.

6 I think that specifically defining drug use as neglect probably came in the late 1980s with the "drug scare" centered on crack and the larger war on drugs (Reinarman and Levine 1997). Laws were changed in similar ways in other places, but I do not know the timing in New York State.

7 Discussions about when the use of corporal punishment should be called neglect were also common, but this issue is extremely complex and beyond the scope of this book. Although issues of inequality and evaluations of who can be a fit parent and who cannot are present in corporal punishment cases, those cases are both less common and bring up issues of cultural differences and immigration that require more discussion than possible here.

8 However, it is important to note that this does not mean that the main allegation/issue in a case at the time I saw it in family court was the same one that first led ACS to be involved with the family. One ACS attorney stated that it was fairly common for attorneys and caseworkers at foster care agencies to lose track of why a case was originally filed. This can make it difficult to ensure that services are provided that address the allegations and can lead to a situation, from the parents' point of view, in which the requirements for regaining custody become a moving target (see chapter 5).

9 In these courts parents must admit their drug problem at the beginning of the case, waiving their right to a trial and allowing a finding of neglect to be entered against them. The case then moves to a dispositional hearing where the parent is ordered into drug treatment appropriate for their situation. They are also given counseling and random drug testing through the drug treatment court itself. These courts aim to get the parent engaged with drug treatment quickly and to use court time to monitor their progress, rather than to deal with the facts of the case. Services begin more quickly in these cases, and they are generally completed more quickly.

10 I did not hear of a single case involving methamphetamine use, and only once or twice did I hear of a case involving heroin.

11 This practice is an important change from how domestic violence cases were generally handled prior to a class-action lawsuit, *Nicholson v. Scoppetta* (the case was filed in 2002 and settled in December of 2004). In this case, mothers who had been charged with neglect for "engaging in domestic violence" and not protecting their children—very often these children were placed in foster care—sued the city over the practice and won. They successfully argued that being a victim of domestic violence did not automatically make them unfit mothers. ACS attorneys and caseworkers were all aware of this decision and cautious about filing against domestic violence victims. Despite this practice constituting an important step toward more adequately helping mothers who have experienced violence, casework practices in these situations remained problematic because some caseworkers continued to hold women responsible, and not all women are willing or able to comply with these conditions (Lee 2015).

12 Mental health issues came up more often in ongoing cases and were less present in new cases. It seems that only very serious cases of mental health (i.e., where a parent was incapacitated or had had a breakdown of some sort) come to the attention of ACS for that reason. I did, however, meet one mother who had her children removed from her care after telling a school guidance counselor she was depressed and overwhelmed. The guidance counselor called ACS. Her case was no longer in court so it is not included in my count.

13 The elements they discussed that matched the list were: prior reports, inadequate housing (health and safety hazards and/or overcrowding), limited or mismanaged financial resources so that needs were not being met, domestic violence or serious conflicts with other adults, alcohol abuse or drug abuse problems in the last two years, serious mental health problem (all elements that would increase a risk score), caretaker recognizes and attends to the children's needs, caretaker views the abuse/neglect situation as seriously as the caseworker (elements that would decrease a risk score). The other risk factors were: the child was with a foster parent or substitute caretaker in the past; children under one year old lives in the family; caregiver has reliable and useful social support; caretaker has limited cognitive skills or a disability; caretaker applies realistic expectations of all the children.

14 Other research has found that prior reports are an important predictor of which children will be removed (Rossi, Schuerman, and Budde 1999).

15 In one she had apparently consumed fluids to dilute her urine, and in the other she gave a sample of urine that was cold.

16 Reports made to get back at people, used as weapons in disputes, or used as methods of continued control in domestic violence situations are common enough that caseworkers complained about them and felt they increased their workload (see also chapter 5).

17 Notice that his argument was that she was probably not using; if there had been more solid evidence of her use he probably would not have asked for the 1028 hearing.

18 A very suggestive comparison to these cases occurred in May 2007 when a three-year-old British girl, Madeleine McCann, was apparently abducted from a hotel room in a resort. Her parents left her and her twin siblings alone in the room while they had dinner nearby. Most of the news coverage, at least in the United States, presented them as loving parents who were victims in a tragedy along with their daughter. The desire for a night alone on the part of a married, white, professional couple was seen as legitimate in a way it never is for the poor women of color involved in child welfare.

Chapter 7 Power in Child Welfare: Compliance and Rights

1 Marilyn preferred a foster care arrangement and a child protective case because the parent is subject to court directives about services, the foster parent's home is monitored, and the agency has more control over the access the parent has to the child and when the child is returned. If a relative files for custody or cares for the child through a private arrangement, the child welfare agency has no control over the situation, and it is then possible for the mother to resume caring for the child without monitoring and services.

2 At this hearing, after their attorneys produced certificates from various programs

(including one from a branch of the caseworker's own agency that she said she had never heard of) and a letter from a counselor, the caseworker protested that she did not "have any idea what they were doing" or if "they were really getting counseling."

3 Another reason was the father's drug history and the fact he had parental rights to other children terminated over ten years prior. In the early stages of the case it seemed they were willing to return the child to the parents, eventually, and even focused on the mother more than the father. Later, it was made clear to the mother that she could separate from him and regain custody. She refused.

4 Their attorneys are the law guardians in most cases, and their social workers are used to evaluate the case to help decide, if the child is too young, what the law guardian's position, including about reunification, should be.

5 This is not surprising because she is a trained social worker and therefore has been taught a therapeutic orientation and methods. One parent advocate at CWOP who has been through the system told me that she did not think that social workers were truly parent advocates and hoped this firm would hire more parents who had been involved in the system.

6 I do not know the source of her anger, but it kept her from unsupervised visits for several months, which delayed reunification. Prior to the supervision change, weekend visits were to start, which is generally the last step before a child is sent home. At the court appearance in which I saw the case, her unsupervised visits were reinstated, but she was told the caseworker would "see how it goes" for a few months before she would get weekends. The mother was visibly angry about the delay, and after the conference the law guardian commented on her "ridiculous" behavior and the anger that the law guardian took to mean she was not progressing properly.

7 Basically, this is a conference held by ACS when they are working with a family and feel that the child is at increased risk despite services or when they feel services are not working. The idea is that all the parties (the parents, caseworkers, and service providers) can discuss an alternate plan to avoid foster care placement. If nothing can be worked out, then a removal will sometimes be made.

8 Interestingly, there was no testimony or questioning from a medical point of view about the child's seizures: how bad they were or how they had either harmed or had the potential to harm her.

9 According to ACS statistics, in 2007, almost 35 percent of parents had their children placed outside their "borough of origin" (i.e., where the child was living prior to removal), and almost 87 percent have children placed outside their Community District. These statistics likely undercount the number of parents whose children are placed relatively far from them. If parents move out of the "borough of origin," children remain in their placements so they might be farther away but would be counted as being in the same borough. I met a few parents in this situation. In addition, in 2006, in 47 percent of cases, siblings were separated, which often meant multiple visiting times (White, Hurley, and Solow 2008).

10 In another case, the parents left a child with a babysitter, and, according to them, she injured the child's arm (it was either broken or dislocated). The child stayed in foster care for about four months before they could convince the judge they had not caused the injury.

11 Out of the nine cases in my data where I know the outcome of the hearing, four resulted in the child's being returned to the parent. Two of these were cases in which a child with a medical problem (cerebral palsy and a seizure disorder) was left

"unsupervised" in the care of an older sibling or a teen babysitter. In the third, an allegation that a father had kicked his young daughter in a park was deemed false. Significantly, this case involved a middle-class white family who was able to hire an excellent private attorney. In the fourth, a father who had been excluded from the home after he broke the mother's arm was allowed to return to the home after it was proven that it had been a one-time incident to which the children were not witnesses, that he was now in counseling, and that neither the children nor the mother feared him. In the other five cases the children remained in foster care. These cases had to do with drug allegations (three cases), one with a young child left home alone when the mother went out with her boyfriend, and a teen mother with a mental health issue.

12 The types of settlements are: (1) an admission, which means that the parent states that all or part of the allegations are true; (2) a "1051A submission," which means that the parent submits to the jurisdiction of the court, waives his or her right to a trial, and allows the court to enter a finding against him or her; or (3) an Adjournment in Contemplation of Dismissal or "ACD," which means that no finding is entered and the parent receives a certain amount of time (usually six months or a year) in which to comply with certain conditions. If the parent complies, after the period is up, the case is dismissed, and no finding is entered against them.

13 On another occasion, a law guardian consented to place his clients with their grandmother temporarily but commented, in court with the grandmother present, that, "unless something's wrong with Grandma" and he had to ask for a remand, their next court appearance could be short.

Chapter 8 Re-creating Stratified Reproduction and System Change

1 For example, one mother agreed to an interview but did not show up. She later told me her welfare benefits had been reduced, she was unable to pay her rent, and her request for assistance with back rent was denied. She had to go to the welfare office and waited most of the day only to *request* a fair hearing. Two weeks later she was evicted. By chance, I ran into her a year later, selling toys on the street. She told me she was still in the shelter system, and her children remained in foster care.

2 Agencies must have a pool of foster parents so they can fulfill their contracts and take in children; thus they often cater to foster parents, lest the parents decide it is too much trouble and they "close their homes." Many parents commented that they felt the caseworker was "on the side of" the foster parent.

3 The rules allow parents to be moved to a family shelter as soon as the children are released (if they have notice and can find a spot).

4 I witnessed one case in family court, for example, in which a mother had an ongoing case solely because of rundown housing that was unsafe for her child who had cerebral palsy. Although she attempted to get much-needed repairs, caseworkers removed her children to foster care on two occasions. On both of them, she requested a 1028 hearing, and the child was returned because there was no cause for neglect.

5 "God grant me the serenity to accept the things I cannot change, the courage to change the things I can, and the wisdom to know the difference."

6 My favorite iteration of this advice came from a parent who had lost custody of her children, regained it, and then worked at a foster care agency. She told a support group that parent advocates "deal with the caseworkers for you so that you don't beat their asses."

References

Anglin, James P. 2002. "Risk, Well-Being, and Paramountcy in Child Protection: The Need for Transformation." *Child and Youth Care Forum* 31 (4): 233–255.

Appell, Annette R. 1997. "Protecting Children or Punishing Mothers: Gender, Race, and Class in the Child Protection System." *South Carolina Law Review* 48 (Spring): 577–613.

Ariès, Philippe. 1962. *Centuries of Childhood*. London: Cape.

Armstrong, Molly. 1998. "Adolescent Pathways: Exploring the Intersections between Child Welfare and Juvenile Justices, PINS, and Mental Health." New York: Vera Institute of Justice.

Ashby, Leroy. 1997. *Endangered Children: Dependency, Neglect, and Abuse in American History*. New York: Twayne Publishers.

Bailie, Kathleen A. 1998. "The Other 'Neglected' Parties in Child Protective Proceedings: Parents in Poverty and the Role of Lawyers Who Represent Them." *Fordham Law Review* 66: 2285–2331.

Bartholet, Elizabeth. 1999. *Nobody's Children: Abuse and Neglect, Foster Drift, and the Adoption Alternative*. Boston: Beacon Press.

Bellingham, Bruce. 1990. "Waifs and Strays: Child Abandonment, Foster Care, and Families in Mid-Nineteenth Century New York." In *The Uses of Charity: The Poor on Relief in the Nineteenth Century Metropolis*, edited by Peter Mandler. Philadelphia: University of Pennsylvania Press.

Bernstein, Nina. 2001. *The Lost Children of Wilder: The Epic Struggle to Change Foster Care*. New York: Pantheon Books.

Berrick, Jill Duerr, Laura Frame, Jodie Langs, and Lisa Varchol. 2006. "Working Together for Children and Families: Where TANF and Child Welfare Meet." *Journal of Policy Practice* 5 (2/3): 27–42.

Besharov, Douglas J., and Lisa A. Laumann. 1996. "Child Abuse Reporting." *Society* 33 (4): 40–46.

Billingsley, Andrew, and Jeanne M. Giovannoni. 1972. *Children of the Storm: Black Children and American Child Welfare*. New York: Harcourt Brace Jovanovich.

Bluestone, Barry, and Bennett Harrison. 1982. *The Deindustrialization of America: Plant Closings, Community Abandonment, and the Dismantling of Basic Industry*. New York: Basic Books.

Bourgois, Philippe. 2003. *In Search of Respect: Selling Crack in El Barrio*. 2nd ed. Cambridge: Cambridge University Press.

Briggs, Laura. 2012. *Somebody's Children: The Politics of Transracial and Transnational Adoption*. Durham, NC: Duke University Press.

Broder, Sheri. 2002. *Tramps, Unfit Mothers, and Neglected Children*. Philadelphia: University of Pennsylvania Press.

Campbell, Nancy D. 2004. "Technologies of Suspicion: Coercion and Compassion in Post-Disciplinary Surveillance Regimes." *Surveillance and Society* 2 (1): 78–92.

———. 2006. "Everyday Insecurities: The Microbehavioral Politics of Intensive Surveillance." In *Surveillance and Security: Technological Politics and Power in Everyday Life*, edited by Torin Monahan. New York: Routledge.

Children's Defense Fund. 2007. "America's Cradle to Prison Pipeline." Washington, DC: Children's Defense Fund. http://www.childrensdefense.org/child-research-data—publications/data/cradle-prison-pipeline-report-2007-full-lowres.pdf.

Chill, Paul. 2003. "Burden of Proof Begone: The Pernicious Effect of Emergency Removal in Child Protective Proceedings." *Family Court Review* 41: 457–470.

Clarke, John. 2004. *Changing Welfare, Changing States: New Directions in Social Policy*. London: Sage.

Clear, Todd R. 2009. *Imprisoning Communities: How Mass Incarceration Makes Disadvantaged Neighborhoods Worse*. New York: Oxford University Press.

Colen, Shellee. 1995. "'Like a Mother to Them': Stratified Reproduction and West Indian Childcare Workers and Employers in New York." In *Conceiving the New World Order: The Global Politics of Reproduction*, edited by Faye D. Ginsburg and Rayna Rapp. Berkeley: University of California Press.

Collings, Sara, and Linda Davies. 2008. "'For the Sake of the Children': Making Sense of Children and Childhood in the Context of Child Protection." *Journal of Social Work Practice* 22 (2): 181–193.

Collins, Patricia Hill. 1990. *Black Feminist Thought: Knowledge, Consciousness, and the Politics of Empowerment*. Boston: Unwin Hyman.

Council on Children, New York City Bar Association. 2007. "The Permanency Legislation of 2005: An Unfunded Mandate—Critical Resource Needs for New York City's Children and Families." New York City Bar.

Courtney, Mark E., Amy Dworsky, Adam Brown, Colleen Cary, Kara Love, and Vanessa Vorhies. 2011. "Midwest Evaluation of the Adult Functioning of Former Foster Youth: Outcomes at Age 26." University of Chicago: Chapin Hall Center for Children.

Daily News. 2006. "Come Clean on ACS, Mayor Mike," January 15.

Derezotes, Dennette M., John Poertner, and Mark Testa. 2004. *Race Matters in Child Welfare: The Overrepresentation of African American Children in the System*. Washington, DC: Child Welfare League of America Press.

Douglas, Susan J., and Meredith W. Michaels. 2004. *The Mommy Myth: The Idealization of Motherhood and How It Has Undermined Women*. New York: Free Press.

Drake, St. Clair. 1945. *Black Metropolis: A Study of Negro Life in a Northern City*. New York: Harcourt Brace.

Edin, Kathryn, and Laura Lein. 1997. *Making Ends Meet: How Single Mothers Survive Welfare and Low-Wage Work*. New York: Russell Sage Foundation.

Ehrenreich, John. 1985. *The Altruistic Imagination: A History of Social Work and Social Policy in the United States*. Ithaca, NY: Cornell University Press.

Erickson, Patricia E. 2000. "Federal Child Abuse and Child Neglect Policy in the United States since 1974: A Review and Critique." *Criminal Justice Review* 25 (1): 77–92.

Eubanks, Virginia. 2006. "Technologies of Citizenship: Surveillance and Political Learning in the Welfare System." In *Surveillance and Security: Technological Practices and Power in Everyday Life*, edited by Torin Monahan. New York: Routledge.

Featherstone, Brid. 2006. "Why Gender Matters in Child Welfare and Protection." *Critical Social Policy* 26 (2): 294–314.

Feige, David. 2006. *Indefensible: One Lawyer's Journey into the Inferno of American Justice.* New York: Little, Brown, and Company.

Feldman, Cassi. 2005. "From Prosecution to Permanency." *Child Welfare Watch* 12 (Winter): 3.

Foderaro, Lisa W. 2008. "Children Left Alone at Home, Worriedly." *New York Times*, August 14.

Folks, Homer. 1902. *The Care of Destitute, Neglected, and Delinquent Children*. New York: Macmillan.

Frame, Laura. 1999. "Suitable Homes Revisited: An Historical Look at Child Protection and Welfare Reform." *Children and Youth Services Review* 21 (9/10): 719–754.

Freeman, Joshua B. 2000. *Working Class New York: Life and Labor since World War II.* New York: New Press.

Gambrill, Eileen, and Aron Shlonsky. 2000. "Risk Assessment in Context." *Children and Youth Services Review* 22 (11/12): 813–837.

Gelles, Richard J. 2000. "Controversies in Family Preservation Programs." *Journal of Aggression, Maltreatment, and Trauma* 3 (1): 239–252.

Gerstenzang, Sarah, and Madelyn Freundlich. 2005. "A Critical Assessment of Concurrent Planning in New York State." *Adoption Quarterly* 8 (4): 1–22.

Gilens, Martin. 2000. *Why Americans Hate Welfare: Race, Media, and the Politics of Antipoverty Policy*. Chicago: University of Chicago Press.

Gillingham, Philip. 2006. "Risk Assessment in Child Protection: Problem Rather Than Solution?" *Australian Social Work* 59 (1): 86–98.

Gilliom, John. 2001. *Overseers of the Poor: Surveillance, Resistance, and the Limits of Privacy.* Chicago: University of Chicago Press.

Gilmore, Ruth Wilson. 1999. "Globalisation and US Prison Growth: From Military Keynesianism to Post-Keynesian Militarism." *Race & Class* 40 (2–3): 171–188. doi:10.1177/030639689904000212.

Ginsburg, Faye, and Rayna Rapp. 1991. "The Politics of Reproduction." *Annual Review of Anthropology* 20: 311–343.

———. 1995. "Introduction: Conceiving the New World Order." In *Conceiving the New World Order: The Global Politics of Reproduction*, edited by Faye Ginsburg and Rayna Rapp. Berkeley: University of California Press.

Goddard, Chris R., Bernadette J. Saunders, Janet R. Stanley, and Joe Tucci. 1999. "Structured Risk Assessment Procedures: Instruments of Abuse?" *Child Abuse Review* 8: 251–263.

Goffman, Alice. 2014. *On the Run: Fugitive Life in an American City*. Chicago: University of Chicago Press.

Golden, Renny. 1997. *Disposable Children: America's Child Welfare System*. Belmont, CA: Wadsworth.

Goldstein, Joseph, Anna Freud, and Albert J. Solnit. 1973. *Beyond the Best Interests of the Child.* New York: Free Press.

Gomez, Laura E. 1997. *Misconceiving Mothers: Legislators, Prosecutors, and the Politics of Prenatal Drug Exposure*. Philadelphia: Temple University Press.

Goode, Judith, and Jeff Maskovsky. 2001. "Introduction." In *The New Poverty Studies: The Ethnography of Power, Politics, and Impoverished People in the United States*, edited by Judith Goode and Jeff Maskovsky. New York: New York University Press.

Goodwin, Michael. 2006. "A Fatal Flaw: Some Families Should Not Stay Together." *Daily News*.

Gordon, Linda. 1985. "Child Abuse, Gender, and the Myth of Family Independence: A Historical Critique." *Child Welfare* 64 (3): 213–224.

———. 1986. "Family Violence, Feminism, and Social Control." *Feminist Studies* 12 (3): 452–478.

———. 1988. *Heroes of Their Own Lives: The Politics and History of Family Violence, Boston, 1880–1960*. Chicago: University of Illinois Press.

———. 1999. *The Great Arizona Orphan Abduction*. Cambridge, MA: Harvard University Press.

Gordon, Robert M. 1999. "Drifting Through Byzantium: The Promise and Failure of the Adoption and Safe Families Act." *Minnesota Law Review* 83: 637–698.

Grossberg, Michael. 2002. "Changing Conceptions of Child Welfare in the United States, 1820–1935." In *A Century of Juvenile Justice*, edited by Margaret K. Rosenheim, Franklin E. Zimring, David S. Tanenhaus, and Bernardine Dohrn. Chicago: University of Chicago Press.

Guggenheim, Martin. 1996. "Effects of Recent Trends to Accelerate the Termination of Parental Rights to Children in Foster Care: An Empirical Analysis in Two States." *Family Law Quarterly* 29: 121–140.

———. 2005. *What's Wrong with Children's Rights*. Cambridge, MA: Harvard University Press.

———. 2006. "How Children's Lawyers Serve State Interests." *Nevada Law Journal* 6: 805–834.

———. 2007. "Parental Rights in Child Welfare Cases in New York City Family Courts." *Columbia Journal of Law and Social Problems* 40: 507–549.

Guggenheim, Martin, and Christine Gottlieb. 2005. "Justice Denied: Delays in Resolving Child Protection Cases in New York." *Virginia Journal of Social Policy* 12: 546–576.

Gutman, Herbert George. 1976. *The Black Family in Slavery and Freedom, 1750–1925*. New York: Pantheon Books.

Hacsi, Tim. 1995. "From Indenture to Family Foster Care: A Brief History of Child Placing." *Child Welfare* 74 (1): 162–180.

Hamer, Jennifer. 2001. *What It Means to Be Daddy: Fatherhood for Black Men Living Away from Their Children*. New York: Columbia University Press.

Hansen, Karen V. 2005. *Not-So-Nuclear Families: Class, Gender, and Networks of Care*. New Brunswick, NJ: Rutgers University Press.

Hays, Sharon. 2003. *Flat Broke with Children: Women in the Age of Welfare Reform*. Oxford: Oxford University Press.

Hill, Robert B. 2004. "Institutional Racism in Child Welfare." In *Child Welfare Revisited: An Africentric Perspective*, edited by Joyce E. Everett, Sandra P. Chipungu, and Bogart R. Leashore. New Brunswick, NJ: Rutgers University Press.

———. 2006. "Synthesis of Research on Disproportionality in Child Welfare: An Update." Washington, DC: Casey-CSSP Alliance for Racial Equity in the Child Welfare System.

http://www.cssp.org/reform/child-welfare/other-resources/synthesis-of-research-on-disproportionality-robert-hill.pdf.

Hughes, Ronald C., and Judith S. Rycus. 2007. "Issues in Risk Assessment in Child Protective Services." *Journal of Public Child Welfare* 1 (1): 85–116.

Humphries, Drew. 1993. "Crack Mothers, Drug Wars, and the Politics of Resentment." In *Political Crime in Contemporary America: A Critical Approach*, edited by Kenneth D. Tunnell. New York: Garland Publishing.

Hutchinson, Elizabeth D. 1993. "Mandatory Reporting Laws: Child Protective Case Finding Gone Awry?" *Social Work* 38 (1): 56–63.

Johnson, Jacqueline. 2011. "Mass Incarceration: A Contemporary Mechanism of Racialization in the United States." *Gonzaga Law Review* 47: 301–318.

Jonson-Reid, Melissa, and Richard P. Barth. 2003. "Probation Foster Care as an Outcome for Children Exiting Child Welfare Foster Care." *Social Work* 48 (3): 348–361.

Kahn, Alfred J. 1961. "Protecting New York City's Children." New York: Citizens' Committee for Children.

Kang, Hyun-Ah, and John Poertner. 2006. "Inter-Rater Reliability of the Illinois Structured Decision Support Protocol." *Child Abuse and Neglect* 30: 679–689.

Kapp, Stephen A. 2000. "Pathways to Prison: Life Histories of Former Clients of the Child Welfare and Juvenile Justice Systems." *Journal of Sociology and Social Welfare* 28 (3): 63–74.

Katz, Michael. 1996. *In the Shadow of the Poorhouse*. New York: Basic Books.

Kaufman, Leslie. 2006. "Response to Child Deaths Suggests a System Poised to Work." *New York Times*, November 17.

Kaufman, Leslie, Mike McIntire, and Fernanda Santos. 2006. "Child Welfare Offices That Couldn't Be Fixed Fast Enough." *New York Times*, January 20.

Kerr, Peter. 1986. "Babies of Crack Users Fill Hospital Nurseries." *New York Times*, August 25.

Kline, Marlee. 1992. "Child Welfare Law, 'Best Interests of the Child' Ideology, and First Nations." *Osgoode Hall Law Journal* 20 (2): 237–425.

Krane, Julia, and Linda Davies. 2000. "Mothering and Child Protective Practice: Rethinking Risk Assessment." *Child and Family Social Work* 5: 35–45.

Kunzel, Regina G. 1993. *Fallen Women, Problem Girls: Unmarried Mothers and the Professionalization of Social Work, 1890–1945*. New Haven, CT: Yale University Press.

Lansner, David J. 2007. "Abolish the Family Court." *Columbia Journal of Law and Social Problems* 40: 637–643.

Lareau, Annette. 2003. *Unequal Childhoods: Class, Race, and Family Life*. Berkeley: University of California Press.

Lawrence-Webb, Claudia. 1997. "African American Children in the Modern Child Welfare System: A Legacy of the Flemming Rule." *Child Welfare* 76 (1): 9–31.

Lee, Tina. 2015. "Child Welfare Practice in Domestic Violence Cases in New York City: Problems for Poor Women of Color." *Women, Gender, and Families of Color* 3 (1): 58–87.

Leschied, Alan W., Debbie Chiodo, Paul C. Whitehead, Dermot Hurley, and Larry Marshall. 2003. "The Empirical Basis of Risk Assessment in Child Welfare: The Accuracy of Risk Assessment and Clinical Judgment." *Child Welfare* 82 (5): 527–540.

Lindenmeyer, Kriste. 1997. *"A Right to Childhood": The U.S. Children's Bureau and Child Welfare, 1912–1946*. Urbana: University of Illinois Press.

Lindsey, Duncan. 1994. *The Welfare of Children*. Oxford: Oxford University Press.

Lindsey, Duncan, Sacha Martin, and Jenny Doh. 2002. "The Failure of Intensive Casework

Services to Reduce Foster Care Placements: An Examination of Family Preservation Studies." *Children and Youth Services Review* 24 (9/10): 743–775.

Lukens, Robert J. 2007. "The Impact of Mandatory Reporting Requirements on the Child Welfare System." *Rutgers Journal of Law and Public Policy* 5 (1): 177–233.

Lyle, Charles Gene, and Elliott Graham. 2000. "Looks Can Be Deceiving: Using a Risk Assessment Instrument to Evaluate the Outcomes of Child Protection Services." *Children and Youth Services Review* 22 (11/12): 935–945.

Lyon, David. 2002. *Surveillance as Social Sorting: Privacy, Risk and Automated Discrimination*. New York: Routledge.

MacDonald, Heather. 1999. "Foster Care's Underworld." *City Journal* 9 (1): 42–53.

Mason, Mary Ann. 1994. *From Father's Property to Children's Rights: The History of Child Custody in the United States*. New York: Columbia University Press.

Mauer, Marc, and Meda Chesney-Lind. 2002. *Invisible Punishment: The Collateral Consequences of Mass Imprisonment*. New York: New Press.

McConnell, David, and Gwynnyth Llewellyn. 2005. "Social Inequality, 'The Deviant Parent,' and Child Protective Practice." *Australian Journal of Social Issues* 40 (4): 553–566.

McDonald, Thomas Porky, Reva I. Allen, Alex Westerfelt, and Irving Piliavin. 1997. *Assessing the Long-Term Effects of Foster Care: A Research Synthesis*. Washington, DC: Child Welfare League of America Press.

McGowan, Brenda G., and Elaine M. Walsh. 2000. "Policy Challenges for Child Welfare in the New Century." *Child Welfare Policy* 79: 11–27.

Michel, Sonya. 1998. "Childcare and Welfare (In)justice." *Feminist Studies* 24 (1): 44–64.

———. 1999. *Children's Interests/Mother's Rights: The Shaping of America's Child Care Policy*. New Haven, CT: Yale University Press.

Mollenkopf, John Hull, and Manuel Castells. 1991. *Dual City: Restructuring New York*. New York: Russell Sage Foundation.

Monahan, Torin. 2006. "Questioning Surveillance and Security." In *Surveillance and Security: Technological Politics and Power in Everyday Life*, edited by Torin Monahan. New York: Routledge.

Moye, Jim, and Roberta Rinker. 2002. "It's a Hard Knock Life: Does the Adoption and Safe Families Act of 1997 Adequately Address Problems in the Child Welfare System?" *Harvard Journal on Legislation* 39(2): 375–394.

Mullings, Leith. 1995. "Households Headed by Women: The Politics of Race, Class, and Gender." In *Conceiving the New World Order: The Global Politics of Reproduction*, edited by Faye D. Ginsburg and Rayna Rapp. Berkeley: University of California Press.

———. 2003. "Losing Ground: Harlem, the War on Drugs, and the Prison Industrial Complex." *Souls: A Critical Journal of Black Politics, Culture, and Society* 5 (2): 1–21.

———. 2005. "Resistance and Resilience: The Sojourner Syndrome and the Social Context of Reproduction in Central Harlem." *Transforming Anthropology* 13 (2): 79–91.

Mullings, Leith, and Alaka Wali. 2001. *Stress and Resilience: The Social Context of Reproduction in Central Harlem*. New York: Kluwer Academic/Plenum Publishing.

Munson, Sara, and Madelyn Freundlich. 2003. "Educating Children in Foster Care." Washington, DC: National Conference of State Legislatures, Children's Policy Institute.

Murphy, Sheigla B., and Marsha Rosenbaum. 1997. "Two Women Who Used Cocaine Too Much: Class, Race, Gender, and Coke." In *Crack in America: Demon Drugs and Social Justice*, edited by Craig Reinarman and Harry G. Levine. Berkeley: University of California Press.

Nelson, Barbara J. 1984. *Making an Issue of Child Abuse: Political Agenda Setting for Social Problems*. Chicago: University of Chicago Press.

Neubeck, Kenneth J., and Noel Cazenave. 2001. *Welfare Racism: Playing the Race Card against America's Poor*. New York: Routledge.

New York City Department of Investigation. 2007. "A Department of Investigation Examination of Eleven Child Fatalities and One Near Fatality. A Joint Report with the Administration for Children's Services. August 2007." New York: New York City Department of Investigation.

Office of the Public Advocate for the City of New York. 2002. "Families at Risk: A Report on New York City's Child Welfare Services." New York: Office of the Public Advocate for the City of New York. Internal report, 44 pages.

———. 2006. "A Dangerous Cycle: Attorney Turnover at ACS Leaves Children Unprotected." New York: Office of the Public Advocate for the City of New York. Internal report, 31 pages.

Ortiz, Ana Teresa, and Laura Briggs. 2003. "The Culture of Poverty, Crack Babies, and Welfare Cheats: The Making of the 'Healthy White Baby Crisis.'" *Social Text* 21 (3): 39–57.

Parton, Nigel. 1999. "Reconfiguring Child Welfare Practices: Risk, Advanced Liberalism, and the Government of Freedom." In *Reading Foucault for Social Work*, edited by Adrienne Chambon, Allan Irving, and Laura Epstein. New York: Columbia University Press.

———. 2006. *Safeguarding Childhood*. New York: Palgrave Macmillan.

Parton, Nigel, David Thorpe, and Corinne Wattam. 1997. *Child Protection: Risk and the Moral Order*. Basingstoke: Macmillan.

Pecora, Peter J., Jason Williams, Ronald C. Kessler, Chris Downs, Kirk O'Brien, Eva Hiripi, and Sarah Morello. 2003. "Assessing the Effects of Foster Care: Early Results from the Casey National Alumni Study." Seattle, WA: Casey Family Programs.

Pelton, Leroy H. 1989. *For Reasons of Poverty: A Critical Analysis of the Public Child Welfare System in the United States*. New York: Praeger.

Pettit, Becky. 2012. *Invisible Men: Mass Incarceration and the Myth of Black Progress*. New York: Russell Sage Foundation.

Piven, Frances Fox, and Richard A. Cloward. 1993. *Regulating the Poor: The Functions of Public Welfare*. New York: Vintage Books.

Platt, Anthony. 1977. *The Child Savers: The Invention of Delinquency*. Vol. 2. Chicago: University of Chicago Press.

Pleck, Elizabeth. 1987. *Domestic Tyranny: The Making of Social Policy against Family Violence from Colonial Times to the Present*. New York: Oxford University Press.

Polier, Justine Wise. 1974. *Everybody's Children, Nobody's Child*. New York: Arno Press.

Polsky, Andrew J. 1991. *The Rise of the Therapeutic State*. Princeton, NJ: Princeton University Press.

Quadagno, Jill. 1996. *The Color of Welfare: How Racism Undermined the War on Poverty*. New York: Oxford University Press.

Reich, Jennifer. 2005. *Fixing Families: Parents, Power, and the Child Welfare System*. New York: Routledge.

Reilly, Thom. 2003. "Transition from Care: Status and Outcomes of Youth Who Age Out of Foster Care." *Child Welfare* 82 (6): 727–746.

Reinarman, Craig, and Harry G. Levine. 1997. "Crack in Context: America's Latest Demon Drug." In *Crack in America: Demon Drugs and Social Justice*, edited by Craig Reinarman and Harry G. Levine. Berkeley: University of California Press.

Risley-Curtiss, Christina, and Kristin Heffernan. 2003. "Gender Biases in Child Welfare." *Affilia* 18 (4): 395–410.

Rivaux, Stephanie L., Joyce James, Kim Wittenstrom, Donald Bauman, Janess Sheets, Judith Henry, and Victoria Jeffries. 2008. "The Intersection of Race, Poverty, and Risk: Understanding the Decision to Provide Services to Clients and to Remove Children." *Child Welfare* 87 (2): 151–168.

Roberts, Dorothy. 1991. "Punishing Drug Addicts Who Have Babies: Women of Color, Equality, and the Right of Privacy." *Harvard Law Review* 104: 1419–1482.

———. 1997. *Killing the Black Body: Race, Reproduction, and the Meaning of Liberty*. New York: Vintage Books.

———. 1999. "Welfare's Ban on Poor Motherhood." In *Whose Welfare?*, edited by Gwendolyn Mink. Ithaca, NY: Cornell University Press.

———. 2002. *Shattered Bonds: The Color of Child Welfare*. New York: Basic Books.

———. 2008. "The Racial Geography of State Child Protection." In *New Landscapes of Inequality: Neoliberalism and the Erosion of Democracy in America*, edited by Jane L. Collins, Micaela di Leonardo, and Brett Williams. Santa Fe, NM: School for Advanced Research Press.

Roberts, Dorothy, Leah Hill, and Eric Pitchal. 2006. "The Racial Geography of Child Welfare System: Community Impact and Response." New York: Fordham University Interdisciplinary Center for Family and Child Advocacy.

Rodriguez, Clara E. 1989. *Puerto Ricans: Born in the USA*. Boston: Unwin Hyman.

Rosner, David, and Gerald Markowitz. 1997. "Race, Foster Care, and the Politics of Abandonment in New York City." *American Journal of Public Health* 87 (11): 1844–1849.

Rossi, Peter H., John Schuerman, and Stephen Budde. 1999. "Understanding Decisions about Child Maltreatment." *Evaluation Review* 23 (6): 579–598.

Ross, Timothy, Dylan Conger, and Molly Armstrong. 2002. "Bridging Child Welfare and Juvenile Justice: Preventing Unnecessary Detention of Foster Children." *Child Welfare* 81 (3): 471–494.

Ryerson, Ellen. 1978. *The Best-Laid Plans: America's Juvenile Court Experiment*. New York: Hill and Wang.

Rzepnicki, Tina L., and Penny R. Johnson. 2005. "Examining Decision Errors in Child Protection: A New Application of Root Cause Analysis." *Children and Youth Services Review* 27: 393–407.

Santos, Fernanda. 2005. "Placements in Foster Care Are at Lowest since Mid-80's." *New York Times*, October 23.

Schechter, Sara P. 2006. *New York Family Law*. Vol. 2. West Legal Studies. Clifton Park, NY: Thompson Delmar Learning.

Schneider, David M., and Albert Deutsch. 1941. *The History of Public Welfare in New York State, 1867–1940*. Chicago: University of Chicago Press.

Scourfield, Jonathan. 2003. *Gender and Child Protection*. Houndmills, Basingstoke: Palgrave Macmillan.

———. 2006. "The Challenge of Engaging Fathers in the Child Protection Process." *Critical Social Policy* 26 (2): 440–449.

Sedlak, Andrea J., Jane Mettenburg, Monica Basena, Ian Petta, Karla McPherson, Angela Greene, and Spencer Li. 2010. "Fourth National Incidence Study of Child Abuse and Neglect (NIS-4): Report to Congress." Washington, DC: US Department of Health and Human Services, Administration for Children and Families.

Sharff, Jagna W. 1998. *King Kong on 4th Street: Families and the Violence of Poverty on the Lower East Side*. Boulder, CO: Westview Press.

Shin, Sunny Hyucksun. 2002. "Need for and Actual Use of Mental Health Services by Adolescents in the Child Welfare System." *Children and Youth Services Review* 27 (10): 1071–1083.

Shireman, Joan F. 2003. *Critical Issues in Child Welfare*. Foundations of Social Work Knowledge. New York: Columbia University Press.

Siegel, Loren. 1997. "The Pregnancy Police Fight the War on Drugs." In *Crack in America: Demon Drugs and Social Justice*, edited by Craig Reinarman and Harry G. Levine. Berkeley: University of California Press.

Smith, Brenda D., and Stella E. F. Donovan. 2003. "Child Welfare Practice in Organizational and Institutional Context." *Social Service Review* 77 (4): 541–563.

Sobie, Merril. 1987. *The Creation of Juvenile Justice: A History of New York's Children's Laws*. Albany: New York Bar Foundation.

———. 2003. "The Family Court: A Short History." http://www.courts.state.ny.us/history/family_ct/History_Fam_Ct.htm.

Stack, Carol. 1974. *All Our Kin*. New York: Basic Books.

———. 1983. "Cultural Perspectives on Child Welfare." *Review of Law and Social Change* 12: 539–547.

Stansell, Christine. 1990. "Women, Children, and the Uses of the Streets: Class and Gender Conflict in New York City, 1850–1860." In *Unequal Sisters: A Multicultural Reader in U.S. Women's History*, edited by Ellen Carol DuBois and Vicki L. Ruiz. New York: Routledge.

Stein, Theodore J. 2000. "The Adoption and Safe Families Act: Creating a False Dichotomy between Parents' and Children's Rights." *Families in Society* 81 (6): 586–592.

———. 2003. "The Adoption and Safe Families Act: How Congress Overlooks Available Data and Ignores Systemic Obstacles in Its Pursuit of Political Goals." *Children and Youth Services Review* 25 (9): 669–682.

Strega, Susan, Claire Fleet, Leslie Brown, Lena Dominelli, Marilyn Callahan, and Christopher Walmsley. 2008. "Connecting Father Absence and Mother Blame in Child Welfare Policies and Practice." *Children and Youth Services Review* 30: 705–716.

Sullivan, Catherine, Paul C. Whitehead, Alan W. Leschied, Debbie Chiodo, and Dermot Hurley. 2008. "Perception of Risk among Child Protection Workers." *Children and Youth Services Review* 30: 699–704.

Swift, Karen J. 1995. *Manufacturing "Bad Mothers": A Critical Perspective on Child Neglect*. Toronto: University of Toronto Press.

Tobis, David. 1989. "The New York City Foster Care System, 1979–1986: The Rise and Fall of Reform." PhD diss., Yale University.

Tolnay, Stewart E. 2003. "The African American 'Great Migration' and Beyond." *Annual Review of Sociology* 29: 209–232.

Tumlin, Karen C., and Rob Geen. 2000. "The Decision to Investigate: Understanding State Child Welfare Screening Policies." Washington, DC: Urban Institute.

Turney, Danielle. 2000. "The Feminizing of Neglect." *Child and Family Social Work* 5: 47–56.

US Department of Health and Human Services. 2010. "Child Maltreatment 2008." Washington, DC: Administration for Children and Families, Administration on Children, Youth and Families, Children's Bureau.

Voices of Women Organizing Project. 2008. "Justice Denied: How Family Courts in NYC

Endanger Battered Women and Children." New York: Human Rights Project of the Urban Justice Center. http://www.vowbwrc.org/pdf/justicedeniedrep.pdf.

Wacquant, Loïc. 2001. "Deadly Symbiosis: When Ghetto and Prison Meet and Mesh." *Punishment and Society* 3 (1): 95–134.

———. 2008. *Urban Outcasts: A Comparative Sociology of Advanced Marginality*. Cambridge: Polity.

———. 2012. "Three Steps to a Historical Anthropology of Actually Existing Neoliberalism." *Social Anthropology* 20 (1): 66–79. doi:10.1111/j.1469-8676.2011.00189.x.

Waldfogel, Jane. 1998. *The Future of Child Protection: How to Break the Cycle of Abuse and Neglect*. Cambridge, MA: Harvard University Press.

———. 2004. "Welfare Reform and the Child Welfare System." *Children and Youth Services Review* 26: 919–939.

Weisman, Mary-Lou. 1994. "When Parents Are Not in the Best Interests of the Child." *The Atlantic Monthly* 274 (1): 43–63.

Wexler, Richard. 1995. *Wounded Innocents: The Real Victims of the War Against Child Abuse*. Buffalo, NY: Prometheus Books.

White, Andrew, Kendra Hurley, and Barbara Solow. 2007. "Watching the Numbers: A Six-Year Statistical Survey Monitoring New York City's Child Welfare System." *Child Welfare Watch* 14: 31.

———. 2008. "Watching the Numbers: A Six-Year Statistical Survey Monitoring New York City's Child Welfare System." *Child Welfare Watch* 16: 39.

Wilkinson-Hagen, Amy. 2004. "The Adoption and Safe Families Act of 1997: A Collision of Parens Patriae and Parents' Constitutional Rights." *Georgetown Journal on Poverty Law and Policy* 11 (1): 137–168.

Williams, Lucy A. 1995. "Race, Rat Bites, and Unfit Mothers: How Media Discourse Informs Welfare Legislation Debate." *Fordham Urban Law Journal* 22 (4): 1159–1196.

Willrich, Michael. 2003. *City of Courts: Socializing Justice in Progressive Era Chicago*. Cambridge Historical Studies in American Law and Society, edited by Christopher Tomlins. Cambridge: Cambridge University Press.

Zelizer, Viviana A. Rotman. 1985. *Pricing the Priceless Child: The Changing Social Value of Children*. New York: Basic Books.

Zerai, Assata, and Rae Banks. 2002. *Dehumanizing Discourse, Anti-Drug Law, and Policy in America: A "Crack Mother's" Nightmare*. Aldershot, UK: Ashgate.

Zetlin, Andrea, Lois Weinberg, and Christina Kimm. 2004. "Improving Education Outcomes for Children in Foster Care: Intervention by an Education Liaison." *Journal of Education for Students Placed at Risk (JESPAR)* 9 (4): 421–429. doi:10.1207/s15327671espr0904_5.

Index

About the Author

TINA LEE is an associate professor of anthropology and the program director for the Applied Social Science Program at the University of Wisconsin–Stout. She earned her PhD in anthropology from the Graduate Center at the City University of New York in 2010.

CPSIA information can be obtained
at www.ICGtesting.com
Printed in the USA
LVOW13s2141080517
533721LV00024B/356/P